Bismillāhir-Rahmānir-Rahīm

In

the name of

GOD

Most Merciful

Most Compassionate

The Creator, the Protector, the Sustainer

The Fast of
RAMADAN

The Inner Heart Blossoms

M. R. BAWA MUHAIYADDEEN

THE FELLOWSHIP PRESS
Philadelphia, Pennsylvania

Library of Congress Control Number: 2005920930

Muhaiyaddeen, M. R. Bawa.
The fast of Ramadan: the inner heart blossoms / M. R. Bawa Muhaiyaddeen
p. cm.

ISBN-13: 978-0-914390-72-5
ISBN-10: 0-914390-72-4

Printed in the United States of America
by the THE FELLOWSHIP PRESS
Bawa Muhaiyaddeen Fellowship
First Printing

The real fast is
the blossoming of the inner heart.
Fragrance must emanate.
The qualities, conduct, behavior, and disposition
that accompany this blossoming make no sound.
Light and fragrance must dawn in the inner heart.
The one point which is God must resplend.
Do fast, but make sure the heart blossoms;
make it fragrant.

The flowering scent must emanate,
and when that space is perceived,
the One who inhales that perfume will come.
The One who perceives that fragrance will come.
He is the Lord.

Muhammad Raheem Bawa Muhaiyaddeen

May God's Eternal Peace and Boundless Blessings be upon him.

May the peace, the beneficence,

and the blessings of God

be upon you.

Āmīn.

Table of Contents

A Note to the Reader..

It is virtually impossible to accurately translate, edit, and compile the words of a master of such calibre as Bawa Muhaiyyaddeen☺. Discoursing in the ancient Dravidian language of Tamil, everything he articulates has over seventy thousand meanings, and in this way he imparts nourishment for all. Every individual who came before him looked upon the vast, bounteous banquet he had furnished as a feast or as medicine, partaking what he or she needed at the appropriate time. Each one's understanding was subtly different, yet befitting that individual. Thus with inner questions answered, mental disturbances cleared, and hearts melted, all turned toward the ultimate questions: *Who am I? What is my origin? Where do I go next?* in their quest to regain mystic union with the One.

And so it is with translating; how does one render this all-sufficing banquet to another? The author himself stated that every translation is but an interpretation, until the one who has to be translated and the one who translates become one with God. The contents of this book are explanations of the author's experiential understanding, depths of comprehension as yet inaccessible to us. Therefore, while we, the translator, editors, proofreaders, artists, and graphic designers strive for this understanding and oneness, we humbly ask the readers to forgive any mistakes we have made. Only Bawa Muhaiyyaddeen's☺ personal injunction to compile this book gave us the courage, resolute faith, and tenacity to undertake and sustain this magnificent project.

We have done our best to present Bawa's words accurately, employing brackets [ ] for any additional words we have inserted, and indicating interpretations contained in footnotes by denoting them as "Trans." Arabic words, Tamil words with profound esoteric meanings, and words spoken in English by the author have been italicized, their meanings (primarily the author's) provided in the glossary. Humbled by insights we have gleaned from the words of this master teacher who referred to himself the "ant man," and perceiving ever more distinctly our own unfinished inner work, we have nevertheless endeavored to present his songs, discourses, and prayers to best of our ability. Those wiser than ourselves may understand and interpret the material differently.

May the peace, the beneficence, and the blessings of God
accompany you
as you partake of this banquet.

...from the worker-ants.

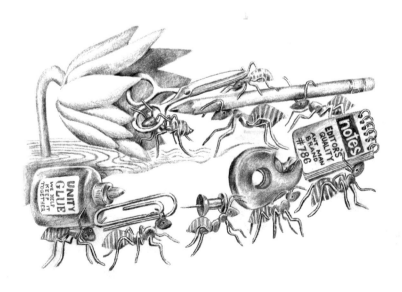

Introduction

In the name of God, Most Merciful, Most Compassionate

God created the human being as the most exalted of all His creations. Endowed with God's radiant Light, His ninety-nine attributes, and seven kinds of wisdom, man is the only creation with the capacity to realize himself and his Creator. When man dedicates his life to God, trusts in God completely, frees himself from elemental attachments, dissolves personal conditioning, and lives in reverent purity, perceiving God alone as sufficient, his inner heart will blossom and merge with God. This book is a guide toward that union.

Although God creates humanity with the potential to live in this manner, human beings often forget, becoming enmeshed in the pleasures of the physical world, while aggrandizing the ego. Although God provides His abundant wealth—land, air, water, nature—as common to all, those driven by self-interest and greed attempt to possess everything they see, touch, taste, and tread upon. Claiming portions of this commonwealth as their own, they create divisiveness and scarcity.

God also unfolds His panoply of *art-work* as a constant reminder to man of His glory and grandeur. Only God can create a living blade of grass; only He can protect and sustain each life. Yet, man forgets. Delving into and glorifying his intellect rather than his wisdom, man ventures to investigate, study, and copy God's masterpieces. Scientifically scrutinizing the blade of grass designed to point man toward God, he claims that it is he who has determined its source of greenness and unique cell structure. Others write poems about the swaying grass or replicate it in their art work, seeking fame and titles for their "masterpieces." In this way, man loses sight of his true heritage and fails to utilize the natural instruments God has provided.

So God has sent special emissaries, the prophets, to provide further tools and to bring direct revelations of His Truth to all mankind. Filled with light and wisdom, each prophet has delivered teachings appropriate to his era, showing man how to return to his inherent state of exalted wisdom and oneness with God. Each prophet—Moses, Jesus, Muhammad, and many others (may the peace of God be upon them)— has brought the same intrinsic message, affirming the existence of the One God who alone is worthy of worship. Muhammad⊕, as the final prophet, transmitted the revelations given to each of the previous prophets, handing man eleven tools—five outer and six inner tasks.

The first outer task is *belief* in the One God. However, perceiving that people were unable to maintain the absolute purity of this belief, he subsequently revealed the second task, *prayer*. For those who persisted in greedily embracing their possessions, he prescribed *charity*, and then *fasting*. Finally, he specified the *pilgrimage of Hajj*, wherein one attempts once more to annihilate the world and focus entirely on God. Since the time of Muhammad⊕, God has sent no further prophets.

In addition to the prophets, divine beings known as *qutbs* have been sent to shed light upon the revelations brought by the prophets. These *qutbs,* fully imbued with the resonance of God's Truth, serve to awaken the inner *qutb,* which is the innate wisdom within each human being. *Qutb-wisdom,* known as *Qutbiyyat,* exists as the vibration and resonance of Truth in all lives. Also referred to as divine analytic wisdom *(pahuth arivu),* it illuminates the right and the wrong in everything. Resonating within, it points man toward God. Yet, man frequently disregards the constant presence of this inner resonance, burying himself beneath a mountain of mind, desire, and illusion. When one meets an authentic *qutb,* the *qutb's* glance, touch, words, and actions synchronize with one's inner resonance, re-awakening the Truth that slumbers within. This experience is one of "finding the shore," of "coming Home."

It is a rare opportunity to find such a being—a true *qutb*—in this world. Muhammad Raheem Bawa Muhaiyaddeen☺, the author of this book, is such a one. Where did he come from, and who was he? Only God knows. Bawa Muhaiyaddeen was first glimpsed in the mid-1930's in the jungles of Sri Lanka, near the holy mountains of Gilani and Kataragama. Two pilgrims from Jaffna came across him sitting under a tree, in meditation. Recognizing something special, they invited him to return with them to be their teacher. He instructed them to return to that same tree, exactly one year hence. They did so, and found Bawa awaiting them there. Promising to appear at their house in Jaffna a few weeks later, he bid them farewell. On the promised day, the two sat and waited. They had not given him their address or even any directions. Finally, as daylight melted into shadows, they looked up and saw him standing in their doorway. This marked the entry of Bawa Muhaiyaddeen into the service of humanity, as we know it.

Over time, people journeyed from all over Sri Lanka in search of guidance from this remarkable sage, eventually joining to form the Serendib Sufi Study Circle. To all who came in search of Truth, he imparted wisdom appropriate to their level of understanding. Meeting his eyes was like gazing into a clear, pure mirror; and if one was willing to look, he revealed the exaltedness of one's true potential, while also mirroring the tendencies and flaws one had to overcome. Bawa Muhaiyaddeen was and continues to be father, teacher, brother, friend, spiritual guide, wise counsel, sanctuary, divine vibration—beyond description.

In the late 1960's, Bawa Muhaiyaddeen was invited to the United States. He arrived in October of 1971, and shortly thereafter a Fellow-ship was formed to record, study, and spread his wisdom and teachings. He spoke of the eternal nature of God, instructing us how to distinguish Reality from unreality. Through spontaneous songs, discourses, prayers, and parables, he taught about essence and illusion, darkness and light, right and wrong, while urging us to shed our differences of color, race, and religion, and unite with God. In 1974, he introduced *dhikr* (then pronounced and spelled *zikr),* the inner declaration and constant remembrance of God: *There is nothing other than You, only You are God; La ilāha, Ill Allāhu.* Travelling between Sri Lanka and the United States, Bawa Muhaiyaddeen ceaselessly instilled the certitude of the Merciful and Compassionate God—the sole Creator, Protector, and Sustainer. Entreating us to acquire God's qualities and to view all lives, all hunger, all suffering and sorrow as our own, he advocated heartfelt worship and charity.

In 1980, as the summer season drew near, we heard rumblings of something new—the fast of Ramadan. We did not know what this had to do with our search for Oneness with God, and so we imbibed Bawa's meticulous, carefully graded instructions and explanations. Many undertook the fast of thirty days with great determination and fortitude, weathering long, unrelentingly hot, humid days without food and water from 3:30 a.m. until 8:30 p.m. Bawa himself, impeccable and aware, monitored the entire proceedings, providing nourishment of every kind throughout the day. To provide nutritious physical sustenance, he personally cooked and served enormous quantities of *khanji*—an eastern stew with grains, nuts, vegetables, and medicinal spices. To provide nourishment for the heart, he tended to individual needs and queries with the utmost love and patience. He nourished the soul through exalted prayers, songs and discourses regarding the nature of God, the nature of man, the significance of the fast, the resistance of the playful mind, and the glorious purity of the path that leads to Oneness—*God-man, man-God.*

Each day, we marvelled at the myriad facets of the *qutb,* our divine teacher who made every day replete. As recorded by an observer:

On the nineteenth day of Ramadan, our father's room quietly filled with his children. At 9:30 a.m., responding to a question about the soul, he used the analogy of choosing between a copper pot and a clay pot in order to illustrate the soul's choices, whether to incline toward God or whether to incline toward the world. "You are sent here complete with God's qualities. Do not waste your lives or forfeit the trust God has in you," he cautioned. In the early afternoon, amidst the flurry of preparing the evening meal, he sang a spontaneous prayer, Those Who Do Not Search For God, Their Minds Will Not Melt.

At 8:15 p.m., just before the time to end the fast, he delivered an exquisite discourse elucidating how the light and revelations of God enter man's soul [See Chapter 3]. An hour later, after he had personally served each individual, he nourished the heart of a child who had patiently waited to request a du'ā', a prayer of supplication worn around the neck. Bawa gently explained to this child that God would grant him the quality of resolute faith, īmān, rather than a material du'ā'.

"What is the best way to get rid of guilt?" asked another child. "To feel guilt is wonderful," Bawa responded. "In the womb we spoke to God. He fed us. We did not kill anyone or eat anyone. We should feel guilty for everything we have done wrong, since coming to this world. Every time we remember what we are guilty of, we should ask forgiveness of God and never do it again. That is the way to get rid of guilt."

As Bawa patiently responded to several further queries, he looked around the room frequently, answering unasked questions with a glance of quiet acknowledgment, a gentle smile that said, Yes! Then, when all hearts were full, each child lovingly paid respects to Bawa and departed for the night. Thus concluded another grace-filled day with our father, our teacher, our friend.

It is impossible to capture the essence of that first Ramadan at the Fellowship House in Philadelphia, a time when seekers of all ages, races, and religions experienced the fast under the guidance of Bawa Muhaiyyadden. When asked by a disciple, Bawa replied, "The significance of Ramadan is to convert you into a real human being." May this book, a compilation of prayers, songs, and discourses from that unique period, guide the reader toward this exalted goal. May Bawa's words resonate within each innermost heart, making it blossom with radiant purity and Truth.

Hussaina

(with grateful borrowing from

Michael Abdul Jabbar Toomey)

How The Words In This Book
May Be Realized

From an explanation by Bawa Muhaiyaddeen

Everything a man of wisdom says has seventy thousand meanings.
At each stage, the appropriate meaning is known.
As wisdom grows and his words are analyzed to a greater extent,
different meanings are understood.
As each connotation is abstracted, the meaning increases in depth.
As one goes further and further inside, a wide open space develops.
This open space will expand and unfold richer understandings.
If a man merely wishes to thrust his head inside,
he will find just enough space to do that.
If he intends to go further within, his body will enter.
If he wishes to go further, his intellect should go inside.
If he wants to delve further, his wisdom should go inside.
If he desires to continue further, his soul should go inside.
As he investigates within and opens up the space, it will seem immense.
If he aspires to go further still, the resplendence of his truth,
the light of his soul, should go inside.
If he persists, he will see the Completeness—the Expanse.
It is a large OPEN SPACE.
If he plunges further within, the complete history
with all its stories will be there for him to understand.
If he delves further still, he will find the *notebook*

that tells him where he came from and who his Father is.
He will be able to read this book.
If he goes further within, he will perceive his Father's Judgment,
God's seat of Justice.
If he searches further within, he will hear the speech of his Father.
If he proceeds further still, he will see the Light of his Father.
If he journeys further, he will know the Secret,
the Mystery of his Father which resplends within him.
When he knows this Mystery, he will realize
that his Father communicates with him on the inside.
He will know the unity, the Oneness,
of the Father within him, and of himself within the Father.
As he goes further, deeper understandings unfold.
Humble men of wisdom can impart such understandings.
The further one goes, the deeper the meaning one attains.

Chapter 1

Balance

July 28, 1980

Faith, certitude, and determination
should dawn;
then the taproot will grow.
The connection to the Sheikh
should remain constant;
wisdom should grow.
The point of discrimination
between right and wrong
should grow;
then it will be easy.
The burden will be light,
the connection will be easy,
and balance can be attained.
You can escape!

Balance

Everything has a limit. The sun has a limit, life has a limit, air has a limit, fire has a limit, hunger has a limit, food has a limit; everything has a limit. If the limit is altered in either direction, if there is too much or too little, there will be an accident. Everything should be done in a balanced manner. That is wisdom.

Whether it is the sexual arts, the sixty-four arts and sciences, or science itself, everything has a limit. Life has a limit. There is a balance. If you exceed that, it will break you. It will break your life, make you wander, and bring you difficulty, sorrow, and illness. The balance must be maintained as you proceed.

Prayer and devotion have a limit and should be pursued precisely in accordance with your growth and development. Proceed with balance in keeping with wisdom. Without wisdom, if you try to reach beyond the limit, something will snap. Everything requires balance. Reflect on this.

I am very old. At different times, in different countries, my age was perceived in different ways. There is no rascal like me in the world. I am the biggest rascal and the youngest one of all. I could change myself and assume a different age. I have changed myself eleven times. This is my twelfth change. After this, the period of destruction could come about. This is my final change.

From my experience, from the aspects I studied, from living through the different ages, I have learned much. I have to bring everything into balance in order to explain these learnings to others. In each period different things needed to be done, and they had to be revealed with balance.

Prayer has a balance.
Balance it according to your own capacity.
Wisdom has a balance consistent with your capacity,
strength, and ability.
Life has a balance consistent with your body and your wisdom.
Sexual joys have a balance.
The sixty-four arts and sciences have a balance.
Science has a balance.
Sight has a balance.
Smell has a balance.
Sound has a balance.
If you exceed this balance, things will break.
Speech has a balance; do not exceed it.
The body has a balance;
it cannot be sustained beyond a certain point.
You have to proceed with balance according to your own capacity.
Balance is the only thing that will not attack you.

Without this balance your mind will be ruined, your eyesight will be lost, your hearing will be impaired, your tongue will blabber because the nerves malfunction, your body will be ruined, and your heart will weaken. You should act with balance according to your own state.

What is your state? What is your balance? What is your life? What are your actions? They should be in balance with each other. Prayer (*vanakkam*), meditation (*thiyānam*), ritual prayers (*tholuhai*), prayer and service performed with a melting heart (*ibādat*), the remembrance of God with every breath (*dhikr*), and the constant contemplation of God (*fikr*) should be done in balance. Sound must be made where sounds must be made. However, if the sound "Huuu" is to be made and instead the sound "Haaa" is made, the balance will be destroyed.

The lion has a particular balance in the sounds it can make. The

4

elephant has a different kind of balance. If you try to trumpet like an elephant, you will die. If you roar like a lion, your heart will burst. God created each creature in a different way: the camel has no bile, the horse has a small lung (īral)[1] and a small heart to enable it to run, and the whale is different in yet another way. Each is created differently for a specific purpose. You should understand each organ of the body. If you understand the four thousand, four hundred and forty-four nerves (narambu),[2] you will understand balance. If you understand the eighty-four kinds of air that dwell within the body, then you can maintain balance. As each air arises, you can balance yourself appropriately. If you understand what exists in the four thousand, four hundred and forty-four nerves you can continue forward with the appropriate balance. Then your breath will flow in keeping with that, and the balance will be accurate. Otherwise, your balance will be lost and a nerve may snap, an artery or vein may burst, and your mind will be ruined.

There are ninety-nine kinds of bile—acid. If you understand which acid flows through which nerve, you can proceed with the appropriate balance. If you deviate from that balance, you will go crazy.

Wisdom disperses in a hundred ways. God's miracles manifest in a hundred ways. That balance [that wisdom] knows what is needed at each time and at each season. It tells you, "At this time this is needed, at that moment that is needed," and so on.

The ocean tides may rise in two and a half hours, and when the winds blow, they recede. In another two and a half hours, the winds may move to the north, and then to the south. You have to proceed with

---

1   **Īral:** This Tamil word is used for all of the following: *lungs, liver, spleen, and other viscera.* A prefix is often used to denote the specific organ (e.g. *ḳal-īral* for *liver*). In this context, however, without a specific prefix, *īral* could refer to any of the organs mentioned above. Trans.

2   **Narambu:** In Tamil, the word *narambu* is used to refer to veins, arteries, nerves, blood vessels, and ducts in the body, which, in Eastern medicine, total 72,000. The author, however, talks about 4,444, or 4,448 *narambu* and it has not been ascertained whether he refers to veins, nerves, or arteries. We have chosen to use the word *nerves* in all such contexts. Trans.

the appropriate balance. You have to move with the tide. If you go against it, it will break you and toss you about. The wind blows in four directions. When water recedes on one side, it swells on the other. And when it swells on the other side, it recedes on this side. The storms, waves, and billows all function in this manner. The blood and the air flow through the body in the same way. Water also flows through the organs like this. You should know the balance, the *point*, and the wisdom. You should understand what is flowing through each part of each nerve and balance yourself accordingly. If you go against the flow, these things will dash against you and hurl you around. Blood, air, fire, water, earth—everything changes course and turns around. If the water is moving in a particular direction, then pay heed to it and move with it. If the water is changing its course because of winds that change every two and a half hours, then you should also change course and move. If you do this, you will be able to maintain balance; otherwise you will be destroyed. This is also an aspect of prayer.

A perfected man, an *Insān Kāmil*, will explain this and teach the Truth, and you should continue onward in accordance with your capacity. You should work toward attaining balance. You should attain that eminent state and know the nerves, the marrow, the two hundred and twelve bones, the forty-eight nerves of the brain, and the nerves of the teeth. You should know how many of these connect to each tooth, where the root is for each tooth, which of these roots are dead, what helps them to function, and how many arteries they have. You have to understand this. You have to know everything about each of the thirty-two teeth. You should know the four segments of the skull. You should know how to position each of these two hundred and forty-eight pieces of bone. If you randomly pull at this and pull at that, it will ruin your balance.

In the inner heart (*qalb*) of man there are 18,000 universes. Within these 18,000 universes, God has placed one single *point* as His Kingdom. In that one *point* He has placed 124,000 prophets, His angels, His archangels, His enlightened beings (*olis*), His divinely wise beings *(qutbs),* His throne *(dhāhuth),* and His judgment. Covering this point are fifteen realms, seven realms below and seven realms above, while in the middle there is a realm which is within that one *point.* The 18,000 universes and the fifteen realms do exist. But what will rule and pass judgment over all these realms is within that one *point,* as an atom within an atom. This wealth of grace *(rahmat),* this grace of God, is placed there as the mysterious morsel of flesh. Within it is Light.

When you attain the state in which you understand all of this, you can act with the necessary balance. You will know how to look at these things. You will know the 18,000 universes, you will know the prophets, the enlightened beings, and the *qutbs.* You will know Allah, His *rahmat,* His throne, His judgment, and His duty. Then you can unite with Him. When you go onward to join Him, you will understand right and wrong, good and evil. Then you can join God's Messenger *(Rasūl)⊕* and the angels. You can unite with the Lord and with His *rahmat.* When you do that, that balance is correct.

Until you reach that state, you should understand what your capacity is, what your intention is, what your prayer is, what your sight is, and what your thoughts are. You should understand what state you are in and what causes you to change. Hunger changes you, illness changes you, disease changes you, pain changes you, ordinary desires change you, base desires *(nafs)* change you, sex changes you, lust changes you, karma changes you, and anger changes you. Therefore, when you are in a state where things can change you, when there are factors that influence and affect you, you should use the balance appropriate to that state. With patience, contentment, trust in God, and complete surrender to God *(sabūr, shakūr, tawakkul,* and *al-hamdu lillāh),* you should balance your life.

Without doing this, if you say, "I am seeing God, I am meditating, I am praying, I am doing the prescribed prayers," it is of no use. What is the point of that? You cannot deviate from balance.

Wisdom is a big ocean. You can copy another's material and speak from it, read a book and speak about it, hear something and speak about it, but this is not wisdom. You should sift through all these things and extract the point. You should go to the other side, connect, and speak to Him. Attain the connection wherein He speaks to you. You see Him, and He sees you. You should attain that balance. Until you attain that balance, you should toil hard, make great effort, work laboriously, and dedicate yourself to God. You should dedicate yourself *(thānam)* to truth and resolute faith *(īmān)*. You should hold on to that resolution *(nithānam)* and maintain that balance. Then you should have total concentration *(avathānam)* and balance. When you go beyond, you will have divine wisdom *(gnānam)*. Only then can you unite and converse with Him.

Without having achieved this state of being,
without this balance,
everything you set out to do will break you.
Your mind will break you,
desire will break you,
lust will break you,
anger will break you,
sex will break you,
sexual games will break you,
maya will break you,
hunger will break you,
and illness will break you.
All these things will break your faith.
Lust will break you,
hatred will break you,
selfishness will break you,
hastiness driven by anger will break you,
treachery will break you,
religion will break you,
race will break you.
They all are weapons that can destroy you.
Since you possess these weapons which can break you, you should understand the balance that is needed to proceed. You should maintain

balance amidst the different kinds of air that flow through the different areas of your body. You should understand how to balance each thing and proceed. Advance without giving in to these things, without getting beaten by them, and without getting caught in them. Such is the balance you must have. Without this balance, whatever you set forth to do will break you. It will destroy your brain and your mind and make you crazy.

I am very old. Using my experience I scrutinize each vein and evaluate its condition—what its function is, how the blood flows through it, at which point the vein has shrunk, and at which point the vein is pressed down. I see that the blood is collecting at a particular point and understand why it hurts. I notice a pricking sensation and much more, but you will not understand this. When I look at the veins, I see many rays, and I observe, "These rays work. These rays do not work. The sun works in this manner. It is related to wisdom and it works like this. This vein relates to desire. This vein functions to create lust and passion. This vein relates to pride. This relates to Satan. This vein relates to gas. This is the vein that relates to earth ties. This relates to ether ties. This connects with maya. This is the vein that serves Satan's anger; it is the vein of treachery. This is the vein of trickery. This is the vein of deceit." You do not understand in which of these the lights, the rays, and the sun function. You should be able to look at them and understand. Until then you should have balance.

When a dog barks, it cries, "Woof, woof, woof." It barks at the dark, it barks at a tree, it barks at a good man, and it barks at a robber. All these things make it bark. Similarly, if your mind and intellect continue to bark, you think, "I am praying, I am going, I am doing this, I am doing my duty." But this is not so. You are doing the same thing as the dog. It does not know what is good and what is evil. It does not understand the *point* and barks at everything because of its hunger.

In the same way, you should realize the *point*. You should know what is right and what is wrong, what is good and what is evil, what is man and what is beast, what is tree and what is shrub. You should know

9

which is shade, which is light, and which is fire. You should understand this and say, "All right, let it come." When a good man comes, you say, "*Anbu*, I greet you with love, come in." To rogues you say, "Go away. You are a rogue," and for Satan, you hold a light in front of him, and he will go away.

In each situation you must know what is to be pushed away, subdued, understood, or studied. If you act without understanding this, there is no use. It will be pointless. Until you come to that final state, you have to maintain balance. When the mind comes and jumps on you, you should find a way to balance it. Leave it alone. Go above it. When water comes to beat against you, observe it coming, balance yourself, rise above it and let it flow by. When the air, the anger, comes to attack you, say, "Oh, it is coming." Quickly leave the branch and hold on to the tree. Let it shake the tree or bend it a little and go away. You should attain that kind of balance with everything. You must understand. This is why you have been given wisdom. This is why you are shown balance. This is why you are given explanations. This is why you are made to understand.

However, your *īmān* is not strong. Your foundation is not strong. You still declare, "I," "I." If your taproot is not strong, you will fall. When your taproot is not strong, what then is your foundation? Your foundation is the secondary roots, the support roots. The taproot of *īmān*, certitude, determination, and Allah is not present. What you have instead are the support roots provided by the mind. Therefore, hunger will come and knock you down. Gales will come and toss you about. Lust will come and roll you around. Passion will come and roll you around. Money will come and toss you around. Titles will come and hurl you about. The "I" will come and heave you around. Like this, many magnificent things will come. You could think, "I am a guru," and that will hurl you around. You could think, "I am a sheikh," and that will toss you about. Everything will come to knock you down. Wealth, praise, titles: these are all things that come and toss you around. They are all secondary roots that will be uprooted by one big storm.

Therefore, you cannot stay in balance.

At this time, you do not have the correct taproot that is absolutely firm and unshakable. Your taproot has not taken hold as yet. The *supreme* root has not yet been established. The support roots exist, but not the *supreme* root. Your thoughts exclaim, "I am studying, I am praying, I am doing prescribed prayers, I do this, I do that, I have desire, I have attachment." This is all that you are doing. These are your support roots. They are of no use. They have no *point*. The *supreme* root has not yet developed. When this *supreme* root takes hold, it will support you. You will be able to bend in different directions whenever different breezes blow. When the wind blows from one direction, you can quickly bend to the other side, and when the wind blows from the other direction, you can bend the other way.

I am telling you about all these things so that you can begin to develop your taproot, so that you may not fall down when different things approach you. You have not firmly planted your taproot. It has developed very little. The support roots, however, have grown a lot. The mind, desires, thoughts, and intentions have spread and taken hold, but the tap root is only two inches to one foot long. Thoughts have taken hold, but the correct taproot, the *supreme* root, has not taken hold. When it does, you will be able to balance. You will be able to bend and let the winds blow by without getting caught or entangled. In this way, you will be able to evade sorrow, hunger, and illness. The tap root will show you the balance. As each thing comes along, the tap root will enable you to be flexible and escape. This state will dawn in you. However, your taproot has not yet taken hold. For ten years now I have been shouting here so that the taproot can take hold. I have been trying to embed this taproot. But if you gain personal fame and begin to discriminate, saying, "I" and "You," you will be hurled around. As soon as the "I" arises, it will knock you over. When you think, "I am a guru," or, "I am a sheikh," you will be hurled around. When you think, "I am learned," you will be tumbled down. Money, learning, titles, lust, desire, and praise will all toss you down. All these things will knock you down. Then you have no balance, no root.

11

You will fall down on the ground. You will not be able to stand upright, so you will fall on the earth. You need balance. You should check on this and develop that root. Each child should do this.

Religions will knock you down, caste will knock you down, and color will knock you down. Thoughts of "my family," "my wealth," "my freedom," "my wife," and "my child" will hurl you around and separate you from others. You should think about this. Contemplate what I am telling you. Faith must develop; the *supreme* root must grow. Only then will our desires be controlled. Thank you. Reflect on this and act accordingly. Do you understand?

When wisdom dawns it will be easy.
Until wisdom dawns, it will be difficult.
Faith, certitude, and determination should dawn;
then the taproot will grow.
The connection to the Sheikh should remain constant;
wisdom should grow.
The *point* of discrimination between right and wrong should grow;
then it will be easy.
The burden will be light, the connection will be easy,
and balance can be attained.
You can escape!

I am a big rascal, a clever rogue. Depending on how you come to me, I will have to give you what you want and escape. If you say, "I want this," I will give it to you and escape. Then when you go and experience suffering, I will say, "That's fine," and escape. I will try to explain things to you, but if you insist that you are right, I will say, "All right, go ahead." Then I have to watch you being tossed about, but I will escape. If you hold on firmly to what I give you, if you hold on to me, then I have to take you with me. But if you say, "I," you will separate yourself. Then I will say, "All right, go, and come back." But if you have fastened yourself to me, I will have to drag you along with me. If you have not latched on, that is fine; the burden is less, and I will say, "Good, go, and come back." *Anbu*—love.

12

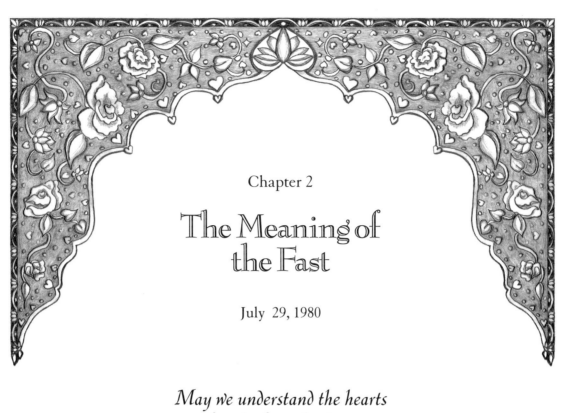

Chapter 2

The Meaning of the Fast

July 29, 1980

May we understand the hearts
of each of our brethren,
understand their
hunger, illness, old age, and death,
and realize their need for
food, clothing, and shelter.
And because they live with us,
bringing them peace
will be the benefit
and the fast.

The Meaning of the Fast

O God!
Through Your benevolence
You have given us Your sustenance and grace (*rahmat*).[1]
Please grant us the intention and yearning
to accept these gifts and live our lives.
Please give us the intention
to offer prayers and service
with a melting heart.

O Grace of all universes!
Please give us
the resolute faith *(īmān),* certainty, and conviction
to accept what You have given
and live our lives.

Even for those who do not do this,
for all those who do not live their lives
trusting You,
O Father, You have amplified Your sustenance,
making it equal
and common to all.

---

1. **Rahmat:** God's grace, mercy, compassion, benevolence—His wealth. Everything in God is *rahmat*. This grace that He bestows is an undiminishing, limitless wealth.

You have created
the world,
Your grace,
and everything
to belong to all.
And You have made man to be the most exalted.
You created him and gave him
Your wisdom,
Your qualities,
and Your grace,
so that he may
live in equanimity, peace, and serenity,
show compassion and love to all lives,
and regard all lives as his own.

But for those who have forgotten Your words,
You have sent down this fast
to help them understand.
You have instituted the five duties
and shown these to be important
through the *Rasūl*,[2]
may the peace and blessings of God be upon him.

This fast
will
bring realization to each heart.
This is why
You made it thrive.
The fast has been here
for two hundred million years,
from the time of Adam ☺ until the present.

---

2. **Rasūl:** The prophet Muhammad ☺.

Your words taught the children of Adam ﷺ,
who are true human beings.
You taught them gradually,
one thing at a time.
But
because they forgot,
lost their equanimity,
did not consider other lives as their own,
and focused on their own bodies and their own hunger
without realizing the hunger of others,
You instituted the five tasks of *Īmān-Islām*.[3]

You handed them to the *Rasūl* ﷺ
as divinely ordained duties *(fards),*
so that man would do what was instituted,
so that he would grow,
realize,
attain clarity,
and make Allah's common wealth
common to all.

You have said that everything,
the earth, fire, water, air, and ether,
the sun, moon, stars, grass, and shrubs,
should belong to all.
You have decreed that each
should be given the sustenance that is his.
But the wealth that You spread out for everyone

---

3. **Īmān-Islām:** A state wherein the pure heart, cutting away all evil, takes on the courageous determination called faith and shines in God's resplendence. When the resplendence of God is seen as the completeness within the heart of man, that is *Īmān-Islām*.

was not disbursed in this way.

Man appropriated this wealth
and made it
his own.
He fell subject to selfishness,
took what belonged
to all lives,
and created scarcity today.

For man to realize what he had done,
You, O God, said,
"O Muhammad, make man realize,
make these into ordained duties,
make them understand these five tasks."
Allah
taught this with His divine grace.

Allah declared,
"These will be the tasks which are the ordained duties.
This common wealth will be made common to all lives.
These are the duties
that will show all lives
how to share the common wealth."

The first duty is to believe in *Allāhu ta'ālā,*
the Singular God who rules and sustains.
Believe in Him and live.
Have faith in Him.
Have certainty and worship Him.
Realize that He has no form or shape
and cannot be contained by anything.
He has no hunger or illness,

no old age or death,
no wife or child,
no house or property,
no wealth or possessions,
no titles, no passion,
no sex or sexual games,
no birth or death.
He existed before the primal beginning.
Know that He is the Supreme Being,
and have faith and certitude in Him.
Know that His wealth is given
equally
to all.
"I have created the nourishment for each life.
Offer prayers and worship
to Me alone."
This is what He decreed.

"I worship him who worships Me.
I think of him who thinks of Me.
I seek him who seeks Me.
I believe in him who believes in Me.
I speak to him who speaks to Me.
If he calls Me once, I call him ten times.
If he cries once, I cry for him ten times."
Thus declared Allah with His words of grace.

He said this to the prophet *Muhammad Mustafa Rasūl,*
may the peace and blessings of God be upon him.
He declared this and instituted the five duties.
The first duty is believing in God.
The second is praying to God
and believing that all things belong to Him.

God decreed this so that everyone may live in
equality,
peace,
and equanimity.

Because man did not realize this,
God introduced another duty,
the third duty of charity.
"Realize this,
and share the wealth you have gathered
with everyone.
Live in equality, everyone!
Live in peace, everyone!
Live as one life, everyone!
Realize the hunger of all lives and serve."
Thus declared Allah.

But once again man forgot.
He claimed things for himself
and created difficulties for everyone.
He caused sorrow and poverty.
He seized land,
took away homes and property,
and made others destitute.

Thereupon, God spoke His divine words of grace:
"Ya Muhammad,
tell the people to fast,
and through this,
make them realize the difficulties of others.
Through the fast,
they will understand their own difficulties,
and realize how they lose strength and courage.

Within a month and ten days,
within these forty days,
they will experience how their bodies change,
lose strength,
and become fatigued.
Upon perceiving this,
may they realize the immense suffering
of those who face this all year round.
Make them realize this.

Make them realize the sorrow and hardship
of those who face hunger and starvation,
year after year,
with no place to live,
no house,
no land.
Make them perceive this suffering through the fast,
and tell them to give others a place to live.
Make them understand the hunger of others
and distribute food.
Make them give unto others house, land, and clothing
similar to their own.
May each life be given what is rightfully its own.
O Muhammad, tell them this," God declared.

But for those whose hearts
had stayed as stone,
God further stated,
"Make them fulfill the fifth duty of pilgrimage, *Hajj*.
Hajj is
to die before death,
to distribute property to wife and children,
to give their extra wealth to others,

to distribute wealth to the poor,
to mendicants, and to travellers.
And after distributing all wealth, they should
come to the holy places of Mecca and Medina
as corpses, while still alive.

"To fulfill the *Hajj,*
tell man to wear death garb.
Let him put the world to death
while he is still alive.
May he do this
and attain the state
of eternal life with Me.
Make him fulfill this fifth duty."
This is what Allah declared
with His words of grace.

These are the five ordained duties.
The fasting we do is one among them.
As long as the benefits of fasting
are not understood,
it will be of no use to fast.
Therefore, understand what the fast means,
and give in charity.
Understand what others need, and give accordingly.
Give peace and tranquillity to others.
Comprehend the hunger of others and help them.
Donate clothing to others.
Comfort other lives as your own.
Bring others peace.
Have patience and tolerance,
and shower others with compassion and love.
This is the significance and benefit of the fast.

However,
being hungry for a month
is not a fast
if we take away
others' property and freedom,
intending to accumulate
more for ourselves.
Because such acts cause others pain,
the fast will not benefit anyone.
All lives must think about this
and give unto others
food, sustenance, house, and land.
We must alleviate the hunger of others,
comfort them,
give them clothing,
and make them peaceful.
This will be the reward of the fast.

Allāhu taʿālā,
the Singular One who rules and sustains,
declared fasting to be the fourth duty.
It was instituted as such on
the path of purity *(dīnul-Islām).*
"These are the
five outer duties of Islam—
important duties,"
God instructed.

My precious jeweled lights of my eyes,
may we understand the benefits of this fast.
May we understand
the qualities, actions, and wealth of God,
the Supreme One.

May we understand the qualities and hunger
of our brethren—those born with us,
and our neighbors.
May we consider our neighbors
as those born with us,
and may we comprehend
their garb and their countenance.
May we bestow peace
and show them the way to equanimity.
These are the benefits of the fast.

Each of you should act
in keeping with these benefits.
To attain the rewards of this practice,
the fast was decreed.
The significance of this fast is its worth.
Its worth is your paradise.
To live in this manner is exalted.
To fast in any other way
will not be beneficial.
To understand this is to fast.
To realize this and act accordingly is to fast.
May we establish this state, and live.
May we understand the hearts
of each of our brethren,
understand their
hunger, illness, old age, and death,
and realize their need for
food, clothing, and shelter.
And because they live with us,
bringing them peace
will be the benefit
and the fast.

Reflect on this,
my precious jeweled lights of my eyes.
Each child, understand and fast.
Understand the reasons for fasting.
Know its truth,
obligations,
and benefits,
and strive to do it in this way.
Understand how to care for your brethren,
and do your duty.

God said,
"O Muhammad!
When I create a tree,
from each of its seeds
I will create a thousand fruits.
To create the fruits,
I will give the tree My grace.
And even if the tree takes the grace for itself,
it gives fruits to all,
without benefit to itself.
In the same way,
I give man the ability to give to a thousand men,
each giving according to his own heart.
If one intends to help others,
I will place the wealth of My grace *(barakat)*[4]
in his hands,
just as I give *barakat* to the tree.
One who is man can distribute it.

---

4. **Barakat:** The primary meaning of *barakat* is grace—a blessing or spiritual in-
    fluence which God sends down. *Barakat* may be found in persons, places, and
    things. Certain actions may also be a vehicle for blessings and God's grace. Trans.

Giving to others
as the tree gives
and making others peaceful,
will be the benefit.
This is the wealth of grace,
the *barakat,* that I give to each life.
I created man, I endowed him,
so he could give to all other lives.

O mankind!
You must understand what I give you.
Through one tree, I give fruits to so many.
In the same way,
through
one
man,
through the *barakat* that I give him,
I can help so many.
Sharing this *barakat* with others
will be the ordained duty.
In all three worlds,
this will be his happiness and wealth.
Man must realize this.

One by one,
each man must understand.
I create a thousand seeds from one seed.
A thousand seeds change into millions of seeds
and help mankind.
They do not claim any portion for themselves
but continue to benefit others, do they not?
Similarly, I have made
one

among every hundred men
to be in that state.
I have given him wealth to share with others,
so that he may look upon others with peace
and bring them
peace and tranquillity.

For every ten million men,
I sent down a prophet to the world.
Through these prophets,
the darkness of man's mind can be cleared.
I sent them to bring peace, did I not?
In the same way,
I have created and placed in the world,
a man,
one in every hundred,
one in every thousand,
or one in every ten million.
And through him I spread
My limitless
wealth of grace,
My *rahmat*.
If he understands My *rahmat*
and does not claim it as his own,
if he gives it to others,
that will be his earnings.
If he does that, I will exalt him.
I will unite with him in paradise.
I will give him a place in My kingdom.
However, if he uses My wealth for himself alone,
that very wealth will result in his attaining hell.
The desires and attachments he fosters will devour him.
That will be the fire of hell."

Thus spoke God.

Therefore,
the sustenance and *barakat*
given to us by the Merciful One
should be shared with others.
Understanding the hunger of others
and helping them,
comprehending their countenance
and sharing with them,
making them peaceful
and comforting them—
this will be our wealth in the three worlds.
It will be the earnings of our prayers.
It will be the exaltedness of our state.
We must trust God,
trust that He will reward our faith
by granting us His grace,
and bestowing on us
the Supreme Treasure of the three worlds.

Each child must think of this.
Understand the duties
you need to accomplish
in the days of your life.
Realize the ordained duties,
the principle and the explanation,
and accomplish them.
Before death and birth come along,
we should realize this
and live accordingly.
We have been born,
and one day death will arrive.

May we understand this before death approaches,
and end earthly attachments.
May we extinguish them before we die
and attain the eternal life of God.
May we attain His qualities and actions
and live eternally.

To keep hell far away from us
in this world and the next,
to make this world into heaven
and the hereafter into heaven,
we should try to dwell in His qualities.
We should strive courageously to do this.
This is resolute faith, *īmān*.

This *īmān*
knows that
all mankind are children of Adam ☺,
one tribe,
one God.
We are one family.
There is but one paradise.
There is but one society of mankind.
Judgment is the same for all.
The Doer is One,
The Questioner is One,
The Creator is One,
The Summoner is One,
The Giver of life is also that very same One.
But
it is we who have created the differences
by using colors, hues, languages, and races.
We have also created religions.

But in truth,
there is only one family,
only one God,
and only one abode that is paradise.

Each of us must reflect on this,
understand,
and seek to live in unity
as one family.
To live in this world as messengers of God,
to live as God's sons in His kingdom,
to attain the qualities and actions
that govern His kingdom,
to be children who have *īmān*,
to become God's children,
we must do His duties,
make the effort to reach the shore,
and search with wisdom.
That will bear good results.

We should search
for the house
that God, our Lord, bestows,
the paradise *(firdaus)* He bestows,
and the heaven He bestows.
We should search for these and attain them here.
This is the victory of our birth—
to receive in this world
the Supreme Treasure of the three worlds.
You must realize and achieve this.
This will be the value of the fast,
the value of the five duties,
and the value of birth.

This is the wealth of great worth,
the wealth that is beneficial.

Each of my children,
live in this way.
Try hard,
realize with faith,
and act accordingly.

My precious jeweled lights of my eyes,
this will be the imperishable treasure
of the three worlds.
This will be the exaltedness of life.
You will be a helper to all lives
and bring peace to all lives.
All lives will bow down and worship you.
This is the state of true man,
the exaltedness of man.
You will receive the wealth of grace.
You will have good virtues and modesty.
It will be good to strive hard and search for this.
This is an exalted state.
This is the exalted wealth of the three worlds.
These are sublime qualities.
This is exalted wisdom.
You will be known as the eminent son
who received the power of Allah's grace.

Each child,
strive hard to achieve this.
Act with faith,
perform your duties with faith,
and before you die,

seek
the imperishable wealth of the three worlds.
Āmīn, Āmīn, Yā Rabbal-'ālamīn.
So be it, so be it,
O Lord of the universes.

All praise is to You,
O Lord of the universes.
Please bestow on My children
that grace,
that wealth,
that explanation,
that peace,
that tranquillity,
and a subtle inner heart.
Āmīn.

Forgive their sins,
bestow grace and wisdom on them,
transform their hearts into paradise,
and so grace them.
Transform their hearts into light,
and so grace them.
Make their hearts have faith
only in Your imperishable wealth,
the Treasure of the three worlds,
and so grace them.
Āmīn.

Reside within their inner hearts,
resonate,
provide explanations from within,
lead them on the good way,

and so grace them.
Lead them on the straight way,
support them,
embrace them to Your breast
and feed them with the milk of grace and honey.
Nourish them
with immeasurable sweet tasting fruits:
fruits of love,
fruits of grace,
and fruits of wisdom.
Give them undiminishing sweet tastes
by bestowing on them
Your sweet tasting treasure,
divine grace-wisdom *(arul gnānam)*,
making them peaceful and tranquil.
Please give them the grace
to understand and serve all lives
as You do.

Āmīn, Āmīn, Yā Rabbal-'ālamīn.
So be it, O Lord of the universes.

May the peace, the beneficence, and the blessings of God
be upon you.
Āmīn.

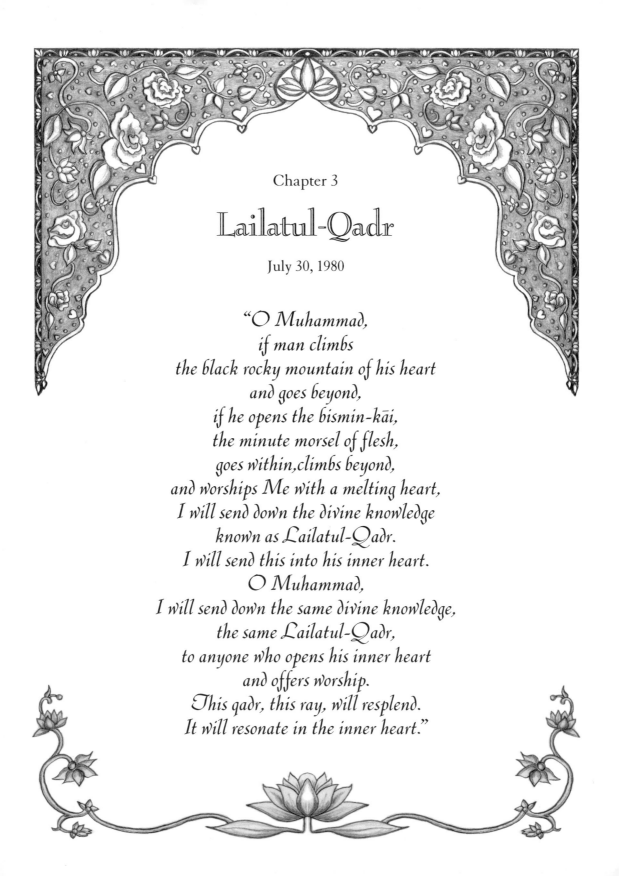

Chapter 3

Lailatul-Qadr

July 30, 1980

"O Muhammad,
if man climbs
the black rocky mountain of his heart
and goes beyond,
if he opens the bismin-kāi,
the minute morsel of flesh,
goes within, climbs beyond,
and worships Me with a melting heart,
I will send down the divine knowledge
known as Lailatul-Qadr.
I will send this into his inner heart.
O Muhammad,
I will send down the same divine knowledge,
the same Lailatul-Qadr,
to anyone who opens his inner heart
and offers worship.
This qadr, this ray, will resplend.
It will resonate in the inner heart."

Lailatul-Qadr

Bismillāhir-Rahmānir-Rahīm.
In the Name of God, most Merciful, most Compassionate.

Allah!
Creator who gave us integrity!
Bestower of tranquillity and peace!
Allah,
Giver of true sustenance *(rizq)*
and grace *(rahmat).*
Within man You placed everything
of this world and the world of souls:
the throne of God *('arsh),*
the gnostic eye *(kursī),*
the pen *(qalam),*
heaven,
and the preserved tablet
(al-lauhul-mahfūz),
which is destiny.

One who is Lord,
You gave us everything:
You gave us completeness,
long life, and death.
Allah,

You are the One who made us complete.
You gave us every wealth,
You gave us Your *rahmat*
and the supreme treasure of the three worlds.
In making us human,
You have given us greatness, glory, and wisdom.
Allāhu ta'ālā,
the Singular One who rules and sustains,
You gave us
the certitude, the reverence,
and the resolute faith *(īmān)*
to worship You.

Allah, Bestower of all gifts,
You are the One
who gave us
a life without death
and a life with death.
You gave us a perfect heaven,
an imperfect body,
and an imperfect hell.
You gave us resplendent wisdom and *īmān*.
You also gave us the darkness of ignorance and desire.
You gave us undiminishing wealth,
the grace-wealth of all the universes,
the *Rahmatul-'ālamīn*.

You gave us this most perfect wealth of
faith,
conviction,
inner patience *(sabūr)*,
contentment *(shakūr)*,
trust in God *(tawakkul)*,

and total surrender to God *(al-hamdu lillāh).*
You gave us this wealth which brings contentment.
You gave us this fortune of grace
and made us complete.

You gave us
the imperfect world
and its hypnotic fascinations.
You gave us ignorant desire and attachments.
You gave us the darkness
of sensory enticements
that bring about
bold, restless, base desires
with their connections
to the world.

You also gave us
the light of love and grace.
You gave us this perfection.

O Giver of all things,
Allāhu,
Lord of all universes,
we have abandoned Your gifts of perfection,
and joyously desiring things that are imperfect,
we walk on the path of destruction.
We follow our minds and desires,
let go of completeness,
and reach out to death.
We follow our base desires and roam the world,
falling prey to sensory enticements,
the darkness of illusion, torpor, lust, anger, and hatred.

Allāhu,
please protect us
who walk the path of evil.
Please destroy arrogance, karma, and maya.
Help us to walk the straight path and bring us peace.
Destroy our fecal arrogance.
Destroy our differences
and lead us on harmonious paths of peace.

Enable us to do charity and to fast.
Give us the faith, the prayer,
and the proper way to pray to You.
Charity, fasting, and the pilgrimage of Hajj—
these duties will be realized by
wisdom, feeling, faith, and awareness,
by actions that realize You,
and by the wisdom that trusts others
as one trusts oneself.
Since the fast
is suitable for
and will be understood by
feeling, awareness, and intellect,
[the first three wisdoms]
this fast was revealed
to the *Rasūl;*
may peace and blessings be upon him.

God revealed the fullness and reverence of this faith
to the *Rasūl* ☙
and said,
"O Muhammad, make your followers understand this.
Tell them to do this task, this ordained duty.
For those who have declared the affirmation of faith *(kalimah),*

and have resolute faith,
this will be an ordained duty.
For those who realize this,
and for those who know Me,
this will be *rahmat.*
If man understands and fulfills this,
if he understands
and does his duty to all lives,
I will give him My wealth,
I will give him My grace,
I will give him the perfection of *īmān*—
the *rahmat* of all the universes.

If man lives like Me,
with unity, tolerance, and equanimity,
this will be the greatest of fasts.
It will be *rahmat.*
It will be the attainment of My throne.
It will be the attainment of union with Me *(ākhir)*.
An undiminishing wealth!
Paradise!
A treasure that will bring happiness!

O Muhammad,
understand, and ask your followers to do this.
Direct them on the straight path of divine knowledge *('ilm)*.
Tell them to study the divine knowledge that is My *rahmat.*
Make them understand this mysterious divine knowledge.
It will make them silent
and patient with everyone.
And when man understands himself through divine knowledge,
he will know himself
and Me.

Make them understand the Wisdom within wisdom.
Make them understand Resolute Faith within resolute faith.
Make them understand Worship within worship and perform it.
Make them understand Charity within charity and do it.
Make them understand the Fast within fasting and accomplish it.
Through divine knowledge,
make them think about the Pilgrimage within the pilgrimage,
the *Hajj* within the *hajj*,
and undertake this task with understanding.
Make them understand the True Man within man.
Make them realize the One who exists as
Perfection within perfected man *(insān kāmil)*.
Make them understand and realize
the Resplendence within Perfection, the *Qutb*,
Make them understand the one who is the *Qutb* within the *qutb*.
Make them realize the Resplendent Perfection
who is the *Nūr* within the *Nūr*.
Make them realize
Allah,
the Treasure
within the *Nūr*.

One who understands
the *rahmat,*
that all of everything
is contained in Allah,
will be one of pure faith, a *mu'min.*
This one of pure faith
will be perfected man,
the resplendence of absolute faith
(dīnul-Islām).
He will never see hell,

never see death.
He will have received
the *rahmat* of eternal life.
He will live
with the compassion
that is life to all lives.
With the name *'Abdullāh,*
he will be a slave to God
and serve Him.
Once he realizes
the proper ways of *īmān,*
he will need none other;
he will remain as God's slave.
Make them realize this state.

When man realizes and looks within,
I will be the *Rahmat.*
If he understands true man,
I will be the True Man within man—
the *Insān* within *insān.*
I will be the Perfection
within perfected man—
the *Kāmil* in *insān kāmil.*
I will be Divine Knowledge
within divine knowledge,
I will be Resolute Faith within resolute faith,
I will be Charity within charity,
I will be the Fast within the fast,
I will be the Pilgrimage within the pilgrimage, and
I will be the Affirmation within the affirmation of faith—
the *Kalimah* within the *kalimah.*
I will be Worship within worship,
I will be experienced as Belief within belief.

I will also be the Eye within the eye,
I will be Wealth within wealth, and
I will be the Light within the Light of God—
the *Nūr* within the *Nūr*.
I will be the Inner Heart within the inner heart,
I will be the Resplendent One within divine knowledge,
I will be the *Qutb* within the *qutb*,
I will be Allah within the *Nūr*,
and as Allah within Allah,
I will serve
and be known as
the *Rahmat* of all universes.
O Muhammad, make your followers understand this.

To those
who have wisdom,
those who have *īmān*,
those who have certitude,
and those who have become slaves,
tell them this, and explain it to them.
And even those who do not comprehend this,
tell them to do the five ordained duties
and attain understanding.
Preach wisdom to them,
and through wisdom,
make them understand."

Furthermore,
God, the Singular One who rules and sustains,
gave these explanations (*ahādith*)—
these words that will be known
as the inner meanings of the Qur'an
and as words of divine knowledge—

to the *Rasūl,*
may peace be upon him.
He explained the meanings of the fast
to the *Rasūl* ☻,
saying, "O Muhammad,
even as I sent down the first *sūrat*[1]
to you on Mount Hira,
I sent down this light and *rahmat.*
I sent it to you as *Lailatul-Qadr.*
When I sent it to you that day,
the first light which descended
embedded itself
in your inner heart.
I sent down the light known as
Lailatul-Qadr
and kept your inner heart open.
I made the heart of an *ummī*
into a heart of *'ilm*—
the heart of an unlettered one
into a heart with sacred knowledge.
I made it into *rahmat.*
I made it remember.
I made it into light.
I made it so that
you
would be understood.

And to you
I revealed

---

1. **Sūrat :** A word used for *chapters in the Qur'an*, of which there are 114. It is also used by the author to refer to the *form of man*. The first *sūrat* revealed to Muhammad ☻ was the *sūratul 'alaq*. Trans.

the *rahmat* that is *Allāhu*
as the light,
the *Lailatul-Qadr*.
I fed this light to your inner heart.
O Muhammad,
if man climbs the black rocky mountain of his heart
and goes beyond,
if he opens the *bismin-k̲ai,*
the minute morsel of flesh,
goes within,
climbs beyond,
and worships Me with a melting heart,
I will send down the divine knowledge
known as *Lailatul-Qadr.*
I will send this into his inner heart.
O Muhammad,
I will send down the same divine knowledge,
the same *Lailatul-Qadr,*
to anyone who opens his melted inner heart
and offers worship.
This *qadr*, this ray, will resplend.
It will resonate in the inner heart.

I made the angel Gabriel hold you tight, three times.
Then after you had crushed the three desires,
earth, woman, and gold,[2]
after you had crushed arrogance, karma, and maya,
desire, anger, sin, and hell,

---

2. **Earth, woman, and gold:** In eastern spiritual thought, the full spectrum of sensory desire is summarized in the phrase earth, woman, and gold. Each word symbolizes a fundamental aspect of desire. Earth refers to the craving for land and power, woman refers to the pursuit of sexual fulfillment, and gold refers to the greed for material wealth. Trans.

after you had crushed all these black stones
that arise from the bile,
I sent down the light known as *Qadr.*
I made it descend and embed itself in your inner heart.
That day, that first time,
I sent the light, I sent the Qur'an.
All the lights I sent down to you after that
were like rays of splendor to your inner heart.
Every sentence and every word was a ray of light.
All these rays were the *Lailatul-Qadr.*
The Light known as *Nūr Muhammad*
accepted each meaning I sent down
and made it its own.

Once established,
it is revealed on the outside
as the *Thiru Qur'an,*
and as the inner Qur'an,
the *Thiru-Marai.*
When it emerges,
each light
is a ray,
a *qadr.*
The ray is the soul.
The soul is light.
The light is *rahmat.*
The *rahmat* is fullness.
This fullness is the light of *īmān,*
which is resplendent.
This resplendence is the *dīn,* the light of purity.
This light of purity is the Life of life, the *Hayāt.*
This *Hayāt* is mysterious.
And I, as the Mystery within the mystery,

will be the One who bestows on all lives
the *rahmat* of
Bismillāhir-Rahmānir-Rahīm—
the limitless grace of
God, most Merciful, most Compassionate.

O Muhammad,
explain the meaning of *īmān* to your followers,
give them divine knowledge,
open their inner hearts,
and break down the rocks of darkness,
the black rocks of sensory enticements.
Break down
earth,
fire,
arrogance,
karma,
maya,
anger,
lust,
selfishness,
pride,
and jealousy.
When man breaks down these black rocks
and crushes them with his wisdom,
when man breaks the hard rocks
with the light of *lām (Nūr)*,
the form of *mīm* that comes into being
will be
Muhammad.

When this *sūrat*, this form of Muhammad,
comes into being,

48

when this state dawns,
worship with a melting heart will grow.
When this worship begins to thrive,
the first *sūrat*
will dawn in his inner heart
as *Lailatul-Qadr.*

When man becomes one of pure faith
and one whose heart is filled
with the resplendence of God *(Īmān-Islām),*
his heart, *aham*, will open.
When all the darkness is destroyed,
the light known as
Ahamad will dawn.
This light will imbibe each word spoken by Me.
When the words are absorbed
and then revealed,
they will be
the power of My attributes, My *wilāyat.*
They will be the *Asmā'ul-Husnā* of the Qur'an,
the ninety-nine *wilāyat.*

One
who has
propriety,
good conduct,
modesty,
good qualities,
patience,
inner patience,
contentment,
trust in God,
total surrender to God,

and the righteousness,
certitude, and completeness of *īmān,*
one who becomes a light within this
and acts with My actions
is
my slave.
He is one of pure faith,
and he is Muhammad.
He is the light, and the Light of God—
Nūr.
He will be *rahmat,*
He will be My wealth of patience,
He will practice patience.

O Muhammad!
Say this
to those who come with *īmān,*
seeking to realize Me.
Of the ordained duties and everything I revealed to you,
the first thing I sent down was the light,
the *Lailatul-Qadr.*
When your followers reach this state,
My words, My explanations *(ahadīth),* and the letters of the Qur'an
will be like souls *(rūh)* and rays of light.
Life will be perfection.
It will be *rahmat.*

He who understands this will be one of pure faith.
He will be *īmān.*
He will be perfected man.
He will be *qutb.*
He will be *Nūr.*
He will be *Nūr Muhammad.*

He will have received Allah's *rahmat*
by being Allah's slave.
When he receives My *rahmat*
he will understand My divine knowledge *('ilm).*
His inner heart will be ever resplendent.
His heart and face
will have the beauty
of having seen Me.
He will do My duty.
O Muhammad,
tell your followers this.

Tell them this,
show them
the explanations of divine knowledge,
and make them realize.
Make them follow this path of wisdom and reach Me.
Through determination, certitude, and patience, make them see Me.
Only then will man achieve good results.
Only then will he understand this fast."
Thus spoke God
to the *Rasūl;*
may the peace of God be upon him.

May all of us understand this.
May we understand
faith, worship, *īmān,*
prayer, charity, fasting,
and the pilgrimage of Hajj.
When we understand
the five outer duties
and the inner duties
and establish resolute faith,

we will become
Muhammad.
Then, when we come out of the cave
and perform prayers with a melting heart,
the light known as *Lailatul-Qadr* will descend.

When this resplendent *īmān*
and *sūrat* are sent down,
the three desires will have been broken down,
and the religions will have been destroyed.
Our inner heart
will be filled
with divine knowledge
and we will be
ummī,
forgetting everything
but replete with Allah's divine knowledge.
Only God's qualities, His divine knowledge, and His words
will be absorbed by the inner heart.
And when they are revealed on the outside,
they will be words of life.
They will be light.
We must understand this divine knowledge,
this *'ilm*.

My brothers and sisters,
children born with me,
Allāhu taʿālānayan,
the Singular One, who rules and sustains,
bestowed this *rahmat* on the *Rasūl* ☺.
In many ways,
in the *ahadīth*
and the Qur'an,

He has placed
His divine knowledge *('ilm)*
as an inner mystery
and has provided the explanations.
We should understand this
and
worship Allah inwardly.
If we do,
we can attain the treasure and *rahmat*.
We will receive that *rahmat*.
Each child must use insight.
We must search for wisdom.
We must study *'ilm* inwardly.
Āmīn,
O Lord of the universes.

Please bestow on us
Your benevolence and Your *rahmat*,
and so grace us.
Please fill these children
with resolute faith.
Please keep open the hearts
of each of my children.
Please keep darkness away from their inner hearts.
Break down the black rocks of darkness and delusion.
Send down the light of *Lailatul-Qadr*
into their inner hearts.

O Allah!
Please give them the intention to worship
on Your path
and offer prayers with a melting heart,
and so grace them.

Āmīn,
O Lord of the universes.
May the peace, the beneficence, and the blessings of God
be upon you.
Go and fulfill your fast.

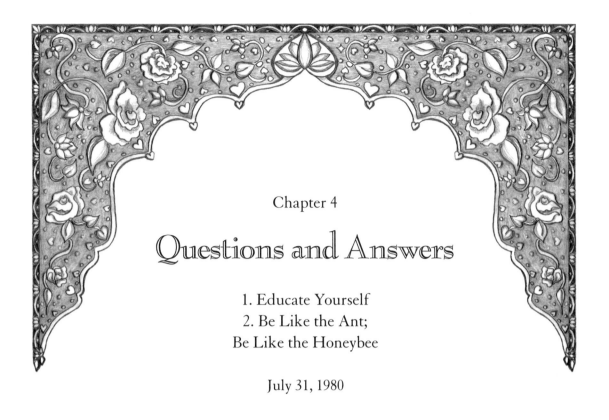

Chapter 4

Questions and Answers

1. Educate Yourself
2. Be Like the Ant;
Be Like the Honeybee

July 31, 1980

*The honeybee scents the honey
and comes directly toward it.
It does not loiter.
It takes the honey and returns to its own locale.
A wise person should do the same.*

Educate Yourself

Question: The last time I was here, I told you about a book I was illustrating. I want to know whether it would be smart to go to different publishers, or whether I should try to publish it myself?

Bawa Muhaiyaddeen: It is only when you hand your wisdom and your research to another person that he will be able to examine it carefully. His wisdom will reflect upon your wisdom, and if the work you have done is something that the world will accept, he will accept your work. Then you can investigate further and do accurate, advanced research.

However, if the man does not accept your work, that's all right. One way to look at the situation is that you should study further and deepen your knowledge. There is also another way to look at the same situation. A dancer, for example, practices his dancing at home. He stands in front of a mirror, dancing away the hours. And as he dances, he praises his own dancing, applauds himself, and continues to dance. But instead of praising himself, the dancer should try dancing on the street. By doing this, he can observe how people respond to his dancing. If his dancing is appreciated, then it may be worthwhile for him to study and practice further. Dancing on one's own and praising one's self is the wisdom of a fool. It is foolhardiness.

In the same way, you have now written a book for others to read, and that is fine. However, if you try to publish your book, you will change into a book-seller. You will have to change into a book-seller. Then your learning will end, your work will end, and your patience will dwindle. You will become proud and arrogant. You will begin to think, "I am a learned one. I am a writer of books," and you will descend to a very low state. You should, therefore, give this up.

The world is teaching you now, but you should be trying to teach the world.

The world is teaching you,
your eyes teach you,
your ears teach you,
your nose teaches you,
your mouth teaches you,
your monkey mind teaches you,
the dog of desire teaches you,
hunger teaches you,
your body teaches you,
illness teaches you,
blood, skin, flesh—everything teaches you.

However, the day you begin to teach them, is the day you begin to learn. Then you can write a story. When you begin to teach them, when you subordinate them and make them your disciples, then you will have learned much.

Educate the eye about all the things it desires, and bring it under control. Educate the ear about all the things it likes, and bring it under control. Guide it toward goodness. Educate the nose about all the things it likes, teach it right and wrong, and make it your disciple, your baby. Educate the tongue that constantly seeks different tastes. It seeks both good and bad tastes. Instruct it well, control it, and teach it to have patience. In this way, teach and control all aspects of yourself. If you reduce each aspect to a baby and teach it, then you will be able to learn. Teach your mind, desire, lust, anger, passion, maya, and pride. Instruct your desires for praise, respect, and gifts; teach them all. Then you will be a learned one, a scholar. Then you will need no advertising. Then everything will happen on its own. Consider everything, and do as you should. That's good. Do you have a question?

Be Like The Ant; Be Like The Honeybee

Visitor : I have no questions. I am just visiting a spiritual teacher.

Bawa Muhaiyaddeen: That is very good. What my brother says is good. However, there is only one teacher who teaches spirituality—God. He is the only Teacher. Four hundred trillion, ten thousand spiritual teachers live in the world, advertising hell. They advertise the four hundred trillion, ten thousand sins, sixty-four sexual games, sixty-four arts and sciences, and the qualities of lust, anger, passion, miserliness, and religious fanaticism. Lust, theft, murder, falsehood, the thirst for intoxicants, the sixty-four sexual games, the games and energies of the rat, cat, dog, horse, donkey, monkey, and elephant, supernatural powers, mesmerisms, miracles, and mantras—all these are taught by teachers. Everything—the dancing, the singing, the enslaving of one life to another, the searching, and the running—is for the sake of the one-span stomach. All these teachers are one-span-stomach teachers. When hunger strikes these teachers, the ten [commandments] fly away and are forgotten. This is false! This is the sort of teachers they are. They are *self-business* teachers.

Only One is a Teacher—God. He alone does not possess any of the earlier mentioned qualities. He has no hunger, illness, old age, death, anger, or sin. He engages in none of the sixty-four sexual games. He has no darkness. He is the Teacher—a Teacher without *self-business*.

He is the One,
the Teacher who is with us
as Wisdom within wisdom,
Eye within eye,
Ear within ear,
Nose within nose,
Tongue within tongue,
Love within love,
Compassion within compassion,
Life within life,

Truth within truth,
and Body within body—
protecting, teaching, and explaining.
He is a Teacher, a Father.
Without differences and without race, He does His duty,
warning us and providing explanations.
Only such a One is a Teacher.
He is God.
He is the *Spiritual* Teacher.

We are not *spiritual* teachers. We are one community, one group of people—His children. We are a *brotherhood* with mothers and brothers. We are all one community, one group of children, one gathering, one family of brothers and sisters. We talk to one another and tell each other about our state of mind. You may tell me something, and I must listen to you and respond. Then, when I tell you something, you have to listen to me, and so on. In this way, we teach and we learn. We come to understand our faults, ascertain what is right and wrong, and then try to do what is right, and avoid what is the wrong. We join together and discuss what is within each of us. We tell each other to do the right and reject the wrong. This is how we learn. In this school, this is the way we understand and learn. This is unity. This is *United Nations, unity,* brothers and sisters in harmony. Through this we try to understand ourselves, learn, and become peaceful. Tranquillity, peace, and equanimity are what we strive for. We say, "We will be peaceful!" This is why we gather here. Each person tells of his inner aspirations and tries to find peace.

When we proceed in this manner and become clear, then our Father, our Teacher, will come. When we attain clarity, the *Original Teacher* will come to us and guide us, saying, "That is correct, this is correct, do this, do that." He will give us the necessary counsel.

What we are trying to do now is to differentiate right from wrong. In each area, we are attempting to look at what is right and wrong and reach a state of clarity. We are not teachers; we are just trying to reach a

60

clear state. One by one, each child must come to this state. On this route, the trees, flowers, and seeds are all gurus that teach us. The eye, nose, mouth, hunger, illness, blood, skin, attachments, and illusion are all teachers that instruct us. We have to understand each of these things. The sun, the moon, and the stars are all teachers. Every pore of the body, the flesh, skin, blood, and marrow are all teachers. We should understand right and wrong within all of this. This is the strength within our learning, the strength within our unity. We assemble here to investigate this learning. We examine what is good. This is what we must do now.

Brother, a tiny ant discerns and picks up things that are not visible to man. An ant comes over quietly, picks up things that have fallen out of man's hand, and eats them very lovingly. It obtains that which slipped away from man, that which man's eye did not perceive. Similarly, God, our Father, is not visible to man's eye at this time. He has slipped away from man.

> God has no form,
> no shape,
> no color,
> no hue,
> no race,
> no religion,
> no differences,
> no "I," no "you,"
> no hunger.
> It is a Power—
> A Power without selfishness.

This Power has fallen away from man. As soon as man said, "I," it fell away from him. Man said, "mine," and it dropped away from him. Man praised himself, and it moved away from him. Everything—all of this Power—left man. The Power slipped away.

Just as the ants find things, we should find this Power. We should move like the ants and detect where this Power is. This is wisdom. Like the ant, wisdom should search, find, and savor it. But first, we have to become small, become like an ant. We must search for the Power like an ant, find it, pick it up and relish its taste. When we do this, we are teachers, men of wisdom, God's representatives. When man recognizes and regains what has fallen away from him, he is "man." He is the son of God, and his qualities, actions, and duties will be that of his Father. This is discernment.

My brother, we should understand this. We have to become very small. If we become [pretentious] teachers, we cannot pick this up. If we become gurus, we cannot pick it up. We have to become extremely small. Then we can find this and take it. We must think about this.

There is another point to consider. In a pond, there is a lotus flower which contains a certain amount of honey. But do the fish, frogs, crocodiles, and beetles of the pond realize this? Do they taste the honey? No, they do not. They do not take the honey and benefit from it. Why? Because they do not know that the honey exists. They eat only the mud and the mire, the mold, the insects, and the germs in the water. They leap around, play, jump, and wander around, but they do not take the *point* that is within the flower. They stir the pond, they come and go, and they catch and devour things within the pond, but they do not discover the honey. They do not taste that which is within. Although the lotus flower is in the pond, although honey exists in the flower, and although there are so many creatures in the pond, not one of them finds the honey and takes it.

Meanwhile, from elsewhere, from a forest on the side of a rocky mountain, comes a tiny honeybee. It buzzes along, "Ree, ree, ree," and takes the honey. There are so many creatures in the pond, so many beetles and insects, yet none of them taste the honey. But the honeybee comes along, does not hurt the lotus flower, does not hurt any other creature, gently sips the honey, and moves on. A wise person should go to God's place in a similar manner. He should fly there, seat himself at the Source, and imbibe the honey. If he does so, that will be the taste.

When you search for a wise man, it is the same. You must realize that this, here, is the world; this is maya, this is the pond—*creation-pond*. Within it are several *points:* crabs, crocodiles, foxes, dogs, fish, beetles, mud-eating creatures, worms, insects, viruses, and micro-organisms. Everything is here, each devouring the other. This is the world. And within this, you should seek a wise man, as the honeybee seeks the honey.

All kinds of people gather around a wise man. This is the world. But what is the use? What is the use of being here like the creatures in the pond? Many creatures live in the pond: crocodiles, sharks, little fish, colored fish, beetles, and micro-organisms. Similarly, so many of us exist in this *creation-pond*. But what is the use in being here? Like the bee, we should know where the honey is, search for it, and take it. We should not look around and get distracted. A person who is on this quest will not look at the multitude; he will take the honey and depart. Though others may be all around, he simply identifies the honey, searches for it, and takes it. Like the honeybee, he will imbibe the honey without hurting the flower, the pond, or the creatures living in the pond. The honeybee sucks the honey and takes it back to the place where it should be stored.

What can the bee do in the pond? The flower does exist in the pond, but what can the bee accomplish by staying there? Similarly, what can one do at the Fellowship? What is the use of joining the Fellowship? What is the purpose of being among this group? Each one catches another and devours him. One virus devours another, one fish catches another, a crab is killed by another, a shark is killed by another, and so on. While each creature continues to catch and consume another, and the pond is churned and disturbed, it is only the honeybee who knows the precise way to extract the honey.

It is the same way in the Fellowship. Although many have gathered here, each one casts aspersions on another behind his back, and each one scolds another. Sometimes they even cast aspersions on the honey, saying, "There is no honey here. This is not a flower, just some other

63

kind of plant." This could happen here because of those who stir up the pond. But do all these people discern the honey? No, they do not. Only the honeybee knows. It heads straight for that *point;* it does not go toward anything else. It does not look around at things in the pond, it does not stop to look at the flower, it focuses only on the honey.

This pond could be like that pond. People who stay here day and night could be like the creatures in that pond. People who stay at the Fellowship could be like that. Some people who have joined the Fellowship could also be like this. They will stir up the pond. However, there may be someone like the honeybee who flies in from elsewhere, extracts only the honey, relishes its sweet taste, and takes it to the place where it should be stored—the heart. If such a one imbibes the honey over and over again and collects it in his heart, he can give the honey to others. He can give it to children, he can benefit from it himself, and he can give everyone a taste of this honey.

This is the honey of grace, the honey of wisdom, the honey of love, the honey of compassion, the honey of patience, the honey of forbearance, the honey of equanimity, the honey of the soul's liberation. Only one who is in the same state as the honeybee can take the honey. It does not matter where he is, whether he comes here or whether he flies in from there; he will be able to take the honey only if he is in that state. Otherwise, there is no point in being here like the crocodiles, sharks, and beetles of the pond. These creatures climb over each thing and fall down, climbing on flowers and falling, climbing on tall objects and falling. They disturb this, and they jump into that.

The same things also happen at the Fellowship. The human beings at this pond may also behave in this manner. If we keep investigating the happenings in the pond, we will be like the crocodiles, beetles, micro-organisms, and frogs who live in the pond but are unaware of the honey. Therefore, if we keep talking about the goings-on at the pond, if we continue to gawk at and inquire into these things, nothing will be gained.

The honeybee scents the honey and comes directly toward it.
It does not loiter.
It takes the honey and returns to its own locale.
A wise person should do the same.
He who searches,
he who has faith,
he who has determination,
he who has wisdom,
he who delights in the honey
will come in the same manner.
Such a man is a wise one,
a clever one,
a believer who has certitude.
He takes what he needs and leaves the rest.
We should understand this.

Do you understand my brother?

Visitor: Very well, thank you.

Bawa Muhaiyaddeen: *Anbu,* love. That is fine. Doctor Thambi, do you understand? My sixty-five year old Doctor Thambi, do you understand? All right, Psychology Doctor Thambi, did you understand?
(All say they understood.)

Bawa Muhaiyaddeen: I haven't understood this as yet. This is what I am studying.
(Everyone laughs.)

Dr. Markar: I will join you and learn.

Bawa Muhaiyaddeen: *Al-hamdu lillāh,* All praise is to God!

Chapter 5

The Call to Prayer:

An Explanation

July 31, 1980

Everyone come!
Everyone join together!
Come here!
Let us give greetings
and praise to God.
Let us meet Him!
Let us converse with Him!
Join the Solitary One!
Come,
everyone come!

The Call to Prayer: The call is made by a *muezzin* from a mina-ret, a roof top, or the doorway of a place of prayer about ten to fifteen minutes before the prayer begins. Once the congregation has assembled in the house of prayer, another call is given inside, before the prayer starts.

The Call to Prayer
An Explanation

Bismillāhir-Rahmānir-Rahīm.
In the name of God, most Merciful, most Compassionate.

Allāhu Akbar
Allāhu Akbar
Allāhu Akbar
Allāhu Akbar
Ash-hadu al-lā ilāha ill-Allāh
Ash-hadu al-lā ilāha ill-Allāh
Ash-hadu anna Muhammadur-Rasūlullāh
Ash-hadu anna Muhammadur-Rasūlullāh
Hayya ʿalas-salāh
Hayya ʿalas-salāh
Hayya ʿalal-falāh
Hayya ʿalal-falāh
Allāhu Akbar
Allāhu Akbar

Lā ilāha ill-Allāh

Bismillāhir-Rahmānir-Rahīm
Al-hamdu lillāhi Rabbil-ʿalamīn
Ar-Rahmānir-Rahīm
Māliki yaumid-dīn

Iyyāka na'budu wa iyyāka nasta'īn
Ihdinas-sirātal-mustaqīm
Sirāt al-ladhīna an'amta 'alaihim,
ghairil-maghdhūbi 'alaihim
wa lad-dāllīn.
Āmīn.
Bismillāhir-Rahmānir-Rahīm.
Qul: Huwallāhu ahad,
Allāhus-samad,
Lam yalid, Wa lam yūlad,
Wa lam yakul-lahu kufuwan ahad.
Āmīn.

As-salāmu 'alaikum wa rahmatullāhi wa barakātuhu kulluhu.
May all the peace, the beneficence,
and the blessings of God
be upon you.

The intrinsic meaning of the call to prayer is:
Allāhu Akbar!
Allah is the Great One!
He is the greatest of all!
He is the Great One!
He is One of unfathomable grace
and incomparable love.
In the world of the soul,
He has placed in fullness
the undiminishing wealth
of divine knowledge (*'ilm),*
the wealth of the hereafter,
the wealth of the soul,
and the wealth of the three worlds.
Allah is the Great One

who has attained
the perfect and complete wealth of
inner patience *(sabūr)*,
contentment *(shakūr)*,
surrender *(al-hamdu lillāh)*,
and the praise
Bismillāhir-Rahmānir-Rahīm—
God, most Merciful, most Compassionate.
He is One who has fully attained
the wealth of creation,
the wealth of sustenance,
and the wealth of protection.
He is *Allāhu,* the greatest.
Allāhu Akbar—He is the greatest!
Lā ilāha ill-Allāhu,
Lā ilāha ill-Allāhu.

This call to prayer is greetings *(salāms)* and glorification *(salawāt).*[1]
For all God's created beings there is none other than Him.
Lā ilāha—other than You there is nothing,
ill-Allāhu—You are God.
Lā ilāha ill-Allāhu.
These *salāms* and *salawāt* resonate
to all parts of the soul *(rūh)*.
They are made to resonate
with the words
Lā ilāha—there is nothing other than *Allāhu ta'ālā*.
Ill-Allāhu—He rules.
He is the Ruler
of the world of souls, this world, the next world,

---

1. **Salāms (greetings) and salawāt (prayer, glorification):** The practice of greeting, praising, and glorifying Allah, the *Rasūl* ☉, the prophets, and the angels is called giving *salāms* and *salawāt* to these exalted beings.

the inner heart, and all created beings.
He is the King,
the Ruler without attachments,
the patient King,
the faultless King,
the unselfish King,
the King without house,
without palace,
without possessions,
without body.
Remaining alone,
He rules over all lives.
This King is *Allāh,*
Allāhu.

Lā ilāha ill-Allāhu—He is the Solitary King
who is Life to all lives,
whose Flag is higher than all flags,
whose Qualities are more exalted than all other qualities,
whose Learning is higher than all other learning,
whose Research is the rarest of all research,
whose Love is more exquisite than all love,
whose Benevolence is more exalted than all benevolence,
whose Patience is greater than all patience,
whose Grace is more exalted than all grace.
And with this wealth of grace *(rahmat),*
He rules over king and beggar without discrimination.
He embraces all lives,
and comforts each inner heart
according to its capacity.
He comforts the mind
and ends its troubles.
He does not forget

even when father and mother have forgotten.
He is the Savior who lifts us out of danger.
He is the Comforter and King.
To Him we say,
Lā ilāha ill-Allāhu—
other than this King, there is no king
with similar qualities.
He is the King.
Therefore we say, *ill-Allāh,*
You are God.

As His house,
He has placed an atom, a *secret room,*
within each inner heart.
Within wisdom
He has placed a secret power.
Within resolute faith *(īmān)*
He has placed a secret wealth.
Within the certitude of each,
He has placed the strength of inner patience.
It exists as Strength within strength,
as the Strength of Faith within faith.
There is no greater strength
than this strength of inner patience.
Of all the weapons given to man,
the weapon of inner patience
will be that which leads him to victory.

Allah has this weapon of victory
that will not hurt anyone,
beat anyone, or kill anyone.
It will do no evil.
God has this weapon of victory.

Thus, there are no wars in His kingdom,
no differences in His kingdom,
and no doubts in His kingdom.
Why?
Because He rules
with the strength of inner patience—
that balance.
God has given this inner patience
as a strength to each human being.
In this kingdom of inner patience,
God's throne and His treasures
exist as the Inner Heart
within man's inner heart.
If man understands this
and realizes the house within this kingdom,
he will never harm anyone in this world.
This is his weapon,
the strength of his kingdom.
With this strength,
he rules all the realms—the 18,000 universes,
the sun, the moon, and the stars.
God has given this house to man as a *secret room,*
as a secret.

God dwells in this room
and protects all lives.
He understands their minds, their inner hearts,
their intentions, and their thoughts,
and comforts them.

Bismillāhir-Rahmānir-Rahīm—
Creation, Sustenance and Protection are His.
Ill-Allāhu—

the One who rules alone
does so unceasingly.

In the call to prayer we say,
Hayya 'alas-salāh!
Hayya 'alal-falāh!
Everyone come!
Everyone join together!
Come here!
Let us give greetings
and praise to God.
Let us meet Him!
Let us speak with Him!
Join the Solitary One!
Come!
Everyone come!
Hayya 'alal-falāh!
Everyone, please come.
Come, come!
Let us come and meet Him, come!
Let us say our *salawāt* to Him, come!
Let us say *salāms* and speak to Him, come!
Do come.
Hayya 'alas-salāh,
Hayya 'alal-falāh.
Everyone please come.
Come and join together.
Let us say our *salāms* and *salawāt* in His Name.
At every minute,
God is inviting us
with 70,000 different voices.
He calls out to us and gives us His *salāms*.
God, His angels, His prophets,

75

His enlightened ones, and His *qutbs*
call out to us
and give *salāms*, saying,
"Come here, come here and look."
Hayya 'alal-falāh!
Come here,
everyone come here and look!
Come, come, come here.
Hayya 'alas-salāh!
Come here,
let us call out
our *salāms* and *salawāt* in His name.
Let us call out.
Let us get together.
Let us gather together in one place.
Come! Everyone come.
The Great Mighty One,
let us speak to Him.
We will call out our *salawāt* to Him.
We will bow down to Him.
Come.
This is how we call out to God;
this is what we say.

Allāhu Akbar —He is the Great One.
Allāhu Akbar —He is the Great One.
We invite Him.
We call out to the Great One who created us.
We praise Him.
Lā ilāha ill-Allāhu,
Muhammadur-Rasūlullāh.
Muhammad is His messenger, His representative.
Rasūlullāh—God fashioned him as His final prophet.

Among all of His prophets,
God gave Muhammad ⊕ the title of *Rasūl,*
and sent him down as the last prophet,
as His messenger, as His representative,
as the *Rasūl,* as *Nūr Muhammad.*

He was sent as
Anāthi Muhammad [the unmanifested],
Āthi Muhammad [the manifested],
Awwal Muhammad [the beginning, the emergence of creation],
Hayāt Muhammad [the *rūh*, the emergence of the soul],
Anna Muhammad—the food, the *rizq* or nourishment for all creations,
Ahamad—the light of the inner heart,
Muhammad—the beauty of the face,
Nūr Muhammad—the clarity of *īmān,*
the Muhammad of perfection
realized as Wisdom within wisdom,
and *Allāh Muhammad*
[the Light of Allah in Muhammad,
and the light of Muhammad in Allah].

In this way
nine Muhammads came
from within Allah,
disappeared in Allah,
and kept resplending in Allah.
God took all nine principles,
made Muhammad ⊕ the *Rasūl,*
and sent him down to earth.
And now when you say the *kalimah*—
Lā ilāha ill-Allāhu
Muhammadur- Rasūlullāh
sallallāhu ʿalaihi wa sallam—

you say,
"Let us follow the *Rasūl* ☉,
let us praise him."
God sent him down as the final prophet,
and to help us follow him,
He instituted the five and six tasks.
We should realize these tasks on the inside
and understand them on the outside.
There are five ordained duties *(fards)* and five daily prayers.
We should understand these five daily prayers.
The *salāms, salawāt,* and call to prayer
are within each of the five daily prayers.
We proceed toward God
and give Him *salāms* and *salawāt.*

Hayya 'alal-falāh!
Everyone come!
God is the Great One!
Everyone come!
Ill-Allāhu—He rules alone.
Come!
Muhammadur-Rasūlullāh.
Come, let us follow him.
Come, he is the *Rasūl* ☉.
Hayya 'alal-falāh.
Come, let us all gather here.
Hayya 'alas-salāh.
Let us say our *salāms* and *salawāts* to Him.

This is the substance of the call to prayer.
There are countless meanings within this.
I am giving you an easy explanation.
People of wisdom

may perceive meanings that are more exalted.
As one proceeds, there are deeper meanings.
This is why we should understand
the five and six tasks.
Six tasks should be realized on the inside.

Not this eye;
there is an inner eye with which to see God.
With this inner eye we must see Him,
we must see the Truth.
This eye does not have outer vision.
It has the inner vision
through which we should see God.

Not this ear;
there is an ear within
to hear God's sounds.

Not this nose;
there is a nose within
to scent and distinguish God.

Not this tongue;
there is a tongue within
with which to speak to God.
It is *īmān*.

Not this hand;
there is another hand, *nambikkai*,[2]
with which to ask God for a blessing.

---

2. **Nambikkai:** In Tamil, the word *nambikkai* means *faith*. The author breaks the word in two parts (*nambu* means *have faith,* and *kai* means *hand*) and uses it to denote *the hand of faith.* Trans.

Not this inner heart;
there is another inner heart
with which to pray and speak to God.

Not this body;
there is another body
with which to go to God,
speak to Him,
and journey through His kingdom.

Not these feet,
but the feet of
Lā ilāha ill-Allāhu,
Lā ilāha ill-Allāhu.
Lā ilāha as the left foot, and [*ill-Allāhu* as] the right foot.
These are the feet with which we journey toward Him.
Leaving this world and traveling,
this journey is the *dhikr*—
the constant remembrance of God
with every breath.
Lā ilāha ill-Allāhu—
Other than You there is nothing;
only You are God.
These are the two legs of faith
that will enable us to travel from this world to His abode.
We should walk toward Him in this state.

Scheduled prayer is done at the five appointed times,
and this is the call to prayer at each of these times.
Of the five ordained tasks, one is belief.
Believe in God.
Pray to God.

Pray to Him alone.
Pray to Him after the call to prayer.
The second is worship—
to know that there is none worthy of worship
other than *Allāhu ta'ālā.*
To an ignorant man,
God is in an unknowable realm,
and for a wise man,
God is in his heart.
To a man who does not have faith, patience, or wisdom,
God is in an unknowable realm.
But a man who has belief, *īmān,* patience, and wisdom
understands God in his own heart.
This is why God
is known as
the God within the heart,
and as the God of an unknowable realm.
For a man without wisdom,
He is in an unknowable realm,
but for a man of *īmān,*
God is in the heart.
We should understand this.

When we know
what the Heart within the heart really is,
we will talk to Him
with our five times of prayer and acts of worship.
Therefore, worship with those inner eyes,
nose, mouth, body, soul,
hands of faith,
and Inner Heart.
This will be true prayer.
When man prays in this way,

everything
will belong to God—
body, eyes, nose, mouth, life.
And when everything that belongs to God
becomes these foundations,
these principles of understanding,
man will have nothing in the world.
What will he have?
Nothing.
He will have no worldly belongings.
He will have neither possessions of the world
nor the hell of the world.
He will have no death,
no possessions,
no anger,
no attachment,
nothing!
Only Allah—that is his wealth.
A man with this wealth has nothing to give in charity.
When he himself belongs to God,
what can he give?

However,
if a man does not strengthen his faith,
if he does not belong to God,
if he gathers hell,
if, motivated by selfishness,
he acquires for himself what is to be shared by all,
then the [third] ordained duty instructs him
to give charity,
to give to the poor.
For such a man, charity is most important.
But a man who has made God his own

has nothing to give as charity.
God alone is His wealth.
A man of *īmān* can only give wisdom and *īmān*.
This is God's wealth.
Apart from this, his hands are empty,
and he has nothing to give.
A man who has taken what belongs to all
must give in charity.
If he cannot give charity properly,
he must fast.
He should try to gain understanding
through the [fourth duty of the] fast
and give to others.
A man who cannot even do this
should finally,
fearing death,
intend and complete [the fifth duty]
the pilgrimage of *Hajj*.
He should die.[3]
The five ordained duties
are the instruments, the means.
From the very beginning,
according to the duty of prayer,
man should know and worship
the only One worthy of prayer.
He should belong to God.
Then, if he prays with that soul,
that inner heart, and those inner means,
the world will be dead to him.
God will be his only treasure.

---

3. **He should die:** The author often speaks of how man must *die before death*.
Man's "I" must die, so that only God exists. Trans.

If that state is not attained,
then,
until we kill earth,
until we kill fire—our anger,
until we kill the waters of creation—the sins of creation,
until we kill air—the base desires,
and until we kill ether—maya, the connections of birth,
prayer at the five prescribed times is necessary.
The five *sections*
[earth, fire, water, air, and ether]
must be killed
at the five times of prayer.
Until they are killed,
these prayers must be performed.
Allāhu Akbar!
Realize that Allah is the greatest,
and worship Him.
Lā ilāha ill-Allāh,
He is Eternal;
other than Him there is nothing.
He is the Judge.
He dispenses justice.
Ill-Allāh—everything is His kingdom.
Trees, shrubs, flowers, earth, sky, the nether-regions—
everything is His.

Lā ilāha ill-Allāhu
Muhammadur-Rasūlullāh.
Through the light of Muhammad,
through the *Rasūl* ☽,
God has proven this to us.
The *proof* is the 6,666 verses,

the 124,000 prophets within that,
and, selected from among them,
the twenty-five prophets,
and the eight prophets of great clarity —
Adam ☺, Noah ☺, Abraham ☺, Ishmael ☺,
Moses ☺, David ☺, Jesus ☺, and Muhammad ☺.
God sent them as *proof*.
Understand this;
follow this.
Come.
Hayya 'alal-falāh!
Come, everyone!
Come and join together here!
Hayya 'alas-salāh!
Come, let us call out to Him
and give Him our *salāms* and *salawāt*.
Let us speak to Him.
Come.
We do not want fights.
We do not want separations.
We do not want differences.
Let us unite in God.
Let us join together.
Come.

This is what the call to prayer means.
We should understand this.
Al-hamdu lillāh,
all praise and praising is to God alone.
Al-hamdu lillāhi Rabbil-'ālamīn,
all praise and praising is to God alone,
He is the Ruler of everything.
He is the Creator

85

and He rules everything that He created.
Ar-Rahmanir-Rahīm,
He is the Sustainer.
He is the Merciful One to all lives.
He is also the Protector.
Bismillāhir-Rahmānir-Rahīm,
He created us.
Rabbil-'ālamīn,
He is the *Rabb,* the Lord.
He is the Creator,
the Ruler,
and the Protector.
Al-hamdu lillāhi Rabbil-'ālamīn,
Ar-Rahmānir-Rahīm.
He is the *Rahmān,* the Compassionate One.
He is *Rahīm,*[4] the One who protects.
Māliki yaumid-dīn,
He is the *Mālik,* the King.
He is the King of perfect purity.
Iyyāka[5] *na 'budu wa iyyāka nasta 'īn,*
He is the One who gives, takes, and bestows,
the Giver who wears the Crown of crowns.
Iyyāka nasta 'īn,
to each He gives what should be given.

---

4. **Rahīm:** The author often brings deeper meanings to a word or phrase by interpreting it through more than one language. The literal translations of the prayers pertain to Arabic meanings, while the author often uses Arabic and Tamil meanings, separately or together. To explain the author's interpretation in such instances, we provide the meanings of pertinent Arabic and Tamil words. In Arabic, *Rahīm* means the Merciful One; in Tamil, *rachi* means to protect, to preserve, to deliver from evil, to save. Hence, Allah is the One who protects. Trans.

5. **Iyyāka:** Pronounced *eeyāka* in Arabic, it means thee, thou, or thine. Hence the literal translation, Thee do we worship. In Tamil, *ee* means give, bestow, grant.

Nasta'īn,
He is the One who gives counsel.
He gives what is good,
He gives what is lawful,
and He is the Protector.
Nasta'īn,
He is the Greatest.
Only what He bestows is wealth.
Ihdinas-sirātal-mustaqīm,
He has written each human's destiny.
He is the One who can bring to an end
what has been written.
He is the One who protects according to destiny.
He is also the One who,
explaining every meaning of one's destiny,
protects and saves.
He is the *Nasta'īn,*
the *Naseeyath,*
the Counselor.
He is the Counsel to your soul
and to your wisdom.
He is the One who gives counsel to your *īmān.*
He gives to everything the counsel that protects.
Ihdinas-sirātal-mustaqīm,
He helps us transcend the hellish [birth] canal.
He is the One who can dispel
our destiny
and take us beyond to reach the shore.
He is the One who can change the writing,
change our thoughts,
lift us out of hell,
and save us from the hell-fire of hunger.
Ihdinas-sirātal-mustaqīm,

He assists us on the bridge
known as *Sirātal-mustaqīm*
and protects us.
He is the One who can change our destiny.

Sirāt al-ladhīna,
He takes us beyond, to the shore,
and rules over us
as the Perfect Light of Purity.
'Amta 'alaihim,
with each of us
He stays within and without,
making us complete.
Ghairil-maghdūbi 'alaihim
wa lad-dāllīn.
He makes all our intentions good *(khair)* and strong.
The One who has *rahmat,*
the One who gives us that *rahmat,*
and the One who takes us to the shore
are the same One—Allah.
That is the Power.

Wa lad-dāllīn,
He is the only One who,
as the Light beyond light,
has cut away all evil.
And having banished all evil,
He protects us.
We must realize this.
This is the *Al-hamdu Sūrat,*
the verse of praise.

Bismillāhir-Rahmānir-Rahīm.

Qul: Huwallāhu ahad,
He who is Allah
is *Ahad.*
He is the *Ahad* for all of everything.
He is *Ahad,* the Mystery in everything.
Allāhus-samad,[6]
to all lives, He is impartial.
He is the Peaceful One.
He is the *Samad,* the same to all lives.
He looks upon all lives
and protects them without any differences.
Lam Yalid,[7]
without ego, without "I,"
He stays with the lowly one as the Lowly One,
with the exalted one as the Exalted One,
and does His duty toward them.
Lam yalid.
He stays small and serves all lives.
Wa lam yūlad,[8]
He is the One on the right side.
All His actions are right.
He does what is right on the right side.
That is His justice.
Wa lam yakul-lahu,

---

6. **Samad:** In Arabic, *samad* means eternal, absolute. Hence, the literal translation God, the Eternal, Absolute. In Tamil, *samam* means equal, even, same. Hence, Allah is the One who treats all lives equally. Also, in Tamil, *samādhānam* means peaceful. Hence, Allah is the Peaceful One. Trans.

7. **Yalid:** In Arabic, *yalid* means begetteth. Hence the literal translation, He begetteth not. In Tamil, *yilivu* means inferiority, lowness in rank. Hence, He stays with the lowly one as the Lowly One. Trans.

8. **Wa lam yūlad:** In Arabic, *wa* means and, and *lam* means not. Hence the literal translation, nor is He begotten. In Tamil, *waladh* means right (as opposite of left). Hence, Allah is the One on the right side. Trans.

on the right side, He is everywhere,
while Satan is on the left.
The entire right side is God's kingdom
whence He dispenses His justice
for heaven and hell.
To those who deviate from the right,
He gives the judgment of hell.
Wa lam yakul-lahu,
His kingdom is on the right.
Kufuwan ahad,
He rules on the right side,
and for all of everything
He is the *Ahad,*
the Mystery,
the Absolute!
He is the *Ahad* to the soul,
to this world,
and to the hereafter.
He is the Mystery.

Realizing this Merciful One,
praising Him,
worshipping Him,
speaking of Him,
speaking to Him,
merging with Him,
and living with Him,
is the exaltation of our lives
and the station of *īmān.*
To realize these, one after the other,
and proceed,
we need to understand the ordained duties.
This is the call to prayer.

I do not know much of the meaning.
I did not recite or learn this;
I am just giving you an explanation.
There could be deeper meanings;
there could be very, very deep meanings.
Āmīn.

As-salāmu 'alaikum wa rahmatullāhi wa barakātuhu kulluhu.
May all the peace, the beneficence,
and the blessings of God be upon you.
Allāhu Akbar—God is the Greatest.

Go and break your fasts. With *īmān,* praise God. Ask for His
forgiveness and ask Him to fulfill your fast triumphantly.
Say, "In the Name of God, most Merciful, most Compassionate,"
and break your fast.
Āmīn, Āmīn.

As-salāmu 'alaikum wa rahmatullāhi wa barakātuhu kulluhu.
May all the peace, the beneficence,
and the blessings of God be upon you.

Chapter 6

A Prayer for My Children

August 1, 1980

One of unfathomable grace,
One of incomparable love,
bestow unto my children
Your undiminishing wealth of grace
to illumine their inner hearts.
Shed on their intentions
the rain of your gaze,
making their inner hearts
blossom into flowers.
And You,
as the Fragrance of the flowers,
reside in their inner hearts
and
guide them on the path of love.
Your fragrance
pervading their every duty,
guide them onward
on the straight path.

A Prayer for My Children

My precious brothers and sisters,
precious jeweled lights of my eyes,
you who were born with me,
lives within my life,
radiant jeweled lights of my eyes,
for you [I pray].

O Lord of all universes,
Merciful One,
Benevolent One,
Mighty One,
Bestower of grace,
bestow
on my brothers and sisters,
on those born with me,
good wisdom,
good words,
and good stations.
According to their focused intention,
guide them on the straight path.
Grant them eternal life.
Unite with them,
and so grace them.

One of unfathomable grace,
One of incomparable love,
bestow unto them
Your undiminishing wealth of grace
to illumine their inner hearts.
Shed on their intentions
the rain of Your gaze,
making their inner hearts
blossom into flowers.
And You,
as the Fragrance of the flowers,
reside in their inner hearts
and guide them on the path of love.
Your fragrance
pervading their every duty,
guide them onward
on the straight path.

Abide with them
in sorrow, despair, sickness, and disease.
Relieve dissatisfied minds.
Dispel their symptoms of illness, suffering, and poverty.
Rid them of their sorrow,
guide them toward the straight path,
give them peace, equanimity, and tranquillity,
and so grace them.

My Unfathomable One,
for Your love there is no equal.
To Your grace there is no end.
For Your qualities, actions, and conduct,
there is no likeness.
My Supreme Lord,

Light of the precious eye,
Resplendence of the inner heart,
Great One, the Creator,
Allāhu!

Bestower of grace on all creations,
grace the inner hearts of true men,
direct their intentions toward the good way,
fulfill their aspirations,
and so grace them.
Āmīn.

Help my precious children.
As Your intent and words have decreed,
their intent and focus is to fast.
The ordained duty of the fast
they do intend.
With certitude steadfast in inner hearts,
they seek the path
that seeks You.

O Allāhu!
May Your resonance dawn
in the hearts and intentions
of these children.
Dispel disease and karmic ailments.
Show them the ways to control base desires.
Remedy their fettersome attachments of this world,
and the illnesses that torment.
Guide them onto the straight path
as is
Your duty.

Throw open,
reveal to them the straight path
from this world to the next.
And keep open for them
the straight path,
the straight way,
between You, the soul, and wisdom.
Āmīn.

Forgive faults of before and after,
and so grace them.
Āmīn.

Grant them the right
to live with You then and now,
and so grace them.
Āmīn.

Grant them Your grace
to extend their living days
on Your straight path.
Āmīn.

Absolve evil and sins
that touched them in the fetal stage,
and so grace them.
Āmīn.

Forgive all their sins:
sins seen by the eyes,
sins heard by the ears,
sins inhaled and experienced by the nose,
sins tasted and relished by the mouth.

All the mistakes made by my children:
sins intended by their hearts,
sins causing pain to others,
sins of treachery,
sins of falsehood,
sins of backbiting,
sins born of selfishness,
sins born of hunger,
sins born of poverty,
sins born of desire,
sins born of cravings,
sins born of blood ties,
sins born of racial and religious differences,
sins born of the possessiveness of "mine" and "yours,"
sins born of anger,
sins born of hastiness and fury,
sins born of the differences of "I" and "you,"
and sins born of the differences of "color" and "complexion."
Pardon all these sins
O Lord of the universes!
Forbear and forgive,
and so grace them.

Direct their intention toward You,
reveal the path,
give them undiminishing wealth
in the here and in the hereafter,
and so grace them.
Āmīn.

To live with love in the world,
to help all lives,
to serve all lives and bestow peace,

grant them tranquillity
in their inner hearts.
Give them wisdom
and compassion,
and so grace them.
Grant them the benevolence that helps all lives,
and so grace them.
Āmīn.

Grant them the grace at every moment
of thought that never forgets You,
and thought that never separates
from You.

Stay with them
as Soul with soul,
as Wisdom with wisdom,
as Spirit merged in spirit,
as Awareness merged with awareness,
as Feeling nestled in feeling,
as Intellect dwelling in intellect,
as Judgment explaining to judgment,
as Subtle Wisdom revealing all
to wisdom.

Give them
penetrating wisdom,
analytic wisdom *(pahuth arivu)*—
the wisdom and grace
of the *Qutb*;
divine luminous wisdom *(perr arivu)*,
the wisdom of Your effulgence and perfection—*Nūr*-wisdom.
And You, as Grace-Wisdom with them,

protect the soul-light and the soul.
End the evils of the body.
Stay within and without.
Grant them perpetual tranquillity and peace,
and so grace them.
Āmīn, Āmīn.

O Lord of the universes!
As You protected the prophets,
as You protected the enlightened ones,
as You protected Truth,
as You protected patience,
protect these precious children,
these jeweled lights of my eyes.
Protect their inner hearts,
protect wisdom,
protect Truth.
Look on them
with Your compassionate eye,
dispelling sins of eyes, nose, and mouth,
forbearing all.
Make their hearts luminous and full
that they may live joyously
in this world and in the next.
Give them this wealth,
this right,
and so grace them.

Give them
the wealth of divine knowledge *('ilm)*,
the wealth of wisdom,
the wealth of the soul,
and the wealth of Your grace.

Give them this,
your undiminishing wealth,
and so grace them.
Āmīn.

Fulfill their aspirations
and their intentions
in a good way,
and so grace them.
Āmīn.

End all future births,
and so grace them.
Āmīn.

End all physical illnesses and poverty,
and so grace them.
Āmīn.

Keep open the path of light,
the path that traverses Truth alone.
Āmīn.

Give my children
direct vision of You,
direct communication with You,
and have them speak to You.
Āmīn.

Establish thoughts of compassion and love,
thoughts never forgotten,
thoughts ever full.
Āmīn.

Grant them
patience,
inner patience *(sabūr)*,
contentment *(shakūr)*,
trust in God *(tawakkul)*,
and total surrender to God
(al-hamdu lillāh).
Grant them this fullness of life,
and so grace them.
Āmīn.

O Lord of the universes!
Give them the grace and light
of Your benevolence.
Protect the precious
jeweled lights of my eyes,
children who have fasted,
children who have not,
children who scold You,
children who forget You,
and children who do not think of You.
Protect them, save them,
and give them Your grace.
Give them the direct way
and bestow Your grace.
Turn them forever toward the good path,
and bestow Your grace.

Since good and evil
are in Your custody,
whatever it is that You intend,
show them that straight path.

Correct their intentions accordingly,
and guide them.
In the same way,
forgive my children everything
they did in the past.
They may have forgotten You,
they may not have intended You,
they may have hated You,
but forgive them,
O Lord of the universes.
Pardon them,
embrace them,
embrace them Heart to heart.
Give them wisdom,
give them the Light of the soul,
render them victory in life.
Dispel the worries and sorrows
of this birth and the next.
Open up the direct path.
Give them an inner heart that protects
other lives as their own.
Give them an inner heart that loves
and helps other lives as their own.
Grant them the grace to serve
as You serve.

O Lord of the universes!
Give them the grandeur of Your benevolence.
And furthermore,
give their eyes the resplendent wisdom
and the light that sees You,
and so grace them.
Āmīn.

Give their mouths
the words to speak to You,
the right to speak to You,
and the directness to speak to You.
Endow them with an inner heart
that does not deviate from
the path of Truth,
an inner heart that avoids
impermissible sustenance
and partakes of tranquil sustenance.
Give them the right to talk to You
voice to Voice,
and so grace them.
Āmīn.

Give them Your grace *(rahmat),*
and the wisdom, fortitude, and truth
to avoid forbidden food
and eat lawful food;
to realize what is bad
and to do what is good;
to avoid misdeeds
and understand Your mysterious secret;
to comprehend the inner heart and body
within the misdeeds;
to follow the path of Your mysterious secret;
to act with goodness;
to live a lawful life
and go on the path of truth,
and so grace them.
Āmīn.

Give them
a way not to see hell.
Instead, give unto them
the eyes and inner heart
to see You,
and so grace them.
Āmīn.

Give them
the eye, inner heart,
and wisdom
to see no evil,
but to see Your *rahmat*,
and so grace them.
Āmīn.

Grant them Your grace
by giving them
resolute faith,
patience,
inner patience,
contentment,
trust in God,
and total surrender to God.
Give them this praiseworthy
wealth of praise,
so they may not perceive evil
but may perceive Your *rahmat*,
the wealth of three worlds,
Your paradise.
Āmīn.

Take them,

my precious children,
to Your feet,
and so grace them.
Āmīn.

Forgive our sins,
and so grace us.
Āmīn.

Lord of the universes!
Give them the right to worship You,
the strength of resolute faith,
and the resplendence of wisdom.
In this way, may they
trust You,
intend only You,
seek only You,
make You their only duty in life,
make You their only helper,
prostrate themselves at Your feet
and worship only You,
and so grace them.

As Helper,
You stood beside each of the prophets
and guided them.
Stand beside us now,
correct our faults,
and show us the right path
when we deviate.
Forgive us and direct us,
protect us from danger at each moment,
open up the good path,
and show us how to live with wisdom,

and so grace us.
Āmīn.

May You give us
the right,
the life,
and the plenitude
that we may reach You,
that we may live with You
without separation in this world
and in the next,
and so grace us.
Āmīn.
O Lord of all universes!

As-salāmu 'alaikum wa rahmatullāhi wa barakātuhu kulluhu.
May all the peace, the beneficence, and the blessings of God
be upon you.

Go now, place the responsibility for your fast in God,
place it in His trust *(tawakkul)*,
and then break your fast.

Chapter 7

Separate from Yourself That Which Separates You from God

August 2, 1980

Until we see
that there is only One
worthy of worship,
only one Father,
the Lord who dispenses justice,
only One who is
the Creator, Sustainer, and Protector—
until then,
our own separations
will separate us from God.

Separate from Yourself That Which Separates You from God

Bismillāhir-Rahmānir-Rahīm.
In the name of God, most Merciful, most Compassionate.

In this month of Ramadan, this month of fasting, the children have undertaken the fast with loving acceptance in their inner hearts. The nature and significance of this fast have been accepted by each, consistent with his or her own wisdom. We will talk about this later. Since the children have accepted the fast, I will provide some explanations of this duty and the way it is to be carried out. I will explain the proper way to break the fast [each day] and receive nourishment.

First, there is the call to prayer. I will give you a brief explanation, because it is a component of breaking the fast. The call to prayer is the time when we dedicate the fast to the Supreme One who fulfills the fast. We offer Him our intention. Every day, between 8:00 and 8:30 PM,[1] we hand over the fast to God. We place it in His responsibility. Each individual surrenders his or her intention to Him. This is why the call to prayer is rendered to the Supreme One. According to one's wisdom and intention, the fast is handed over to the One of unfathomable grace and incomparable love. The fast is placed in the responsibility of this Gracious, Loving One, and He is asked to accept the fast.

God is the Greatest. The call to prayer announces this.

---

1. **8:00 and 8:30 p.m:** Each evening, in the month of Ramadan, the fast is broken after sunset. The time varies each year. In Philadelphia, in the year 1980, sunset was between 8:00 and 8:30 p.m. Trans.

Allāhu Akbar

Allāhu Akbar

Allāhu Akbar

Allāhu Akbar

Ash-hadu al-lā ilāha ill-Allāh

Ash-hadu al-lā ilāha ill-Allāh

Ash-hadu anna Muhammadur-Rasūlullāh

Ash-hadu anna Muhammadur-Rasūlullāh

Hayya 'alas-salāh

Hayya 'alas-salāh

Hayya 'alal-falāh

Hayya 'alal-falāh

Allāhu Akbar

Allāhu Akbar

Lā ilāha ill-Allāh.

God is the greatest.[2]

God is the greatest.

God is the greatest.

God is the greatest.

Other than You there is nothing, only You are God.

Other than You there is nothing, only You are God.

Muhammad is the messenger of God.

Muhammad is the messenger of God.

Come to prayer, come to success (salvation).

Come to prayer, come to success (salvation).

God is the greatest.

God is the greatest.

Other than You there is nothing, only You are God.

---

2. The following is a literal translation for those unfamiliar with the call to prayer. However, the author has often stated that every word has more than a thousand meanings. In this and other chapters the author elaborates the explanations for each line of the prayer. Trans.

As-salāmu 'alaikum wa rahmatullāhi wa barakātuhu kulluhu.
May all the peace, the beneficence, and the blessings of God
be upon you.

In this month of Ramadan, this [call to] prayer is offered with great devotion. In all parts of the world, in the Islamic religion, this month is called the "Fast." According to the intention of each, the fast is offered to the Great One and He is asked to fulfill the intention. Each prophet, in his time, introduced the fast to the people in a different way. The prophets Adam ☺, Noah☺, Abraham☺, Ishmael☺, Moses☺, David ☺, Jesus ☺, and Muhammad ☺ did this. The fast also exists in the Hindu religion, but it has a different name—*Viratham*. People give their intentions to God, placing them in God's responsibility—this is called the fast. As wisdom develops, further explanations of the significance and purpose of the fast emerge. May we realize this.

Allāhu Akbar means Allah is the Greatest. We call out to Him three times in our intentions. In all prayers it is customary to have one, two, or three "sounds" that call out to God. When one calls out to God, it should be done with a melting inner heart *(qalb)*. Those who do not realize this may first say the words with their mouths. The next time they should say them with awareness. If He does not hear it when spoken in words, [it is said] He may hear the sound when it is said with awareness. Finally, these words have to be said with a melting inner heart. They are, therefore, said three times, one after another. These sounds signify that we undertake the fast in the name of the Supreme One—"We are doing this in Your name, for You. Please accept it. Please fulfill our intentions." Religions talk about these thoughts, motives, and intentions. These are the precepts of religion. They are understood as the *laws* within the *shariat* of each religion.[3] They call this the Fast.

---

3. **Shariat:** Derived from the Arabic root *shara'a—to introduce, enact, prescribe—* the literal meaning is the law. *Shariat* is the first of five steps of spiritual ascendance. In this step, one discriminates between good and evil, and tries to live life according to the good. Trans.

113

Then they say, *Lā ilāha ill-Allāh*. It is a word[4] that melts the heart. *Lā ilāha*—everything that is created dies. Everything changes. All created beings will change and die. They have a limit, but there is One who has no limit. He is God, *ill-Allāh*. We say, *ill-Allāh*, You are God. *Ill-Allāhu* resonates in an inner heart, in a tree, in air, in fire, in water, and in earth. This resonance reverberates in the sky, sun, and moon.

The resonance of *Lā ilāha* is one breath [the author sings *Lā ilāha* slowly and very melodically]. Two breaths flow through every being. One breath relates to the world and the body. This sound of *Lā ilāha* [rising with the left breath] cries out to all the spirits within the body except the pure spirit. Another sound, *Allāhu,* then softens the inner heart and resonates from the heart, giving counsel. *Lā ilāha, ill-Allāhu*— the breath flows on the right side and joins the heart. The breath rises, and descends on the right side as God's breath, as Light.

God is the Solitary One
who functions alone.
He rules alone
without body,
without form,
without color,
without hue,
without religion,
without race,
without differences,
without shape.

---

4. **Word:** The literal meaning of the *Kalimah* is the *word*. The *Kalimah* is the testimony of faith in which a person affirms, There is nothing other than You, only You are God *(Lā ilāha ill-Allāh)*. This recitation, or remembrance of God, cuts away the influence of the five elements, washes away all the karma that has accumulated, dispels darkness, and makes the heart beautiful and resplendent. This *Kalimah* washes the body and heart of man, making him pure. It makes his wisdom emerge, and impels this wisdom to know the self and God.

Not controlled by anything,
as King to all kings
and Beggar to beggars,
He rules.
He rules without a house.
He has no deeds [of ownership]
and yet, ruling alone,
hoists His sovereign flag everywhere.
He has no body
yet is intermingled in all bodies.
He has no book or story
yet is understood as the story in everything.
He has no wife
yet has given birth to all children.
Without the attachment of blood-ties
He protects all children.
He stays within and without all lives
performing selfless duty.
He is the Lone Ruler.
To kings, He is a King,
to beggars, He is a lowly Beggar,
to His lovers, He is a Lover.
If we call Him once,
He calls out to us ten times.
If we trust Him once,
He trusts us ten times.
If we love Him once,
He loves us ten times.
If we come forward
and intend Him once,
He takes ten steps toward us.
He is the Beauty of Compassion.

The body, its organs, the thoughts, and the eyes focus on this, infer correctly, and intend Him. This Energy and Power is intermingled in the nerves and skin. The angels Gabriel ☺, Michael ☺, *Isrāfīl* ☺, *'Izrā'īl* ☺, *Munkar* ☺, and *Nakīr* ☺ are also mingled in the body, in earth, in Adam. God has said, "Believe in Me, My angels, My archangels, and My prophets. Believe in the Day of Judgment, and the Day of Questioning *(Qiyāmah)*. Believe in the angels since they exist as the body within the body: Michael ☺ for water, Gabriel ☺ for wisdom, Muhammad ☺ for earth, *'Izrā'īl* ☺ for fire, and *Isrāfīl* ☺ for air." In the grave, the angels *Munkar* ☺ and *Nakīr* ☺ look into and judge the karma we accumulate. Every day, these two angels on our shoulders record the right and wrong in what we do—our speech, our perception, and our thoughts. They stay with us, doing their work. God has asked us to believe in these angels.

God has provided the fast
to help us
attain forgiveness for our mistakes,
to perceive and pursue the straight path without deviation,
and to dispel from the body the arrogances
of self-importance, karma, maya, "I," and "you."
The fast also enables us to understand how it feels
when arrogance decreases, strength diminishes,
worries abound, and the body shrinks.
Having experienced this, and realizing that other lives
must feel the same, we should
help and feed others,
trust and understand other lives as our own,
realize their condition, and help them.
These purposes are integral to the fast—
one of the five ordained duties in Islam.

Belief in God and worship of God are the first two duties. Lack of surrender to God in these states led to the decree of three further duties:

116

charity, fasting, and the pilgrimage of *Hajj*. Until all of this is understood and wisdom develops, these are practices each observes according to his or her intention. We should realize that this is not just a fast. We should understand the inner purposes and principles of the fast, and connect ourselves to God.

There is a reason for each of the five daily prayers. At the first prayer, the early morning prayer *(subh),* we should cut away our connections to earth. At the midday prayer *(zuhr)* we should abandon the connections to creation—maya. At the afternoon prayer *('asr)* we cut away connections to base desires, mind, and cravings. At the sunset prayer *(maghrib)* we cut away the connection to death. At the night prayer *('ishā')* we connect ourselves to Allah and merge with Him, regaining the unity that existed in the world of souls. These are the purposes of the five times of prayer. For Sufis of resolute faith *(īmān)* and certitude, this is the significance. God reduced fifty times of prayer to these five, and gave them to man to help him cut away all attachments.

We should understand this in our ritual prayer, inner worship, and service to God. After we have connected with God, our bond to our own and other lives will be the same. Our hunger and others' hunger will be the same, as our sorrow and that of others will be the same. So too, our troubles and others' afflictions will be the same. In this state, the plenitude of 124,000 prophets will be like gold within us. The inner heart of one who has attained this will be the Light that has received Allah's grace *(rahmat)*. The words of Allah given directly to the Prophet ﷺ and the revelations *(wahy)* given to the 124,000 prophets will fill his inner heart. God's explanations will remain understood in that heart, and the prophets and God will live with him. In this way, the 124,000 prophets, the Qur'an, the Bible, Judaism, and all the religions will reside in the house of his inner heart, which will be the throne of a pure one *('arshul-mu'min),* the throne of God *(dhāhuth)*. God will be the Ruler on this throne, dispensing His judgment. From God's judgment, laws, rules of moral conduct, and His words will continually flow to man. Then man will teach these words to his children— the children he now serves without attachment.

Such a man will be like the lotus flower that rises above the water. He will also be like mercury, moving along, not attaching himself to anything. In the paradise of his inner heart, God's throne and God's judgment will continue to provide explanations. He will have the peace and equanimity that comes from helping all lives attain peace. His will be a life of helping others. He will strive hard to help his children find peace in their inner hearts. His life will be devoted to the service of lives dedicated to God. Duty, free of all attachments, will be his duty. He will not find fault with the world, but just as the sun moves in the sky circling the earth, the soul and wisdom of such a man will circle the 18,000 universes. He will never look for faults in any situation, but will only render his duties and bring peace to other lives. He will be God's representative, God's slave, doing his duty as God does. We should establish this state in our lives and attain clarity in everything, according to our wisdom. We should thus realize clarity in our life, in our mind, in our desire, and in our anger. We should control and govern all of these and merge with God. We should do this by cultivating the inner heart that unites with all lives, and by developing the wisdom and inner heart that stand united in peace and equanimity, bring comfort to other lives. Those who attain this clarity, perceiving the clarity of God, are chosen by Him to be His representatives.

The duty of such people is to consider all lives as their own and serve them. In order to accomplish this, the fast, ritual prayers, faith, worship, charity, the pilgrimage of *Hajj*, good, and evil were revealed as Wisdom to the wisdom of man. This was done so that each could ascend step by step, climb what had to be climbed, and reach clarity. Just as we grew from infancy, we have to grow on the path of God. Until we develop fully, each one of us should live according to our wisdom. Then, if by climbing, we gradually attain greater and greater clarity, we can merge with God. Until we become one with our Father, until we attain that Oneness and do our duty, we have to ascend one step after another, doing different things on the path—fasting, ritual prayer, worship. Everything that has connections to us, everything connected to earth, must die. Connections to earth, desire, maya, and arrogance must die. When this happens, we will not die. The connections of this body, everything intermingled in it, belong to earth. Once everything belonging to earth dies, we will be a Light in the kingdom of God, the hereafter. This Light has no death.

We came from the world of souls as a ray of God. We came to this house to study and understand God's secret and our secret. The soul will understand this secret, for it is something that the soul must know. The body will die, but the soul has no death. But if the "I" dies before the body dies, *'Izrā'īl* ☮, the angel of death, will not seek us out. It is this "thing" that has a limit, that faces death, questioning, reckoning, judgment, justice, and equity. This questioning is known as the Day of Death and the Day of Judgment. If we succeed in setting right this house, then we will have victory in this world, the hereafter, and the world of souls. God will make us His representatives.

However, if we do not successfully attain this exaltation in the three worlds, we will be sent to kingdom of hell once more. God has instructed us, and has given us many ways to accomplish this according to our wisdom. He has told us to rise up step by step with perception, awareness, intellect, judgment, subtle wisdom, analytic wisdom, and Divine Luminous Wisdom *(unarvu, unarchi, pudthi, mathi, arivu, pahuth arivu,* and *Perr Arivu).* He told us to try to climb up with these seven wisdoms. People of all kinds, big ones and little ones, do this in different ways with total conviction and determination. We each do it differently according to our wisdom, but whatever we do, we must gain understanding through it. We should study the meaning of whatever we intend, act upon it, and learn from it. We should probe deeper and deeper, continue to study, and go within. As we proceed further and further, we will experience greater wisdom, explanations of Truth, and liberations of the soul. Through the fast, different examples, and different paths, God has shown us how to accomplish this.

To fulfill the intentions of each, the fast that we call Ramadan is undertaken by different religions in different months, different days, and in different ways. Different names are used, and different practices have been followed at different times. But no matter how many or what the different practices are, God is One; judgment is given by One, paradise and heaven are bestowed by One, and the Questioner is One—our Father, the Lord who created us.

No matter what religion, creed, or race we may be,
until
we know that there is only one God,
only one family,
until
we realize that we are the children of Adam ☺ with one Father,
until
we defeat the enemies within us,
until
we overcome the enmity among our brothers and sisters,
until
we eliminate the differences that separate us
and see ourselves as one,
as one family, one Father, one Truth,
until
we see that there is only One worthy of worship,
only one Father, the Lord who dispenses justice,
only One who is the Creator, Sustainer, and Protector—
until then,
our own separations will separate us from God.

We will thus be parted from God's Truth. We will have separated ourselves through race and religion. These separations separate us from God's Truth, His intention, and His Kingdom. They keep us from connecting with Him. In whatever way we pray, worship, understand, or study, as long as we see separations in our hearts, separations in our brethren, separations of color, separations of race, and separations of religion, it means that we are sundering ourselves from our Father and from Truth. We separate ourselves then from the good and from God's Kingdom, separating ourselves from the One who has no separations. As long as we have these separations, there is no use in our studying, no purpose in our understandings. The One who rules the divine kingdom has no separations. He has no doubt, no color, no religion, no race—no separations.

Judgment, Truth, Creation, Protection, and Sustenance are His only divisions. His judgment consists of sending the soul, calling it back, and questioning it. But He Himself has no separations. Only when we realize this, will we unite with Him and attain His Kingdom. Only then will He embrace us as His sons and daughters, drawing us near and giving us His kingdom and His treasures.

Until that wisdom and realization dawn, we have to study Truth and knowledge in many ways. This is why different religions show us different ways. Through these, we should understand and gain clarity. Only then can we pray and forge the connection between our Father and ourselves—ourselves and our Father.

> This [connection] cannot be bought with money.
> It cannot be bought with land.
> It cannot be bought with property.
> It cannot be bought by seeking another's approval.
> It cannot be bought with tricks and treachery.
> It can only be bought with something that is perfectly pure.
> It can be bought with a perfectly pure inner heart.
> It can be bought with a perfectly pure soul.
> It can be bought with perfectly pure wisdom.
> It can be bought with perfectly pure duty.
> It can be bought with perfectly pure actions.
> It can be bought with perfectly pure qualities.
> We can only attain God and His Kingdom
> by staying perfectly pure.

Know with certainty
that this cannot be reached in any other way.
Each child must understand this.

We should cut away from us the pride, jealousy, treachery, "I," "you," religion, and race that exist within our inner hearts. Each one of us should separate away from us that which keeps us separated. Doing this, we should merge with God.

Compassion should be our very essence and beauty. Our inner hearts must be like the water that provides for all animals—snakes, cows, goats and pigs—quenching thirst, cleansing filth, and comforting. Just as the water gives to each what it needs and remains clear, so too must our inner hearts remain clear. Only then will our duty and truth be correct. If we are like fire, with our differences, colors, races, and religions, then we will burn everything. The fire burns everything that falls into it, both gold and garbage. It will burn what is good and also what is evil. If we have arrogance, anger, hastiness born of fury, and differences, they will burn up all God's goodness, consuming good qualities and all our rightful deeds. Everything we do seeking approval and acceptance by others will burn up like fire.

Instead, we should be like the water and the earth, remaining calm and serene with patience, inner patience, trust in God, and total surrender to Him, saying, "All praise is to God alone—*Al-hamdu lillāh*." My precious children, only with these qualities can we progress in life, attaining clarity in wisdom, goodness in faith, and truth and unity in God's intention. Only then can we reach God's kingdom. Each child, in order to do your duties and progress, you should strive to find the supporting wisdom, belief, determination, *īmān,* and certitude. You should try to do this day after day. Your success will come from this.

Have only the beauty of compassion.
Keep open your inner hearts and minds.
Tap your own hearts and God's door will open.

Tap, tap your hearts.
Dispel karma that pursues what is unlawful.
Then tap your hearts and see!
Ask forgiveness for your faults;
open God's Kingdom and ask.
This is the way to experience success in the Kingdom.
This will give victory!
Āmīn, Āmīn, Āmīn.

As-salāmu ʿalaikum wa rahmatullāhi wa barakātuhu kulluhu.
May all the peace, the beneficence, and the blessings of God
be upon you.

Go and break your fasts. Ask God to fulfill your intentions.
Ask Him to do this.
May God fulfill your intentions.
Āmīn, Āmīn.

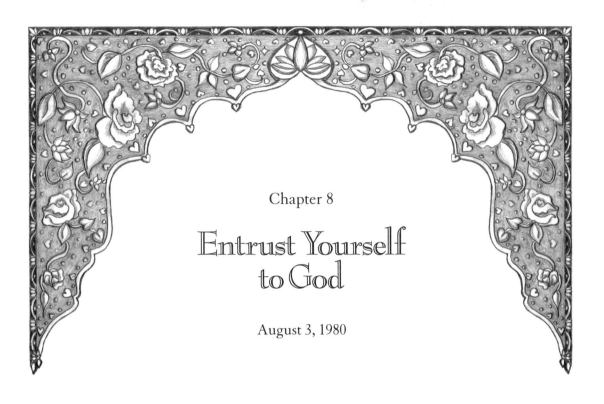

Chapter 8

Entrust Yourself to God

August 3, 1980

May we live our lives
trusting God's intentions
unconditionally.
May we worship Him
with an immaculate heart.
May we place our inner heart
within His intention,
bow down to Him alone,
and entrust ourselves to Him.

Entrust Yourself to God

Bismillāhir-Rahmānir-Rahīm.
In the name of God, most Merciful, most Compassionate.

One of limitless grace,
One of incomparable love,
Allāhu!

We must make
our intentions, beliefs, and yearnings
His responsibility alone.
We should ask Him to forgive
the faults we commit in our lives.
We should ask for forgiveness.
We should ask for
a prayer of supplication *(du‘ā’)* on our behalf.

Each of us should entrust our intentions to Him alone.
We should make them the responsibility
of *Allāhu ta‘ālā,*
the Singular God who rules and sustains.
When we do this, asking for forgiveness,
God, our Father, will forgive us and grant us His grace.
With each breath ask for pardon.
Say, *Astaghfirullāhal-‘azīm—*

God, please forgive all our faults and correct us,
astaghfirullāhal-ʿazīm, astaghfirullāhal-ʿazīm.

Say this three times and ask for His forgiveness.
The two angels will note that pardon
and thus will
our faults be absolved by God,
the Singular One who rules and sustains.
It will be written down as having been forgiven.
On the Day of Judgment
we will be awakened in our graves again.
We will be handed a list
of our "good" and our "bad,"
and according to this list
God will dispense judgment and justice.
We should believe in this day with certainty,
and believe fully in Allah,
and in the many ways that He fulfills
every intention and yearning.

Worship, serve, and pray to the One God,
believing in Him,
remembering Him with every breath *(dhikr),*
and maintaining focused contemplation of Him *(fikr).*
Perform charity, fasting, and the pilgrimage of *Hajj,*
moving step by step;
then surrender completely to our Father,
giving Him all responsibility,
making Him the source of all wealth.
And until we attain His wealth,
make Him responsible for our duties and intentions,
ask forgiveness for all our faults,
and ask Him for a prayer to make us pure.

To help us attain this state,
God has revealed many instruments,
and so graced us.
We should perform the ordained duties *(fards)*,
complete them triumphantly,
ask for His forgiveness,
and ask Him to pray for us,
so we may attain perfect purity.

To provide a path,
God has sent down
one instrument after another through His prophets.
He has provided us proof beyond proof
and made us understand these instruments.
All of us should understand these means.

We should intend *Allāhu*
and have faith in Him
so that we may
perform our duties and attain purity,
dispel the darkness of the inner heart,
fill the inner heart with
Allah's Light, grace *(rahmat)*,
and benevolent qualities,
and attain a life of freedom forever.

May God accept our duties,
forgive our faults,
accept us,
and bestow His grace.
Āmīn.

May we live our lives trusting His intentions unconditionally.
May we worship Him with an immaculate heart.
May we place our inner heart within His intention,
bow down to Him alone,
and entrust ourselves to Him.

May we offer Him
the praise of trusting Him completely *(tawakkul)*
and surrendering to Him *(al-hamdu lillāh)*.
May we say,
"*In shā' Allāh* —if God wills,"
and "*Ma shā' Allāh* —as God wills."
For all that is happening,
and for all that is to happen,
may we praise Him and trust Him.

May we complete our life victoriously.
May we leave this world,
go beyond the next world,
and enter the world of souls.

May we receive Allah's *rahmat*.
May we attain His
imperishable wealth of the three worlds—
Rahmatul-'ālamīn.

In our life,
each of us should understand
and follow the commandments brought down
and explained to us by the prophets.

With each breath
let us praise Him.

And with the next breath
let us ask forgiveness for the breath
that intends evil.

In that state
May God, our Father,
utter His benevolent words,
protect us and grace us.
Āmīn, Yā Rabbal-'ālamīn.
So be it,
O Lord of the universes.

Surrender your intentions and fasts to Him; entrust them to Him,
and break your fasts.
Āmīn. May it be so.
May all the peace, the beneficence, and the blessings of God
be upon you.

Chapter 9

Forgive My Children and Grant Them Your Grace

August 4, 1980

O Allah,
give them Your love, Your Light,
and Your qualities,
and so grace them.

Whether they intend You constantly
or whether they do not,
forgive them,
and so grace them.

Pardon the faults
committed by these little ones,
and so grace them.
Āmīn.

Forgive My Children
and Grant Them Your Grace

O Allah,
O Merciful One,
to those in the world
who intend You
and to those who do not,
to those who desire You
and to those who do not,
to those who scold You
and to those who speak ill of You—
You are God,
showering compassion
on all.
You are *Allāhu*.

One without anger,
One without sin,
One without haste in any situation,
O Peaceful One,
give us Your serenity,
and so grace us.
Give us Your actions and conduct,
and so grace us.
Āmīn.

Immeasurable, Endless One,
Indivisible, All-Pervasive One,
Light of the inner heart,
Plenitude of intention,
Resplendence of wisdom,
Noble One within the state of resolute faith,
Intended One to those intending prayer and service,
Giver to those who seek,
Bestower of
compassion and love on all lives—
bless us according to Your intention,
and so grace us.
Āmīn.

Forgive us our faults,
and so grace us.
End the sufferings we undergo
through base desires, cravings,
and attachments,
through wealth, women, and earth.
Give us Your inner patience and plenitude.
Grant us the discernment of Your wisdom.
Bestow peace and equanimity,
and so grace us.

On those who dedicate themselves to You
and afflict their body,
on those who focus and intend the fast in Your name,
on those who give up the welfare of the body,
trust in Your beneficence,
and intend the fast as
You decreed—
please bestow Your benevolence.

Fulfill their intention and endeavour.
Complete their search,
and so grace them.

Make their inner hearts resplend
without darkness,
and give unto them what they seek.
Grant them the grace, wisdom,
and peace they intend,
and so grace them.
Āmīn.

O Lord of the Universes,
protect them with Your benevolent grace,
and so grace them.

In this earth-world, the soul-world,
and the divine kingdom,
be their Helper.
Take them to the shore,
make them follow the good way,
and so grace them.

God, most Merciful One,
Lord of the universes,
Bestower of equality and peace
on all lives,
Benefactor of compassion,
You look upon all lives with
Your eye of compassion,
and bestow Your grace.
Give unto them Your words of love
and words of grace.

Destroy, in their inner hearts,
the arrogance, karma,
and maya of birth.
Show them the path that runs straight;
show them a life of tranquillity
and help them attain peace.
Take them away from the suffering of hell,
and so grace them.

Protect them from the vehemence
of fire, water, and air,
and so grace them.
Enable them to experience tranquillity
in a serene life,
and so grace them.

Crown with victory
their life of freedom
in this world,
and let them receive
permanent life in the hereafter.
Give them Your love, Your light,
and Your qualities,
and so grace them.

Whether they intend You constantly
or whether they do not,
forgive them,
and so grace them.

Suffer the faults committed
by these little ones,
and so grace them.

When they consider the past and the future
and make mistakes,
forgive them,
and so grace them.

Pardon the sins they committed
when they were lacking in wisdom,
and so grace them.

Forgive past faults
present faults,
and future faults,
and so grace them.
Forgive transgressions committed in ignorance,
protect and support them,
and so grace them.

God, *Allāhu!*
Lord of the universes,
One of unfathomable grace,
One of incomparable love,
Your grace has no equal,
Your love has no flaw, no end.
O Mighty One,
You protect all lives
in this state.
Ill-Allāhu—You are the One
with the singular resonance.
One who rules alone,
One who shows compassion
and love to all lives,
Benevolent One,

All-Powerful God,
Allāhu!
Protect us and connect us to the
good path,
and so grace us.

Grant us Your grace
never to be touched by hell,
never to be touched by sin,
never to fall into anything else
but You,
never to seek any other help
but You,
never to intend any other joy in our inner hearts
but You,
and never to seek or accumulate any other wealth
but Your wealth.
Please grant us the grace to attain
Your grace-wealth—Your *rahmat,*
to receive the wealth of the three worlds,
and to perform Your duty in Your kingdom.

O Lord of the Universes,
Benevolent One,
shield us at all times.
Support us day and night.
In our sleep and in our waking,
protect us,
and guide us on the right path.
Āmīn.

Grant us Your grace
that we may never let go

of Your grasp.
Āmīn.
So be it,
O Lord of the Universes.
All praise is to God.

As-salāmu ʿalaikum wa rahmatullāhi wa barakātuhu kulluhu.
May all the peace, the beneficence, and the blessings of God
be upon you.

Go and fulfill your fasts. Those who have not eaten, go and eat.
May God fulfill your intentions.
Āmīn.

Chapter 10

May We Live Together As One Family

August 5, 1980

God has shown us
the principles of understanding
in several ways
so that we may gain wisdom.
If we understand this,
we can live as one family.
As one family
we can worship one God.
We can live in unity
as one life,
one body,
one heart,
and attain tranquillity.

May We Live Together As One Family

Bismillāhir-Rahmānir-Rahīm.
In the name of God, most Merciful, most Compassionate.

Other than God,
Allāhu ta'ālā Nāyan,
the Lone One who rules and sustains,
there is none worthy of worship.
All praise and praising are to Allah alone.
Āmīn.

The Giver of the soul
and the Taker of the soul
is Allah.
The Giver of true nourishment,
the Cherisher,
the Bestower of benevolence,
the grace-wealth *(rahmat)* of all universes
is He.

God will always be as One.
For all of Adam's ☺ children,
God is the only One.
We must know Him and attain
the purity of resolute faith *(īmān)*.

145

In order that we may
all join together as one family,
worship only one Father,
believe only One,
and trust only One;
that we may unite and live as one
with our inner hearts steeped in oneness;
that misunderstandings at one time
of prayer may be settled
before the next;
that we may establish inner patience,
contentment,
trust in God,
and total surrender to God
(*sabūr, shakūr, tawakkul* and *al-hamdu lillāh*),
attaining victory in our life;
and that we may strengthen our certitude
on the straight path—
God has given us 100,000 affirmations.

He has created us
and given us His wealth of grace.
He has given us house and land,
cattle and livestock,
property and wealth.
He has given us the wealth of our eyes,
the wealth of our ears,
the wealth of our mouth,
the wealth of our nose,
the wealth of our wisdom,
the wealth of our tongue,
and the wealth of our hands and legs.
He gave us this wealth.

He gave us His perception,
He gave us things He created,
and He gave us the wisdom
to know
and speak with understanding.
He has given us a place,
a body,
and
a life.
He has given us seven kinds of wisdom
that can understand:
perception,
awareness,
intellect,
judgment,
subtle wisdom,
analytic wisdom,
and Divine Luminous Wisdom
(unarchi, unarvu, pudthi, mathi,
arivu, pahuth arivu, and *Perr Arivu).*

He has given us seven kinds of perception
with which to analyze,
the wisdom with which to understand,
and seven channels:
two ears,
two eyes,
two nostrils,
and one mouth.
He created a form that would understand everything,
made it into an eminent head,
and within that eminence He placed seven organs
that would make things evident.

And with this head
He sent us down to earth.

The Praiseworthy One
known as
the Lord of all universes
planted us here as
most exalted beings.

He created
horses, dogs, lions, tigers, bears,
and other animals.
He created the birds
and all the reptiles
in different colors and hues.
He gave them many different sounds,
but all of these sounds
are contained within man's sound.
The sounds of all animals—
dogs, foxes, cats, rats, birds, snakes, scorpions—
are all compressed within man,
so that man may learn from them
and conduct his life with that knowledge.
God created man as the leader
who can bring peace to each heart
by being a father to all
and a friend to each life,
comforting each one
and relieving all distress.

God, who created man as exalted and wise,
God, who created man as the leader of all beings—
may we trust in Him completely.

The One who gave us the wealth of
eyes, ears, nose, mouth, hands, feet, and body,
the One who gave us this wealth through
light, sound, scent, and taste,
the One who gave us this wealth
so we may experience and understand—
may we praise such a One,
worship only Him,
join Him,
and live as one with Him.

Just as the connections of
earth, fire, water, air, and ether
intermingle, unite, and live in us,
may we unite with all human lives
and live as one family.
May we worship only One
with service,
īmān, clarity, certitude,
peace, and equanimity.

May God reveal
the qualities of peaceful living
that He placed in man.
God is the One that is exalted in man,
He is the One that is wise in man,
He is the One that is love in man.
He has given man the *rahmat*
that can make all lives bow down to him.
We must realize this and perform each duty.
When we conduct our duties in this way
our arrogance, karma, maya,
and the pride of "I" and "you"

will be destroyed,
and we will attain peace.

It is for this that
the fast,
five daily prayers,
prayer with a melting heart
(*'ibādat*),[1]
and charitable acts
were ordained as duties by God.
He did this so we could,
within the composition of our bodies,
realize these obligations on the path of justice.
Through the prophets He told us about the duties.
Each child must understand this.

God has pointed out to us
that we cannot achieve peace of mind
until we attain peace as one family.
God has given us proof that
man will not experience peace in himself
as long as he does not find peace
in considering all lives as his own.

If man does not perceive all lives with compassion,
He will not feel compassion in his heart
and attain equanimity.
One who does not see justice in himself

---

1.   **'Ibādat:** In Arabic, *'ibādat* means *prayer, acts of worship, service*; from the verb *'abāda* "to serve" and *'abd* "servitor." Praying to God with a melting heart is *'ibādat*. When the inner heart melts into liquid, when it melts like wax in prayer to God, when that state is achieved, it is *'ibādat*. This is prayer. It is prayer to the One.

will not see justice in others.
One who does not perceive forbearance in himself
will not perceive forbearance in others.
One who does not comprehend patience in himself
will not comprehend the patience of others.
One who does not understand himself
will not understand others.
One who does not experience unity within himself
will not experience unity in others.
One whose wisdom does not
respect and love each life within
will not
display love for others without.
In this condition, serenity will never be his.

If man does not find peace in himself,
he will never find peace
in the world,
in his children,
in his wife,
in his property,
in his house,
in his titles,
or in his wealth.
He will never find peace.

One who does not see patience and tolerance
in himself,
one who does not consider others' hunger as his hunger,
others' sorrow as his sorrow,
and others' troubles as his troubles,
will never end hunger, disease, old age, and death.
One who remains stone-hearted

will never experience tranquillity and peace
from birth until death.

One who does not see purity in himself
will never see purity in others.
One who does not see unity in himself
will never see unity in the world.

Through the 124,000 prophets,
Allāhu taʿālā Nāyan,
the Singular One who rules and sustains,
has instructed us
to live together as one family,
to realize that there is but one God,
and to know the Day of Judgment
and the Day of Reckoning
within ourselves.

If man understands the Day of Judgment
and the Day of Reckoning
within himself,
if he understands that judgment in himself,
if he realizes it and corrects his faults,
he will behold peace in the world,
and tranquillity in himself.
He will love Allah,
worship Allah,
place his inner heart in God's responsibility,
attain tranquillity and peace in the world,
become the master of his grace-wealth
and wisdom-wealth,
wear the crown,
and know himself to be

one who has received God's grace.
All lives
will bow down to him, serve him,
and come to his aid in times of sorrow.

God sent us each prophet
to feed us
wisdom, fortitude, and *īmān,*
so we may follow the right path.
To understand what they fed us
and to live our lives accordingly,
we were provided
the fast, ritual prayers, *'ibādat,*
wisdom, fortitude, divine wisdom,
and teachings.
God has shown us these principles in several ways
so we may gain wisdom.
Through awareness we must comprehend
the fast, ritual prayers, worship,
love, patience, and compassion.
So that we may study every aspect of these,
they were ordained as the five duties.

If we understand this,
we can live as one family.
As one family
we can worship one God.
We can live in unity
as one life,
one body,
one heart,
and attain that tranquillity.

153

To attain that tranquillity,
the truths and ordained duties were revealed by God.
And even though the world claims to have four religions,
each prophet was the messenger of but one God.
If we analyze the teachings of the prophets with faith and truth,
we will realize that there is but one God for everyone.
Step by step, the same God gave His teachings
to them
and to us.
It is to comprehend this
that we undertake these duties.

My precious jeweled lights of my eyes,
the duties were ordained so that we may
know them to be the principles of understanding,
and live accordingly.
They were given to us
so we may
bow down to God,
foster unity,
show compassion, love, and patience,
feed the hungry,
perceive a hungry face and offer protection,
reassure the ill, bring them peace,
and comfort the troubled.

God revealed these principles
so that we may cultivate compassion for others
and flourish.
The fast, *'ibādat,* ritual prayer, wisdom,
and divine wisdom
will bring us serenity on the path of peace.
May we understand this,

bow down to God,
and live as one
with justice and good conduct
on the exalted path.
The principles were provided
to help us proceed along this route.

My precious jeweled lights of my eyes,
to analyze and understand each thing
is wisdom.
The principle you put into practice
is not important;
learning the truth within the principle is.
What you worship is not important;
attaining clarity and realization within it
is prayer.
Whatever you do,
learn the truth within the action.
To understand that with clarity
is prayer.
When each principle is practiced like this,
doing it is not the obligation.
You must understand the obligation
within what you do.
May you clearly understand
the benefit of each duty
and undertake each principle.

My precious jeweled lights of my eyes,
the ordained duties exist in this way.
May you realize each one.
Āmīn.

May the benevolence of God fulfill your intentions.
Go and break your fast.
May He bestow His *rahmat* on you. May He fulfill your intentions
and grant you His grace.
Āmīn, Āmīn.

As-salāmu 'alaikum wa rahmatullāhi wa barakātuhu kulluhu.
May all the peace, the beneficence, and the blessings of God
be upon you.

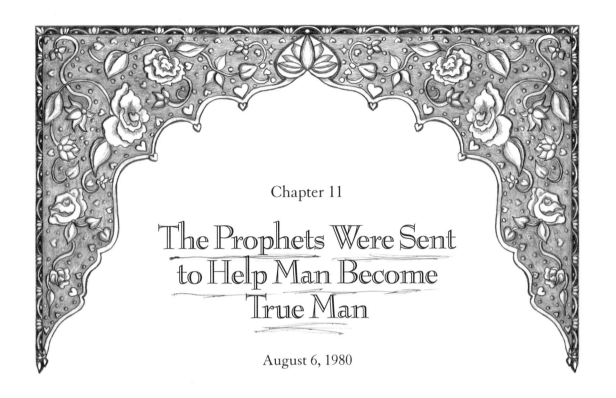

Chapter 11

The Prophets Were Sent to Help Man Become True Man

August 6, 1980

Man forgot it all;
he hurt other lives
and succumbed to selfishness.
He sought things out for his own ends
and changed into the worst of animals.
So God sent each prophet
to help man become true man,
to help him become exalted,
to help him understand his kingdom
and his King.

GOD

The Prophets Were Sent to Help
Man Become True Man

Bismillāhir-Rahmānir-Rahīm.
In the name of God, most Merciful, most Compassionate.

May all our praise and glory be to God alone.
And may God's praise and glory be true man *(insān)*.
May we all walk on the path of God's grace.
Āmīn.

May we receive His benevolence.
In this world and the next
may we receive the wealth of the three worlds.
In death and in life may we be liberated,
attain Allah's wealth of grace *(rahmat)*,
and so live our lives.
Āmīn.

Precious jeweled lights of my eyes, the here and the hereafter are aspects of our life. To understand both and live our lives, *Allāhu ta'ālā,* the Singular Ruler, has instructed us in many different ways. He has taught us through His created beings, through trees, flowers, and leaves. He has made us understand through the numerous four-legged creatures. He has taught us through the birds, fish, reptiles, scorpions, jungle-animals, city-animals, grass, shrubs, and flowers.

159

Through them all,
He makes us understand His limitless *rahmat*.
He teaches us through water, fire, earth, air,
sun, moon, clouds, lightning, thunder, rain,
stars, planets, lights, and colors.
These creations make us realize,
"No one else can do this.
The One who does all this is God!"

Believe only in Him—the One. He has established all these things as common wealth. He has created them to belong to man and animals. He has created grass, water, air, trees, plants, and fruits as our common wealth, belonging to all. However, only man lives in selfishness. Whatever man touches, he takes for his own. Whatever he sets foot on, he claims as his land, his country. Whatever he sees, he desires and gathers for himself. His every intention is for control and possession, for snatching another's freedom or hurting another's life. Man lives as one who hurts the lives of others. Whatever he sees, hears, smells, or tastes, he appropriates. He takes everything into his possession. Through millions of created beings, God tries to teach man to live in peace, equanimity, and tranquillity. But because of his self-interest, man does not realize this.

God teaches man through many different things, but his mind, darkness, cravings, and base desires have not left him. Man most exalted, has therefore, changed into man most degraded. For this condition, this state of being, God sent 124,000 prophets, saying, "Man does not learn from My creations; he does not realize the truth from these examples and explanations. Instead, he tries to control all living creatures and claim them for his own purposes. If he sees a creature, he takes it for himself. Whatever he sees, he appropriates. He plucks away the freedom of all lives. He plucks away the peace of all lives. He snatches away the tranquillity of all creatures. He takes on all the attachments of the world.

160

"Go to these sinful men and teach them this:
My creations belong to all.
All lives have freedom.
My kingdom is to be peaceful for all.
I created each being with rights,
peace, and equanimity.
Tell mankind,
and make them attain clarity
through everything I created—
the sun, moon, stars, water, fire, air, earth,
trees, grass, and shrubs.
I created them so all lives can thrive in freedom.
I created My kingdom for each life
to live in peace, equanimity, and tranquillity.

"The world-kingdom, soul-kingdom, divine-kingdom, and hell-kingdom—I assign mankind to these kingdoms according to way they live their lives. To the hell-kingdom, I apportion those of hell. Through their own sins and what they rear, they subject themselves to this. In the soul-kingdom, the achievers of soul-liberation dwell in liberty, with liberation in this world and the hereafter. They live in freedom.

"To an achiever of hell, all the pain returns from the lives he hurt, the lives he killed, the lives he ate, and the lives he subordinated. Everything he nurtured devours him now. Everything he hurt, hurts him now. Everything he looked at, looks at him here. Everything he relished, relishes and consumes him. Everything he sought devours him in the hell-kingdom. Make man realize this. Make man understand and live his life accordingly."

This is what God told the prophets before he sent them down to earth. He revealed these principles, examples, and explanations and told the prophets to teach each individual in a way that he or she would understand. The prophets that were sent down in this manner numbered 124,000. Many divinely wise beings *(qutbs)*, saints *(auliyās)*, messengers *(ambiyās)*, angels, and archangels were also sent down. Lights and sounds were sent down and made to resonate.

But man forgot it all;
he hurt other lives and succumbed to selfishness.
He sought things out for his own ends
and changed into the worst of animals.
So God sent each prophet
to help man become true man,
to help him become exalted,
to help him understand his kingdom and his King.
He sent down the appropriate words and grace.
He revealed the instructions of grace and their effulgences.

Through the final Prophet ☽, God sent the 6,666 verses as well as the five and six ordained duties. He explained the history of each prophet and the teachings given to each; then he told the Prophet ☽, "Ya Muhammad, I am sending you as the final Prophet. Go and teach the people."

According to this command, one of the five and six duties is the fast. God has to instruct us through the fast because we live our lives without awareness. Through studying the fast, may we realize its real meaning and purpose. We must find a way in which we, and others, can attain peace. These, among others, are some purposes of the fast.

My precious jeweled lights of my eyes, each of my children, whatever you do, go within it. Whatever you see, creep into it and look again. Distinguish *wrong* and *right*. Whatever you think, go within and reflect with wisdom, questioning, "What is wrong, what is right?" Whatever you intend, go within and perceive what is good and what is evil. When you understand with wisdom and realize, you will have resolute faith *(īmān)*, purity, and a pure life.

In this state, we should be resolute and extract each principle with understanding. We should know and adopt the right way to live our lives. When we walk and move one foot forward, placing it on the ground, the other foot lifts up automatically, does it not? If one foot slips, the other foot plants itself firmly on the ground, and our hands reach out to support the body, keeping it from falling, do they not? In the same way, inner patience, contentment, trust in God, and complete surrender to God *(sabūr, shakūr, tawakkul, and al-hamdu lillāh),* will constantly intertwine and operate within us. In our conduct, wisdom and *īmān* should prevail. When *īmān* slips, it should be supported and caught by wisdom. When wisdom falters, it should be assisted and held by *īmān* and belief. We should uphold this state in everything we do in life, saying the *Bismin*[1] before we proceed. If we say the *Bismin* and live our life in accord with it, we will never do what is unlawful *(harām),* and we will never see hell. We will realize the straight way.

Ours should be a body of inner patience, contentment, trust in God, total surrender to God, wisdom, *īmān* and trust. When we live with such a body, one foot must automatically lift up when the other meets the ground. Such is the intention. On the path of the soul we move forward saying, *Lā ilāha ill-Allāhu*—other than You there is nothing, only You are God. When the breath, feet, and *īmān* move forward in this manner, hell will be far removed from us, sins will be burned away from us, and desires will try to run away from us. Allah, Allah's messengers, prophets, angels, and archangels will surround and protect us. With this guardianship we can go to our Father's divine kingdom. If, in everything we do, we live in this way, the angels, archangels, prophets, and enlightened beings will surround us, and we will experience no danger. We will then walk in safety and protection.

---

1. **Bismin:** An abbreviated version of *Bismillāhir-Rahmānir-Rahīm*—in the name of God, most Merciful, most Compassionate. To say it with true meaning is to acknowledge God as the Creator, Protector, and Sustainer of all lives. Then, realizing that He knows all, place all responsibility in His keeping, and live in peace.

Each child must think of this.
Adhere to the straight way.
Walk on it with *īmān,* certainty, and trust,
letting each breath and footstep
synchronize with *Lā ilāha ill-Allāhu.*
When you place your left foot forward, say, *"Lā ilāha,"*
and when you place your right foot forward, say, *"Ill-Allāhu."*
Our breath and feet should move together.
Belief, determination, and *īmān*
should surround and safeguard each step we take.
This will be the protection in a resolute life.
Our sins, birth-karma, arrogance, and maya will leave us.
Each child, reflect on this and live!
Āmīn.
As-salāmu 'alaikum wa rahmatullāhi wa barakātuhu kulluhu.
May all the peace, the beneficence, and the blessings of God
be upon you.

My precious jeweled lights of my eyes,
go now, and break the fasts that you intended in God's name.
Say the *Bismin;* say, *"Bismillāhir-Rahmānir-Rahīm—*
in the name of God, most Merciful, most Compassionate."
Intend God and say, *"Al-hamdu lillāh—*
All praise is to God!"
Give Him your intentions,
give Him the responsibility,
and do your duties.
Āmīn.
As-salāmu 'alaikum wa rahmatullāhi wa barakātuhu kulluhu.
May all the peace, the beneficence, and the blessings of God
be upon you.

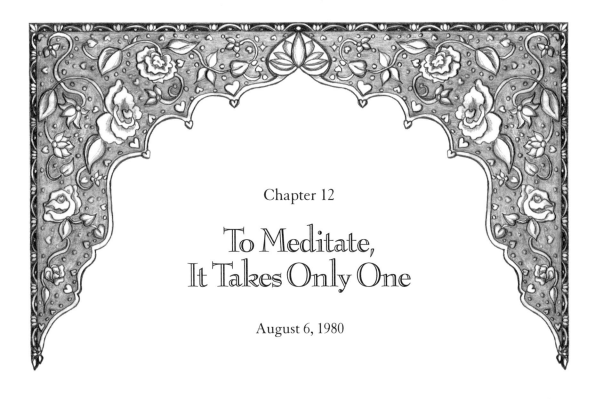

Chapter 12

To Meditate, It Takes Only One

August 6, 1980

Meditation.
God alone should meditate on God.
God's inner heart alone should meditate on God.
God's speech alone should speak to God.
God's qualities alone should merge with God.
God's prayer alone will reach God.
Only God can worship God.
This is why there must be
only One
for meditation.

To Meditate, It Takes Only One

All the searching
and all the running,
the one-span stomach it is for!
All the dancing,
all the singing,
and one becoming another's slave,
all the searching,
and all the running,
the one-span stomach they do it for!

One becoming another's slave,
the searching,
and the running
my dear one,
the one-span stomach it is for!

Whether one travels from here to New York, from New York to Canada, from Canada to Chicago, or from Chicago to Pennsylvania— it is all for the sake of the one-span stomach. Wherever you may run, it is always for the one-span stomach. Well, go ahead and take care of the stomach, but do one more thing. There is something else you must do. Listen!

For meditation, it takes only one.
For pleasure, it takes two.

For a corpse, it takes four.
O dear one,
this is the way of the world.

Meditation.
God alone should meditate on God.
God's inner heart alone should meditate on God.
God's speech alone should speak to God.
God's qualities alone should merge with God.
God's prayer alone will reach God.
Only God can worship God.
This is why there must be only One for meditation.
There is no "I" and "you."
The duality of "I" and "you" is not meditation.
Only He can meditate on Him.
This is the state in which we should meditate.
He becomes us, we become Him—this is meditation.
This is why there is only one for meditation—
One God.

For pleasure, there must be two. To increase the world, a man and a woman are necessary. Two are needed to enlarge the body and enlarge the world. For a corpse, there must be four. Four people are needed to carry the coffin, or four wheels are needed to wheel the body away. This is the explanation.

None of these mean very much. There is not much to say about the "husband-wife work." Instead, reflect upon meditation. What is meditation? It will be wise to reflect on this. There is not much use in running to different places. Getting married, expanding your body—there is no point in doing that either. There is no use in increasing the population of the world or in expanding your belly to accomplish this. There is no point in running about either. There is no point in accumulating more and more. Only meditation is of value. Pursue this. Do you understand?

Someday, everyone will leave us and we will have to be alone. Therefore, we should practice being alone now, saying, "We are going to be alone one day. Everyone will carry us to the cemetery and leave us there—alone. They will gather together, carry us to the grave, and leave us alone." If we practice being alone right now, it will be easier later on. We can then leave unperturbed, saying, " I was alone then, and I am alone now. There is no reason to be distressed!" However, if we take a group of people with us wherever we go, then we will have to cry when we get there. We will be lonely and say, "Where is my child? Where is my wife?" We will look around for them and it will be very difficult. Remain alone; you have to be alone later on. Practice now for what is to come later. That will be good. All praise is to God!

All right. What's next?

Chapter 13

May God Fulfill
Your Intentions

August 7, 1980

May God
fulfill your intentions
here and in the hereafter.
May He give you His blessings of grace,
guide you on the straight path,
make your yearnings and intentions
complete,
and so grace you.
Āmīn.

May God Fulfil Your Intentions

Bismillāhir-Rahmānir-Rahīm.
In the name of God, most Merciful, most Compassionate.

One of unfathomable grace,
One of incomparable love,
Allāhu!
To Your magnitude and grace
there is no equal.
To Your love
there is no end.
My Creator, Supreme One!
You gave me
my precious eye
and the light of my eye.
For all who trust
and believe in You,
You will bestow
paradise in Your kingdom.
For all who intend You,
You will bestow Your blessings,
and so grace them.

One without anger.
One without sin.

173

One without jealousy.
For those who say He exists,
and for those who say He does not,
for those who realize,
and for those who do not,
He is the Mighty One, the Giver of love—
ill Allāhu!

For those who intend Him,
He intends them first.
For those who seek Him,
He seeks them first.
For those who take one step forward to seek Him,
He takes ten steps forward first.
For those who worship Him,
He praises them.
As One who understands the intentions
and yearnings
of yesterday,
He bows to all lives and helps them.
He is the Giver of love,
the Protector,
Allāhu ta 'ālā Nāyan,
the Singular One who rules and sustains.

He bows to all lives
in His kingdom,
in His grace,
in His Truth,
and in His wisdom.
Through His benevolence
He bestows grace.
Through His compassionate love

He helps all lives,
showering them with compassion, patience,
tolerance, and equanimity.

The Lord,
the Helpful One,
the Merciful One,
the Creator,
the Protector,
the Life-Giver,
the Beckoner,
may all lives bow down,
worship Him,
intend Him with yearning,
and search for Him.
May He bestow on them
His benevolence
and His grace-wealth *(rahmat)*,
and so grace them.
Āmīn.

O Intenders!
In your fast
and in your charity,
merge with
His belief,
His intention,
and His certainty.
In your ritual prayers,
prayers with a melting heart *(ibādat)*,
constant remembrance of God *(dhikr)*,
prayers,
charity,

fasting,
and the pilgrimage of Hajj,
merge with the qualities and actions
of the Limitless One.
Allāhu is the Mighty One,
the Bestower of grace
who protects and sustains the intentions
of all who worship Him.

Whatever actions you perform
upon intending Him,
may He bestow the
grace and benevolence
that will elevate them,
and fulfill your intentions.
Āmīn.

May He
help you in every way,
bestow His grace on you,
protect and preserve you,
and so grace you.
Āmīn,
O Lord of the Universes.

May He
fulfill your intentions
here and in the hereafter.
May He give you His blessings of grace,
guide you on the straight path,
make your yearnings and intentions
complete,
and so grace you.

According to His intentions
may you accept and pursue
His commandments, His rules,
His wisdom, His fortitude, and His patience.

May God bestow His grace
on each of you who join His path.
May He fulfill your intentions
and so grace you.
Āmīn.
Lord of all Universes!

As-salāmu 'alaikum wa rahmatullāhi wa barakātuhu kulluhu.
May all the peace, the beneficence, and the blessings of God
be upon you.

Children who are fasting, fulfill your fast according to your intentions and God's intentions. Then after your fast is over, we will talk some more. Tonight is the twenty-seventh night of the fast. It is called the night of *Lailatul-Qadr*, the night on which a ray of light *(qadr)* descended. We will talk about this after you complete the fast and fulfill your intentions. We will talk about how this *Lailatul-Qadr* descended to the *Rasūl* ☙ on this day, and of its benefits and significance.

As-salāmu 'alaikum wa rahmatullāhi wa barakātuhu kulluhu.
May all the peace, the beneficence, and the blessings of God
be upon you.
Go and fulfill your intentions.
According to your yearning and search,
may God grant you His wealth.
May the Merciful One bestow upon you
the *rahmat* that is yours.
Āmīn. Āmīn. Āmīn.

177

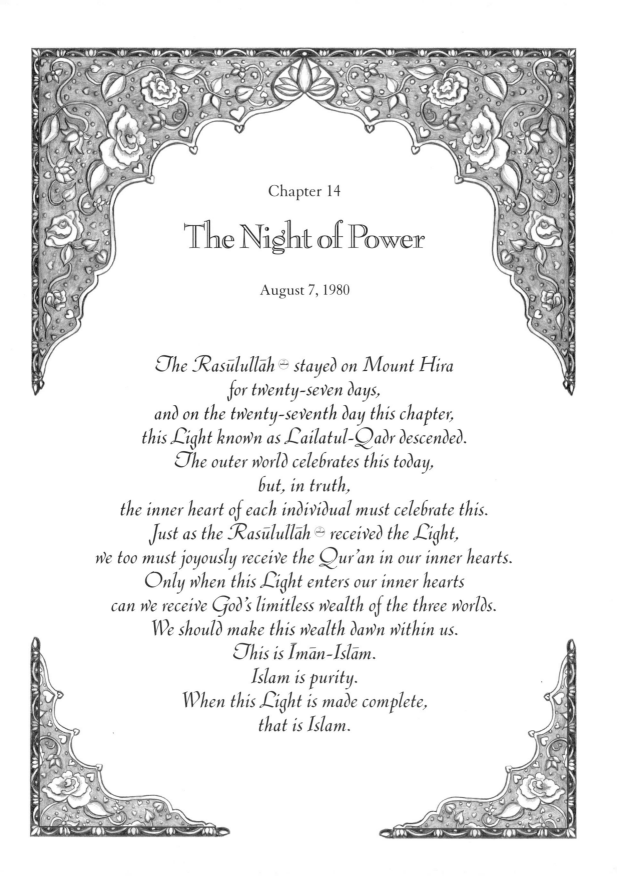

Chapter 14

The Night of Power

August 7, 1980

The Rasūlullāh ☺ stayed on Mount Hira
for twenty-seven days,
and on the twenty-seventh day this chapter,
this Light known as Lailatul-Qadr descended.
The outer world celebrates this today,
but, in truth,
the inner heart of each individual must celebrate this.
Just as the Rasūlullāh ☺ received the Light,
we too must joyously receive the Qur'an in our inner hearts.
Only when this Light enters our inner hearts
can we receive God's limitless wealth of the three worlds.
We should make this wealth dawn within us.
This is Īmān-Islām.
Islam is purity.
When this Light is made complete,
that is Islam.

The Night of Power

As-salāmu ʿalaikum wa rahmatullāhi wa barakātuhu kulluhu.
May all the peace, the beneficence, and the blessings of God
be upon you.
May all praise and praising be to God alone.
May He be our Bestower of benevolence and grace-wealth *(rahmat)*.
May praise and praising be rightfully His and His alone.
May this One of unfathomable grace and incomparable love
bestow His benevolence,
and so grace us.
Āmīn.

May all the peace, beneficence, and blessings of God
be upon you.
To all the children who fasted in the month of Ramadan
with focus, intention, faith, and trust,
in God's name, and with great certitude;
to those who carried out this fast of Ramadan in their inner hearts;
to those who executed it with their bodies and inner hearts;
to those who rendered it with their inner hearts and intentions;
to those who fasted, and to those who did not fast due to illness;
to those whose hearts melted
as they acted in accord with God's intention;
and to those who have faith;
may God bestow His wealth of three worlds in this month of Ramadan.

May they receive Allah's *rahmat* in their lives, in their souls,
and in the hereafter.
May Allah bestow on us His wealth of the three worlds,
and so grace us.
Āmīn.

May He give us a life free of illness,
an inner heart free of sorrow,
and a peaceful life free of distress and agitation.
May He give us inner patience, contentment,
trust in God, and total surrender to God
(sabūr, shakūr, tawakkul, and al-hamdu lillāh).
May He grant us this patience, this eminent gift,
which is the scepter of His kingdom.
May He give us His beautiful qualities,
and so grace us.
Āmīn.

May He give us peace and equanimity in our inner hearts,
and a tranquil life in this world and the next,
and so grace us.
Āmīn.

May He lengthen our lives,
purify our living days,
make our inner hearts radiant,
strengthen our *īmān,*
and give us the certitude
to worship *Allāhu ta'ālā*
soul with Soul,
and so grace us.
Āmīn.

O God,
Lord of all the universes!
May He bestow wisdom and light
on our inner hearts, faces, bodies, and intentions.
May He manifest His resplendent beauty and light
in our faces, hearts, and bodies,
and so grace us.
Āmīn.

May He grant us His benevolent grace
so we may live in purity, remain in purity,
and leave the world in purity;
so we may live in this world as light,
recede as light,
and disappear in Allah's throne and *rahmat*
as light.

My precious jeweled lights of my eyes,
may God grant us His grace
to not see the hells we have seen in this life
after we die.
May God grant us the fortitude and purity
in this very life
to leave hell peacefully behind
and dwell in heaven.
Āmīn.

May we always attain happiness and tranquillity
within God's benevolent grace.
For those who see Him here,
for those who see Him, His prophets,
His enlightened beings, and His *Rasūl* ☉,
for those who have seen them in their inner hearts,

realized them in their inner hearts,
and spoken with them in their inner hearts,
it is said that God,
the Singular One who rules and sustains,
will have kept hell far away from them.
May God keep hell far away from us
in this world and in the next,
and so grace us.
Āmīn.

May He give us His wealth, exalted qualities,
inner patience, compassion, forbearance,
and the qualities and actions of His benevolence,
and so grace us.
Āmīn. Āmīn.

O Lord of the universes,
may all the peace, the beneficence, and the blessings of God
be upon you.
All praise is to Him.

Bismillāhir-Rahmānir-Rahīm.
In the name of God, most Merciful, most Compassionate.

My precious jeweled lights of my eyes, we will now talk about the purposes of your intended fast. Allah Himself must come and speak of His *rahmat.* Just as God Himself came to the *Rasūl* ☉, answering questions, He will have to come and provide the explanations. Allah Himself must speak Allah's words. In this month of Ramadan, on this twenty-seventh night of the fast, God sent the Qur'an known as *Lailatul-Qadr* to the *Rasūl* ☉. Now, God Himself must talk about that *rahmat.* May we all reach out our hands and receive and understand that *rahmat. Āmīn. Āmīn.* First, we will talk a little about *Muhammad Mustafar-Rasūl* ☉ who

184

came as a child to Āminah ☺. We will relate a portion of his story, and how he was sent down to the world as the son of Āminah ☺ and 'Abdullāh.

In the city of Mecca, Āminah ☺ and 'Abdullāh lived together, poor and childless. When Āminah ☺ was in this state she had three dreams about *Allāhu ta'ālā Nāyan*. In these dreams God told her, "Āminah☺, you are going to have a child. This child will be the wealth of the three worlds. I have placed in its hand the keys that open the three worlds. I have created this child to be a Light that is greater than all the prophets in the world of souls *(awwal),* the hereafter *(ākhirah),* and this world *(dunyā).* I have created this as a Light for the beginning and the end. Keeping this Light in the realm of pure souls *(arwāh),* I summoned all the other lights and souls, saying, 'Look at this Light, everyone! Who will accept this Light?'"

When the mountains, oceans, and shores were asked this question, the Light engulfed all the other lights, and everyone replied, "O Allah, this Light swallowed all our lights. We cannot keep this Light with us. It engulfs us." God asked all the lights, the prophets, and enlightened beings once again, but this intrinsic, radiant, Divine *Nūr*-Light over-powered all the other resplendent lights. When God raised the question once more, the earth rose saying, "O Allah, I will accept this Light." Then God, the Singular One who rules and sustains said, "O Earth, this Light dawned from Me; I brought it out of My inner heart. It dawned from My inner heart, emerged, and bowed down to Me saying, *'Bismillāhir-Rahmānir-Rahīm*—in the name of God, most Merciful, most Compassionate.' It uttered this name and this *rahmat.* This Light will understand things that others do not comprehend. This is the Light that you now accept.

"O Earth, this Light is perfectly pure! And since you said that you would accept this Light, I am giving it to you as an entrusted property. You will have to return this entrusted property—this pure Light—to Me, later on. I will entrust this Light to every life that is created out of you, and you will have to be both mother and father. I will name you

Adam. From you, I will take your earth and your light—the essence within earth—and create Adam and Eve. On their foreheads, I will impress the Light that you accepted. The Light in their foreheads will be *Nūr Muhammad*. This is the *rahmat* that sees Me. I will place it in the gnostic eye in the center of the forehead (*kursī*). With this *kursī* they will be able to understand the throne of God (*'arsh*), the seat of God (*kursī*), the divine pen (*qalam*), heaven, and the inviolate preserved tablet (*al-lauhul-mahfūz*).

"With this Light you can understand the eighteen thousand universes, all the hells, and the seven heavens. This will be the beauty (*zīnat*) and Light of earth. It will be this Light that I place in the forehead of each human being created from you. The beauty of this Light will the beauty of God in man.

"This Light will be there as wisdom, as inner patience, as contentment, as *rahmat,* and as the wealth of the three worlds. You will receive this Light; you said that you would accept it. However, if at the very end, you do not return this entrusted treasure to Me in its absolute purity, you will have caused your own ruin. O Adam, I am giving it to you now."

Then through this Light, this *Nūr*, God made the earth, fire, water, and air repeat the affirmation of faith (*kalimah*).[1] And having done this, He created Adam☉ out of earth and pressed the Light into His forehead. This is the *kursī,* the gnostic eye in our forehead, which keeps the inner heart, face, and forehead radiant. After God created Adam☉ and the Light, He created us, the family of mankind. He expanded the family, and as the family increased, He decided to have Āminah☉ give birth to Muhammad☉ [this Light] in a final form.

---

1. **Kalimah:** The *Kalimah* is the testimony of faith in which a person affirms, *There is nothing other than You, only You are God (Lā ilāha ill-Allāh)*. This remembrance of God cuts away the influence of the five elements, washes away all the karma that has accumulated, dispels darkness, and makes the heart beautiful and resplendent. This *Kalimah* washes the body and heart of man, making him pure. It makes his wisdom emerge, and impels this wisdom to know the self and God.

For the children of Adam☻, God created one hundred and twenty-four thousand prophets, with Muhammad ☻ as the final prophet. God made Muhammad ☻ witness His principles. Then He showed Āminah ☻ these principles and said, "Āminah, I am giving you this child, My Intrinsic Light, as the final one. He will be the wealth of the three worlds. In the hands of this child, I will place the key that can unlock the world of souls, this world, and the hereafter. When this child is born, name it Muhammad." This is what God said.

Āminah ☻ experienced the same dream three times, and she told 'Abdullāh what she had perceived. Then one day while 'Abdullāh was with Āminah ☻, the child arrived as a light and entered Āminah's ☻ abdomen. Four months later 'Abdullāh died while away on business. The celestial beings, angels, and archangels announced, "Āminah's☻ child has become an orphan. It will be born poor, and without a father." But the sound of God, the Singular One who rules and sustains, was heard: "Muhammad is not an orphan. He will be a child with the wealth of the three worlds. He will be a leader to you all, a light to resolute faith (*īmān*), purity and completeness to the light of perfect purity (*dīn*), and a leader to the children of Adam. All of Adam's children will be Muhammad's followers. Such is the wealth I have given Muhammad. He is not an orphan."

In accordance with God's sound, nine months passed; the tenth month arrived, and Āminah☻ began to deliver the child. Then God, the Singular One who rules and sustains, resonated, "Āminah☻, a child will be born unto you today. This child will be one who has received the wealth of the three worlds in its hands." As soon as Āminah☻ heard this, the Light known as Muhammad was born.

It was born clothed in white silk of the greatest purity. There was no blood associated with childbirth, and no evidence of delivery by a female. It was born with no blood connections, clothed in purity and silken clothing. Heavenly maidens, celestial messengers, and angels arrived to deliver the child. At the moment of delivery Āminah☻ was made unconscious, and the child was supported by [other] hands before it touched the ground. The child appeared amidst a delivery that had no signs of childbirth, and was immediately taken to heaven. The eight heavens had been decorated and the seven hells had been locked shut. The heavenly maidens and angels carried the child and showed him around the seven heavens. They bathed the baby in the beautiful wisdom-waters of heaven. The heavenly maidens called out, *"Dīn, dīn,"* and the angels and archangels recited prayers. The prophets and enlightened beings stood there resonating greetings and prayers *(salāms* and *salawāt)*.

The child was taken around the eight heavens dressed in an exquisite silken robe. A crown known as *darsul-ambiyā'* was placed on his head, and he was told, "You are the archetype of all prophets in heaven. You will be the Light known as *Nūr Muhammad.* You will go to earth and reveal My principles. As the final prophet, I will confer on you all that I have given to the other prophets. Make everyone into [one family with] one father and one mother. Make them realize Me. I will give you one purpose, one *īmān,* and one *kalimah* known as *Īmān-Islām.*[2]

"May you make all lives attain peace through this *kalimah.* May you end all duality, and create oneness. May you establish the certainty that Allah is One. Prove to the people that I am the only Father, and that all the children of Adam are one family. Make everyone pure and resplendent. The *kalimah* I give you is one of Light. If the *kalimah* is embedded in man's inner heart, he will always be a perfect light. I am giving you the Light that is the *kalimah;* may you fill each heart with this Light. The pure Light of the *kalimah* originated from Me and emerged through you. *Ya Muhammad,* you bowed down to Me saying, *"Bismillāhir-Rahmānir-Rahīm,"* acknowledging Me as the Creator, Protector, and Sustainer. Because of this, you are the one to give everyone this completeness. As you made Me realize Myself, stay within all inner hearts,

---

2. **Īmān-Islām:** A state wherein the pure heart, cutting away all evil, takes on the courageous determination called faith and shines in God's resplendence. When the resplendence of God is seen as the completeness within the heart of man, that is *Īmān-Islām.*

fill them with light, and make them realize Me. I am placing you as Light, as *Ahamad*, within their hearts *(ahams)*. But in the world, I have created you as Āminah's child. I have filled you with the Light that is Muhammad. I have given you this beauty in the eyes, forehead, nose, cheek, lips, and mouth. In the children of Adam, this will be the beauty *(zīnat)* of the face. When this beauty and the heart become clear, these children will merge with Me. They will be My children. They will be the princes, the rulers of My kingdom. Go to these children, and make My judgment and faith dawn in them.

"O Muhammad, tell them to believe in the prophets, enlightened beings, angels, and archangels. Make them believe in the Day of Questioning *(Qiyāmah),* the Day of Judgment, and the day of death. Tell them to believe this. Show them that I am the One who will dispense judgment. Make them understand the six principles clearly. The principles, and the sun, moon, stars, earth, fire, water, air, and ether have been given as common wealth to belong to all. Make them realize this. Reveal this to every inner heart. I have given all My *rahmat* as wealth that belongs to all. Tell them to preserve this as common wealth.

"May everyone share the common wealth, live as one family, eat off the same plate, live together, and unite as one. With no differences between king and beggar, rich and poor, help them to live together as one family, worshipping Me. Make them live together through good times and bad. If one is hungry, let another appease that hunger. If one is in difficulty, let another come in and help. If one is sorrowful, let another offer comfort. If one is agitated, let another embrace him heart to heart and pacify him. In death, in birth, in sorrow, in good times, and in bad times, let others embrace, help, and offer comfort. Tell your followers this. Reveal this *kalimah* and make them develop a pure inner heart. To this end, I am giving you the *kalimah* that is perfect purity.

"Establish this state. Prove to them that Allah is the only wealth. Tell them that I have placed My *rahmat,* My limitless grace, in the trees, shrubs, grasses, water, air, sun, and moon. I have filled everything with My grace. Tell your followers to understand and share this *rahmat* with others while partaking of it. I have distributed this common wealth equally to all lives. This common wealth must not become one's personal possession. No one must take control or possession of it, claiming it to be their own. If they do this and hurt another life at *'asr*,[3] ask them to embrace each other in unity and give *salāms* before the *maghrib* prayers. Tell them that jealousy and treachery should not exist on the path of purity *(dīnul-Islām)*. There should not be even an atom of a blemish in perfect purity. Convince them of this.

"I have so instructed the prophets that they may help man to progress from one step to the next. Since the time of Adam I have taught one hundred and twenty-four thousand prophets, giving them step by step explanations. Now, O Muhammad, I am giving you the teachings in their entirety—each story in its complete form. I am placing My story within you, and I am also giving you your story, which was within Me. Go and reveal these stories!" God gave Muhammad ☺ many more explanations. We cannot talk about them in detail now. I will just establish certain points.

[Returning to Muhammad's birth]

Then the heavenly maidens stood in front of Āminah ☺ as she quickly opened her eyes and was handed the baby. Āminah ☺ exclaimed, "O wealth of Allah, my grace-wealth of all the universes *(rahmatul-'ālamīn)*, wealth given by Allah, treasure that comes to me as the wealth of the three worlds, you will be the complete wealth for this world and the soul-world. God has given me a treasure that will bestow compassion on all lives." Āminah ☺ took the baby in her arms, hugged it to her breast and kissed it, saying, "Come, precious jeweled light of my eyes." She kissed the baby and placed it in her lap. The heavenly maidens joined both hands in prayer, bowed down in reverence, and kissed the child. The angels, archangels, and prophets in the divine realm kissed the child. The enlightened beings kissed the child on the forehead, kissing the

---

3. 'Asr: Of the five daily prayers, the *afternoon prayer* is the *'asr* prayer, followed by the sunset prayer of *maghrib*.

Light. Upon kissing the child, everyone left the baby in Āminah's ☺ hands and disappeared.

Āminah ☺ raised the Light known as Muhammad, and though they were poor and owned no property, their hearts were not impoverished. Abū Tālib, the uncle, took care of Muhammad ☺. In those early days, the *Rasulullāh* ☺ would not drink anything other than mother's milk. The town of Qulay, meanwhile, had experienced a severe famine for twelve years, and many poor women now came to Mecca to serve as wet-nurses and earn a living.

One of these women was Halīma. Driven by poverty, she had left her two children behind and arrived in Mecca, hoping to nurse a baby and earn money to support her family. But Halīma could only nurse with one breast, as one of her breasts had always been dry. She walked all over Mecca seeking a job as a wet-nurse, but was unsuccessful, while other healthy women procured employment. Finally, someone suggested that Halīma visit Āminah ☺. At Āminah's ☺ house, Abu Tālib asked her, "What is the matter? Why are you here?" Halīma replied, "We came here from the town of Qulay, fleeing a twelve year famine. We have had no rain in years. Many of us came here to earn money as wet nurses, and everyone but me is now employed. I was told that there is a child here, and so I came." Abu Tālib replied, "My brother's child is here. My brother is dead. His wife Āminah ☺ has a child. They are poor, with no money or property. All they have is Allah. This is their condition. If you wish, you can offer them your milk, but they have no money to offer you."

Halīma started to grow perturbed: "God gave everyone else wealth and fancy houses, but He has directed me to this poor house to feed a little child. What should I do?" She reflected on this with her husband. "We do not know what Allah has in store for us. We do not know what *rahmat* He has reserved for us. Let us at least look at the child once before we leave," they thought to themselves. And so they said, "Bring us your child. Let us at least see him and hug him before we leave."

Abu Tālib went to Āminah ☺ and informed her that a wet-nurse had come to see the child. As Āminah☺ carried Muhammad☺ outside, the Light shone on Halīma's face, and her face blossomed with youthfulness, transforming her from a thirty-five year old to a sixteen year old. Reaching out to the child with great emotion, saying, "This is very wondrous," she hugged and embraced the baby to her bosom. She was immediately transformed into a sixteen year old maiden. Her body became robust, her dry breast filled, and milk started to flow from both breasts. Halīma told her husband, "My body has changed. My breast is no longer dry." She held the baby close in order to feed it.

Muhammad☺ did not drink from the breast her own two children had suckled, but moved instead toward the breast that had been dry. God's voice was heard saying, "O Muhammad, when I created you I had already created Halīma. I kept her breast dry and untouched by saliva. I have released it for you now. You can drink this milk." Then Muhammad☺ placed his mouth on her breast, and due to his perfect completeness, Halīma's inner heart trembled with joy. She knew that she had received the wealth of the three worlds. Her inner heart had the completeness of this knowledge. "I do not need any other wealth, I have received the wealth of the three worlds," remarked Halīma, as she bowed down to Āminah☺, continuing to feed the child for a long time. After a while she told Āminah☺, "We have received *rahmat;* God has given us this. But I do have two children to take care of in the neighboring town. Allow me to keep this child with me until he no longer needs milk. I will take him to my hometown, raise him, and return him to you."

Āminah☺ replied, "If such is God's intention, you may certainly take the child." Muhammad☺ smiled, and Āminah☺ said, "Let me hold him once and then you may take him." The child looked at Āminah's☺ face and beamed. Āminah☺ and Abu Tālib kissed the child, and the baby smiled again with such beauty that it seemed to spread through all the three worlds. Blue clouds tumbled into his eyes as he smiled; his lips turned as rosy as corals, and his mouth shone like pearls. Āminah☺ hugged the child joyously and handed him back to Halīma saying, "All praise is to God. Only God will understand this mystery. God, the Giver of this child, will also protect him ."

The camel that had brought Halīma from Qulay was an old, broken down beast, starved, emaciated, and merely skin and bones. Halīma's husband held on to its reins, while Halīma placed the baby on the camel and climbed up herself. In an instant, the camel burgeoned in the most amazing way, filling out and becoming very young and beautiful. It was a wondrous sight. Halīma exclaimed, "We have received the most complete treasure! The camel is transformed, and our journey of six months will now last only one month!" Halīma's husband tied a cloth hammock under the camel's belly and climbed into it; Halīma and Muhammad ⊕ rode on top; and the camel, carrying all three, set off on the journey.

Fifteen days into the journey, the camel halted at the place where 'Abdullāh⊕ had died. God's sound was heard, "O Muhammad, your father is buried here." The child looked intently at the spot, smiled, looked again, chuckled, and looked once more. The camel stood very still for twenty minutes, gazing at the burial spot. Then, it lifted one foot and moved forward.

As they journeyed onward, the trees on either side, parched and dry from the drought—olive trees, date palms, and other fruit trees—started to sprout, blossom, bear fruit, and ripen. The trees were soon laden with juicy fruit. What a wonder this was! On both embankments, fruit appeared on once barren trees. Halīma and her husband were amazed. The fruits, when eaten, had seventy kinds of flavors. Wondrous events were taking place all around. As soon as they reached the town of Qulay, it began to rain. The trees in Qulay began to miraculously bear fruit. The famine had ended!

Everyone came to see the child, bringing money and wealth. Money poured in as people flocked to see, kiss, and embrace the child. When the sick embraced the child, their diseases were cured. When the lame carried and embraced the child, they were able to walk immediately. When the blind came, they regained their sight. When the dumb arrived, they began speak. When those who could not smell came, they regained their sense of smell. When the deaf came, they regained their ability to hear. When those with handicapped arms or legs arrived, they were cured. Many miracles happened in the town of Qulay.

The king thought to himself, "Halīma brought back a child, and we might lose our kingdom on account of him. This child might capture our kingdom. This child cures incurable diseases. Every kind of illness—asthma, cancer, karmic illnesses, and leprosy—is cured. As soon as the child laughs, diseases are cured. As soon as the child is carried, bodies are transformed." The king and his ministers decided to see the child for themselves. They carried the child and became youthful instantly; their bodies began to transform.

The king thought, "This child will capture my kingdom. I should try to take him away." He asked Halīma, "Will you give us the child? We will raise the child in our kingdom, in our palace. We will give him a lot of wealth." But Halīma replied, "I have accepted this child as the wealth of the three worlds. I will not give him away." The king offered Halīma the child's weight in gold, but she refused. Once more the king cajoled, "We will give you the child's weight in precious stones," but his offer was turned down. For a year, the king tried every means of cunning and trickery to seize or hurt the child, but was unsuccessful.

Meanwhile, the famine had come to an end, but fear had arisen in Halīma's heart. She wondered, "What will the king do to my child? O Muhammad, I cannot live without you." At this time, Halīma was still feeding Muhammad ☺ from her right breast and her own two children from her left breast. Her milk flowed in abundance. The year drew to an end, and the child had to be returned to Āminah ☺, who longed to see him. But Halīma, fearing what the king of Qulay might do, was unwilling to undertake the journey. The child, who could now speak, spoke softly, "While Allah exists, nothing will happen to me. Mother, while His protection exists, you need not fear. Do not feel sad. There is not a creature that He does not protect. Therefore, do not be afraid." Halīma enquired, "Shall we take a lot of people with us on our journey? They can protect us." The child replied, "No, we will take only God with us. Let us take God alone with us." And so it was that Halīma, her husband, and one-year old Muhammad ☺ set off on their journey.

As they travelled between Qulay, Mecca, and Medina, they rested under a banana tree. Halīma climbed off the camel and sat under the tree, nursing the child as he lay on her lap. While she was nursing, black clouds rolled across the sky, and a large cloud tumbled out, scooping up Muhammad ☺ and taking him away.

Halīma was distraught. She beat her head and chest, shouting, "O Muhammad, where did you go?" But there was nothing she could do. She beat herself, rolled on the ground, and shrieked, "What will I tell Āminah? O God, you plucked my child away from me. Where has this child gone?" She screamed, cried, and shouted, beating her head and chest.

An Arab walking by at this time enquired, "O husband and wife, why do you cry? Even the camel is crying! What is the matter?" Halīma replied, "My child known as Muhammad, Āminah's son, was given to me by Allah as the wealth of the three worlds. When we received this wealth, all our poverty and illness came to an end. We were on our way to return the child to his birth-mother, but a black cloud fell onto my lap as I sat nursing the child. I saw the cloud, and when I blinked again, I could not see my child." "Is that so?" asked the man. "Well, you cannot see your child now. But come with me. There is a big temple further along. If you beseech the deity in the temple, you will get your child back. The deity will tell you where the child is."

So they went to the temple, walked up to the statue of the deity, and reverently pleaded, "O deity, a cloud came down while I was nursing and took my child away. I don't know where my child went. Please tell me where my child is. Please return my child to me." The statue did not speak. The man who had accompanied them said, "Mention your child's name, say his name." Halīma said, "Muhammad, the child's name is Muhammad." Immediately the statue broke into pieces, with the arms, head, and legs falling apart and tumbling to the ground. The man who accompanied them was very astonished. "What is this?" he exclaimed, "This is a great deity, a great god who bestows favors and speaks to us, but it shattered into pieces on hearing your son's name. If god himself falls down in this manner, what danger can ever befall your son? Nothing will happen to him. Why should you cry? There is no need to cry. Resume your journey. Go on. You will find your child as you proceed."

Further ahead, they found the child lying on a silken carpet in an orchard. A five-headed snake had spread its hood to protect the child from the sun, and the child lay there smiling. The townspeople voiced their amazement: "Who is this radiant child in our orchard?" The trees were rapidly flowering and bearing fruit—bananas, oranges, and lemons. All the townspeople gathered around the orchard to witness this wondrous sight, but the snake did not permit anyone to come near the child. When Halīma approached the orchard and saw the child, the sound of God was heard saying, "Halīma, this child of grace, this child of *rahmat,* had to be brought here because the angels and heavenly maidens wanted to see him. This is why the child was brought here. Nothing will ever happen to Muhammad. Why do you cry? Do not let anything disturb you. You came here fearing the king, but there is none who can kill Muhammad. Allah is protecting him."

As Halīma approached the child, he smiled and waved his hands and feet in delight. The snake moved away, and Halīma took her child and proceeded toward Mecca. She handed the baby to Āminah☙, and the mother joyously smiled, hugged, and kissed her child. She kept the baby with her for a few days and then returned the child to Halīma's care.

Four years passed, and one day Halīma was planning to go out with her two children. Muhammad☙ said, "I need to go with you too." The two older children were going out to graze the sheep and goats, and Muhammad☙ wanted to join them. Halīma said, "O son, Muhammad, you are my life. You should not go there. There are rocks, thorns, animals, and snakes."

[The author says: There is a long song about this, but I cannot sing it now. I will just give you the meaning and the explanations.][4]

Muhammad ☺ replied, "No. If the thorns hurt them, why shouldn't they hurt me? If they can go out among snakes, why shouldn't I. Am I different? If it is difficult for them, why shouldn't it be difficult for me? That is not the way it should be, mother." Muhammad ☺ opened his mouth and sang these words as a song. The sound of his voice echoed all over this world and the soul-world, and was heard by the angels and archangels. Everyone heard the voice and sound of Muhammad ☺, and upon hearing it they praised Allah with resonant greetings and prayers *(salāms and salawāt)*.

Halīma could say nothing in reply, and so she sent Muhammad ☺ outside with her two children. She placed the child in a jeweled blanket, telling her children, "Take your younger brother with you. Here is some food for the child. Place the food in a shady spot, and make sure you feed him at the appropriate time. Don't let him walk. Don't let him run. Be very cautious! He is my life. He is your life, and mine. No harm should befall him. Take great care of him."

Thus Halīma entrusted Muhammad ☺ to the care of her two children as they set off with the goats. The children led the goats to the grazing pasture and then, spreading out the blanket for Muhammad ☺, they began to feed him. As the child smiled and played, the sheep and goats did not graze, but drew steadily closer to the blanket. The wolves, birds, and beasts of the forest flocked around, rustling and squawking. Every living creature in the area drew close, surrounding Muhammad ☺. The two children tried unsuccessfully to chase away the animals and send them out to graze. Once the animals caught sight of Muhammad ☺, they stood still, gazing at him.

The angels Mīkā'īl ☺ and Isrāfīl ☺ came along at this time, carrying a sword and a jug of water in their hands. They were so enormous that the children who had gathered around quickly ran away. Muhammad ☺ stood up, ready to follow the others, but the two beings held him and

---

4. **Song:** A book entitled *A Song of Muhammad* has been published by the author.

hugged him saying, "O Muhammad, come." They carried him to an Uva tree, and making a cot appear beneath the tree, they placed Muhammad ☻ on the cot. Then they tore open his chest and took out his bile. The child smiled and played as the two beings removed his bile. "O Muhammad, treasure of the three worlds, *Allāhu taʿālā* asked us to give you His greetings. He told us to give you the name of *Rahmatul-ʿālamīn*—God's grace-wealth of all the universes," they said, as they sprinkled water from the jug and rubbed it over Muhammad's ☻ body. His chest healed completely, with no sign of a scar or tear.

Upon seeing the angels, the two children ran away and watched the entire proceedings in hiding. They ran home crying, "They tore open Muhammad's chest. Two rogues came and did this." Halīma shuddered, cried, beat her chest, and ran as fast as she could, screaming, "O Muhammad, who killed you?" She ran to the date palms and appealed to them, "O date palms tell me who killed my son, Muhammad." The date palms replied, "Halīma, no one will kill your son. No one will hurt him. Do not cry. Go to your son."

Halīma ran onward and saw a flock of pigeons fluttering by. "O wild pigeons," she shouted, "Did you see who killed my Muhammad? Have you seen where he is? Tell me who killed him! Tell me!" The pigeons replied, "Halīma, no one will kill your son. Your son is Muhammad, the Light of all the universes. God Himself protects your son. Why do you cry? Calm yourself and proceed."

Halīma walked on, calling out to the mountains, but was met with the same response. Herds of deer passed by and Halīma appealed to them. "Yes, we do live in the jungle, but no one murdered your son. We did not see anything," they replied. Further along she saw some wolves who said, "The entire forestland is our domain. No one will kill your child. If we see your child we will bow down in reverence. We will only worship Him, we are not killers."

Then Halīma went to a well and asked the water if it had seen her son. "Go that way," directed the water, "Your child is there." When Halīma walked onward, she saw the blanket. She picked up the blanket, kissed it and exclaimed, "O son, where are you?" Looking around, she saw the child under the Uva tree, smiling and looking at the sky. She went over and carried him, hugging him close. "Who killed you? Who cut you open?" she asked. The child looked at the sky and replied, "No one killed me. I was looking at Allah. Then, two of His messengers came along, and I looked at them. No one hurt me." "What did they say, my son? I heard that they tore open your chest!" Halīma enquired, examining his body, but finding no wounds. "Son, what happened?" she asked. The child smiled, "They told me that Allah had given me the name of *Rahmatul-'ālamīn*. They gave me His greetings." Then the child opened his mouth to sing, and on hearing his sound, all the trees and plant stems unfurled in joy. Halīma said, "Muhammad, open your mouth again and let me look." The throne of God *('arsh),* the seat of God *(kursi),* the divine pen *(qalam),* heaven, the 18,000 universes, this world, the hereafter, the angels, the archangels, the enlightened beings, Mecca, Medina, Halīmah, Āminah☺, and 'Abdullāh☺ could all be seen within his mouth. All the land and oceans could be seen there. Halīma exclaimed, "I am within your mouth. Everything is within your mouth. It's all there!" She hugged him and cried. She lifted him up, embraced him, carried him home. and told her children, "Children, you and I, this world and the next, are all inside Muhammad's mouth. The 18,000 universes and the eight heavens are there." Turning to Muhammad☺, she said, "Son, open your mouth and show them!" Then, everything was seen within his mouth—everything in this world and the soul-world. "What a wonder!" they exclaimed.

(Precious jeweled lights of my eyes, I am giving you a few explanations.)

In Muhammad's ☺ sixth year, Āminah☺ died. Muhammad☺ grew up with Halīma and later came to Mecca. For a while, he traveled with businessmen to places like Rome and Yemen, working with people such as Abu Jahl and other traders. At this time, a very wealthy woman named Khadījah☺ fell in love with Muhammad☺. (There are many, many secrets in this, but I will not speak about it now).

Khadījah ☺ said, "I trust in this Light known as Muhammad!" She was twenty-eight years old and had been married before; Muhammad ☺ was twenty-five. 'Abu Talib took his son to see Khadījah ☺. She welcomed them with great respect, and in their honor spread out money, gems, and everything she owned. She pleaded with 'Abu Talib saying, "I desire your son. Please speak to him and make him agree." 'Abu Talib replied, "We will ask Muhammad and decide."

Then the sound of God was heard, "This is what I have destined for you. Accept this! This is permitted."

There was a secret about Muhammad ☺: His body could never be seen. Khadījah ☺ never saw it; 'Ā'isha ☺ never saw it. He had a canopy of clouds to protect him, and when he walked on the earth, stones, or sand, there were no footprints. There were never any traces of urine or feces; the earth swallowed up everything and kept it secret. As he walked along, the earth hid everything without a trace, and people in search of clues found none. This is the way it was—a secret. On Muhammad's ☺ shoulder there was a light (rānjaniyam) which shed light on this world and the world of souls. With this light, he could see in front and behind. This light, which enabled him to see all of everything, was within a minute morsel of flesh.

Such was the Muhammad ☺ that married Khadījah ☺. He soon made her distribute her wealth to the poor. She had been a very opulent lady, but her wealth was rapidly given away. If she had a handful of wheat, it was given away to the hungry. Only when there were no hungry people at the door was she permitted to cook that handful of wheat. And even after the wheat was cooked, Muhammad ☺ would look around to see if any beggars approached. Only then would he eat. They spent their lives in this manner, until Muhammad ☺ grew to be forty years old.

God's sounds and rahmat continued to come to him. He could perceive God's sounds, resonances, angels, and archangels. With his eyes, he could see Gabriel ☺, Michael ☺, Isra'fil ☺, and all the other angels, but each time he saw the angels he felt a little apprehensive. Even so, he knew that he had to leave the house and go into the forest toward Mount

200

Hira to worship God, the Lone One who rules and sustains. He had heard the message, "Go to Mount Hira! Go to the mountain! Go to the mountain!" He sat on the mountain for twenty-seven days, praising and worshipping God, and on the twenty-seventh day this *sūrat*,[5] this chapter, called the *Lailatul-Qadr* was sent to him while he was praying. This [same period of time] has now become the period of the fast.

For twenty-seven days, Khadījah☺ brought Muhammad☺ food in the late evening, at the time of the *'ishā'* prayers, past the *'asr* and *maghrib* prayers. Sometimes Muhammad☺ would eat at the *'asr* time, and sometimes he would not. And so it went until the twenty-seventh day when God, the Singular One who rules and sustains, sent down the *sūrat* of *Lailatul-Qadr,* the *Sūratul-'Iqrā*. That *sūrat* was a ray of light. It was the first one to descend. Gabriel☺ brought down this chapter saying, "O Muhammad, on this day of your fast, due to your melted-heart prayers (*'ibādat),* God, the Singular One who rules and sustains, has asked me to give you this *sūratul-'Iqrā*. He asked me to give you this Light." Muhammad☺ asked, "I am illiterate, how will I recite this verse?" Gabriel responded, "Say it! Accept this Light! God has asked me to give you this!" "But I have not studied anything, I do not know how to say it!" Muhammad☺ exclaimed.

On the first attempt, God said to Gabriel☺, "Hold him tight!" Gabriel☺ held him tight, and Muhammad☺ felt as though all his bones were being crushed and all his nerves were being compressed. He cried out, "How will I recite this verse? I don't know how to say it!" Angel Gabriel☺ said, "God told me to give you this Light. This is the *Lailatul-Qadr,* the Light, the resplendence. God has instructed you to receive this Light." Gabriel☺ held Muhammad☺ tight for the second time and told him to recite the verse. "I don't understand anything! Something is happening to me! I don't understand!" Muhammad☺ cried, unable to repeat the *sūrat*. The third time, Gabriel held him very tight and pressed

---

5. **Sūrat:** A word used for *chapters* in the Qur'an, of which there are 114. The first *sūrat* revealed to Muhammad ☺ as a ray of light was the *Sūratul-'alaq,* also known as *Sūratul-'Iqrā.* Trans.

his body hard. Then, with a crushing sound, the rocky stones—arrogance, karma, maya, all his attachments, and the world—were completely crushed, and the Light entered within. "Now, say it!" Gabriel⊕ instructed, and it was then that Muhammad⊕ recited the *sūrat*.

This was the twenty-seventh day of Muhammad's⊕ prayers on Mount Hira. Today (the twenty-seventh day of Ramadan), commemorates the day when the Light came down to the Messenger of God *(Rasūlullāh)*. Of the 6,666 chapters, this was the first chapter to descend as Light. It is known as *Lailatul-Qadr*. God told Muhammad⊕, "Today I am giving you this perfect Light of My divine kingdom *(ākhirah)*." At that time Muhammad⊕ was illiterate and did not comprehend anything, but after the Light entered him, each verse became complete, and he was able to accept every revelation that came to him through Gabriel⊕. Muhammad⊕ then saw and understood everything—the 18,000 universes, the throne of God, the seat of God, the divine pen, heaven, the good and bad, the permissible and impermissible, the mystery *(sirr)* and the manifestations *(sifāt)*, hell and heaven. The 6,666 chapters came down to him in this way. He was given *īmān* and the *kalimah*. The *kalimah* established that there is only one God, one family of brothers and sisters, one Lord for the world of souls, this world, and the hereafter, and none worthy of worship but *Allāhu ta'ālā*, the Singular One who rules and sustains. For those of wisdom, Allah is within their knowing, and for those who have no wisdom, He is in the unknowable realm. For those of wisdom and *īmān*, God is in the heart. For those without wisdom and *īmān*, God is in the unknown world, in a place they cannot understand. All of this was explained to Muhammad⊕, and the fast originated according to this explanation.

After the Light known as *Lailatul-Qadr* descended, the *rahmat* of God—all that had been sent through the prophets—was taught to Muhammad⊕. God explained the history and significance of each prophet, and handed him the key of *īmān* which opens the three worlds: the world of the souls, this temporal world, and God's divine kingdom. Through the *kalimah*, he was given this key of *īmān*, and with the keys of *alif* and *lām*,[6] hearts were unlocked. With the key of *Lā ilāha ill Allāh Muhammadur-Rasūlullāh* (Other than You there is nothing, only You are God, and Muhammad is Your Messenger), with this key of *īmān,* the inner hearts of men were opened.

He opened locked hearts by inserting the key of *Lā ilāha ill-Allāh,* the key that acknowledges, "You alone are God!" Hearts were made pure and filled with *īmān.* God showed man that unity can be attained through living a life of equality, peace, tranquillity, and equanimity, which is achieved by considering all lives, all hunger, and all sorrow as one's own.

Allāhu ta'ālā Nāyan defined the purpose of Islam. Islam is *brotherhood*—the unity of brothers and sisters. Even though we [mankind] have been here for thousands of years, we need brotherhood. And what is brotherhood? If someone is sorrowful, you experience that sorrow within you. If someone has joy, you experience that joy within you. If someone is hungry, you experience that hunger within you. If someone is troubled, you experience that distress. In this very life, embrace one another, attain unity, and live as one family with one father and one mother. This is Islam. This is the *kalimah.* This is *Īmān-Islām.*

Those who establish this resolute faith *(īmān)* in the proper manner, attain purity *(Islām).* This is known as *Īmān-Islām. Islām* signifies perfect brotherhood. It means embracing another to the heart—bending the neck to one side and embracing another, and then, without straightening up, bending it to the other side and embracing on the other side. Two hearts embracing as one, lungs embracing lungs, and chest embracing chest. In a direct embrace, two hearts unite. In a face to face embrace, two faces become one. When two hands join, this is the unity of brothers and sisters. When two pairs of eyes meet, they experience each other's feelings and become brethren. This state of being is known as *Islām.*

Allāhu ta'ālā Nāyan taught this to the *Rasūlullāh* ⊕ step by step, and

---

6. **Alif and lām:** *Two Arabic letters* which represent *Allah, and Allah's Light (Nūr).*

gave Islam the perfection and purity of *Īmān-Islām*. This state [of perfect purity] is known as *Islām*. We have been given what is necessary to attain this perfection—the precepts, the explanations, and the fast performed by the *Rasūlullāh* ☮. The melted-heart prayer *('ibādat)* performed by Muhammad ☮ is called the fast. He immersed himself in prayers and praise to God, perceived Allah to be his only nourishment, and with dedication, offered himself completely to God. This is called fasting. We should comprehend this state with conviction and, starting today, accept and practice this fast. We must realize this.

My precious children, jeweled lights of my eyes, this is called the fast. However, since there are those who do not perform this fast properly, do not perform *'ibādat* correctly, do not realize that there is none worthy of worship other than *Allāhu ta'ālā Nāyan,* do not attain a state of equality, peace, and brotherhood, and do not strengthen their intention and faith through the understanding that God alone is worthy of worship, God instituted further principles.

He said, "O Muhammad, I created everything in common for you and your followers. I created the sun, moon, stars, trees, plants, fruits, grass, shrubs, and milk (from goats and cows) to be shared by all, without selfishness. Make your followers look at these examples. Water, fire, air, oceans, and land were created to belong equally to all. I explained this to the 124,000 prophets. This "common wealth" was claimed by individuals, saying, "I, I." Those who failed to strengthen their *īmān* took possession of the wealth of others. I gave ocean-lives their freedom, and I gave forest-lives their freedom, providing houses, trees, caves, and other necessities. For the reptiles and the ants I created openings and homes; I gave termites places to live, and I gave snakes places to inhabit. I protect each being by providing body, shelter, and nourishment *(rizq)*.[7] Tell your followers this.

---

7. **Rizq:** That which is given as *true nourishment* by God. All the food that comes from the world is straw and hay for our desires, but the atom of nourishment provided by God is our real sustenance, *rizq*. It is the food for *īmān*—beauty that comes directly from God.

"The grass, shrubs, trees, and plants are useful in many ways, are they not? They sacrifice themselves for the sake of human beings. They live their lives in accordance with what I have said. The sun gives its rays to humans, the moon sheds its light on humans, the stars offer their light to humans, the trees give their fruit to humans, and the grass gives of itself to humans and cows. Everything I created as *rizq* is to be shared by all. And to man, who can partake of all this *rizq*, I bestowed wisdom of the greatest grandeur. I gave him judgment, subtle wisdom, analytic wisdom, and divine luminous wisdom, *(mathi, arivu, pahuth arivu,* and *perr arivu)*. I gave the animals perception, awareness, and intellect *(unarchi, unarvu, pudthi);* but to man I have given four more wisdoms. Make your followers realize this. Just as I have given to the trees, grass, and fish, I have given to every man the *rizq* that he must distribute. Each individual may receive the *rizq* in a variety of ways, but sharing this with others is *Īmān-Islām*. Distributing to others that which has been given to you is *Īmān-Islām*. It is sharing that arises from the inner heart. I have bestowed My *rahmat* so that man can share what has been given—without hurting another, without seeing another go hungry—by feeding the poor, by embracing inner heart to inner heart, and by embracing chest to chest.

Man must understand this *rahmat* if he is to be *Īmān-Islām*. Instead, man takes this *rahmat* for himself. He mouths the words "*Īmān-Islām,*" only to take possession of another's wealth, another's life, another's house, another's freedom, and another's happiness. O Muhammad, tell your people this. Tell them to offer charity. Make their *īmān* realize that I am the only Wealth, the wealth of the three worlds. Make them comprehend that I am the only One worthy of worship, and the One who decrees judgment. Let my common wealth be shared by all.

"But the stone-hearted, who have attained only a quarter-*īmān* or half-*īmān*, have changed into beings of base desire, worshipping statues, cows, goats, dogs, foxes, snakes, donkeys, cats, rats, horses, and pigs as gods. They also made fish and certain birds—chickens, roosters, peacocks, and crows—into gods. In this way, because they did not establish *īmān* correctly, they turned ghosts and demons into gods. O Muhammad, talk to these people, make them develop pure hearts; melt the *kalimah* and give it to them so that they may progress. Filter the *kalimah* and give it to them. Make them drink this *īmān;* it will illumine their inner hearts." Thus spoke God.

But even at this time, there were some who accepted this and some who did not. Many had a fraction of faith and an abundance of doubt. To these people, God gave further explanations. Because they hurt others, claiming all wealth and material for themselves, they were asked to give in charity. God decreed the five appointed duties. The first duty is faith, the second is prayer, and the third is charity. "Ask them to share what they have," God said, "And [fourth] for those who do not yet understand, ask them to fast. Make them gain understanding through the fast, and then have them share their wealth with their brethren." The fifth duty is the Hajj, to die before death, to give up base desires and cravings, to give away wealth and titles to the poor, and then proceed toward Mecca and Medina to fulfill the Hajj. "Tell them to meet Me attired in death-garb and in the death-state. Trusting in Me, let them put the world to death, and come forth to see Me. Tell them to put to death the possessions of the world, to give back to the world what belongs to the world, and to give generously to brothers, sisters, the poor, and the needy. Tell man to come alone to receive My Wealth. Tell him to bring his inner heart to accept My Wealth. Tell him to bring his resolute faith and perfect purity to receive My wealth of the three worlds. O Muhammad, tell your people this, so that they may receive the undiminishing Treasure," said God. These are the five ordained duties.

In those days [when the duties were instituted] people slaughtered animals constantly, killing cows, goats, and chickens as they pleased. As a result of these random killings, fifty to sixty million animals were killed every day. Then *Allāhu ta'ālā Nāyan* told the *Rasūl* ☺, "O Muhammad, I am the Bestower of compassion upon all lives. Go now and enable those of pure *īmān* to have compassion toward other lives. For those who accomplish this, I have created many kinds of *rizq*. They must know, however, that the qualities of whatever they consume will develop within them. The sins of their actions will collect within them. Currently, their actions create rivers of blood that flood the world. They turn living beings into rivers of blood. In each place, one thousand, two thousand, or ten thousand beings are slaughtered, and blood flows across the land.

"O Muhammad tell them that this is not permitted, it is *harām*. Allah is the One who decrees judgment. Therefore, trust Him, and sacrifice the animal in the permitted manner *(qurbān)*. Do it in the manner prescribed by Allah. First, sacrifice your inner hearts, your base desires, your cravings, and the evil in your thoughts. Make yourselves pure, and then try to sacrifice the animal. And how should this sacrifice be performed? Instead of forty chickens, kill one goat. Instead of forty goats, kill one cow. Instead of forty cows, kill ten camels. Kill them in the proper manner, and share them with everyone. To kill a chicken correctly, one must have a knife of specific length, grip, and sharpness. To kill a goat, the knife blade should be one-span in length and have a specific handle. To kill a cow, the knife blade should be one cubit[8] long, and very sharp. To kill a camel, the knife blade must be over one cubit in length and also extremely sharp.

The person who slaughters the animal must be someone who performs the five daily prayers. Two helpers (who also perform the five prayers) should hold onto the animal while the *kalimah* is recited and water sprinkled on the animal. Then, the person who kills the camel should look at the camel and place the knife on its neck, saying, "*Subhānallāhi, wal-hamdu lillāhi, wa lā ilāha ill-Allāhu wallāhu akbar, wa lā hawla wa lā quwwata illā billāhi, wa huwal-'aliyyul-'azīm*—Glory be to God, and all praise is to God, and none is God except God, and He is most Great. None has the majesty or the power to sustain except God, and He is the Majesty, the Supreme in glory."

This *kalimah* should be recited before offering the animal in sacri-

---

8. **Cubit:** Ancient measure of length, approximately equal to the length of the forearm.

fice, and then, within three strokes, the camel must be killed. The carotid artery should be severed. The animal should not throw up or scream. If it throws up or emits any sound, it is impermissible *(harām)*. While the camel is being cut, it should be looking at the person, and the person should be looking at it. Once the animal is killed, the person, continuing to look at the animal, must recite *dhikr*[9] and pray to God, until the soul leaves the body. The *kalimah* should be recited once again as the knife is washed. Then, another animal may be killed. Once again, *dhikr* should be performed until the soul leaves the body. The *lebbe,* or *muezzin* (the one who does the call to prayer in the mosque), should be the one who kills the animals.

The reason behind this *qurban*, this prescribed method of slaughter, is this: The *lebbe* has about ten to thirty minutes of free time between each of the five daily prayers, and if this method is observed, only five or six animals can be slaughtered in thirty minutes. Thus, instead of one hundred million, only six animals will be killed; and no slaughter will be permitted after the evening *maghrib* prayers. In the morning, after prayers, the *lebbe* has to attend to the affairs of the mosque until 9 a.m. Then, after he has eaten, he can only slaughter animals between 9 and 11 a.m., because he has to give the call to prayer before noon. After lunch he has another two hours before the next prayer, and after the late afternoon *'asr* prayers, he has no time for any more killing. Thus, in a day, he can slaughter approximately twenty-five animals. The slaughter of a half million animals was thereby reduced to twenty-five. Sacrifices, killings, and sins were lessened, and the animals that were killed were intended to be shared. The *Rasūlullāh* ☸ stated this to be God's decree. When people of wisdom reflect, this is the explanation. We should understand the purpose of *qurban;* it was decreed in order to reduce slaughter. In those days, one thousand, four hundred years ago, vegetables were not easily available. Meat, dates, milk, ghee (clarified butter), and

---

9. **Dhikr:** The *remembrance of God. Dhikr* can be recited, appealing to God through any one of His ninety-nine qualities. The most exalted *dhikr* of all is to declare, "There is none other than You, You alone are God—*lā ilāha ill-Allāhu.*

bread were the basic foods. Under these circumstances, had Muhammad ☺ instructed the people not to eat meat, they would have killed him. People did try to kill him at other times, but this instruction would have created a great furor.

Therefore, Muhammad ☺, in his wisdom, introduced God's commandments gradually. He instructed man to look at the animal and to pray until its soul left the body. He specified this so that man would have to look at the animal's flowing blood, its rolling tears, and its twitching body, which would cause even a stone-hearted man to melt. In some animals, tears flow out of their eyes; others look as if they are crying, and the bodies of many animals twitch until the soul leaves, while blood flows from them in streams. It was anticipated that the hearts of hard-hearted men would melt on seeing these sights, and that they would stop performing *qurban* altogether.

Millions of people have stopped performing *qurban;* unable to watch the animals die, they stop the slaughter. This method was prescribed in accord with God's commandments, in order to reduce the killings. When a hard-hearted man performs *dhikr* as he watches an animal die, he will begin to acquire mercy, especially if the goat, cow, or camel is one that he himself has raised. This is why *qurban* was decreed as one of God's commandments. This is why God gave Muhammad ☺ the specifications of the *qurban*—to face the *qiblah,*[10] to perform *dhikr,* to look at the animal, and so forth.

However, this practice will be effective only for men of wisdom. Only a pure inner heart will melt with compassion, shudder at the sight of another's blood, tremble at another's sorrow, and quiver at the knowledge of another's hunger. This trembling of the heart at another's distress is known as pure *Īmān-Islām.* The hearts of those who have pure *īmān* will melt at the sight of another's sorrow, and they will shower their compassion and offer comfort instantly. Those in this state are called *Īmān-Islām.* They are known as people with resolute faith, *īmān.*

---

10. **Qiblah:** The direction in which all Muslims pray, facing Mecca.

God has declared those who possess such compassion, affection, unity, forbearance, and equanimity to be *Islām*. He gave these explanations to the *Rasūlullāh*⊕.

When man tries to fulfill the commandments of God, he realizes that God sent down countless principles, and the true wealth of the three worlds exists as a mystery *(sirr)*. Divine knowledge *('ilm)*, the wealth of three worlds *(mubārakāt)*, and the limitless wealth of God's *grace (rahmat)* is purity. A man who has received these treasures of purity will be the life in all lives, the illness in all illness, the happiness in all happiness, the hunger in all hunger, and as such, will serve and embrace all lives. He will do this with inner patience, contentment, trust in God, and surrender to God. With the conviction that everything happens as God wills, he will trust God and embrace all lives. This is *Īmān-Islām,* the meaning and essence of the fast. We should attain this.

Precious children, jeweled lights of my eyes, each one of us must understand and accept this on the path of God. We must understand *Īmān-Islām*. Our inner hearts should understand the teachings of the 124,000 prophets in their entirety. God created 124,000 prophets, and of them He first clarified twenty-five, and then from among them, He clarified eight more prophets. Finally, He put together all their histories, condensed them into one, and gave the entirety to Muhammad⊕ as perfect completeness. This is known as the *Thiru Marai,* the *Thiru Qur'ān,*[11] and the Qur'an. This perfect completeness is called Qur'an. It is true scripture—*Satthiya Vetham*. Truth is the scriptural code. God's words are the code; purity is the code. Those who have filled their inner hearts with these scriptural codes are the pure ones—*Īmān-Islām*. They

---

11. **Thiru Qur'ān:** This is the original inner *Qur'ān* inscribed in the heart, containing the essence and secrets of all three worlds: the soul-world, this world, and God's divine world. It is the manifestation of the conscience of God in every age, to every nation, revealing to mankind the means of attaining Him. God is Reality immanent in man, and the voice of God, the revelation that proceeds from the *Nūr,* (God's Light, Divine Luminous Wisdom) is called *Thiru Marai* or *Thiru Qur'ān*.

trust God, and they love God. May we think about this.

Precious children, jeweled lights of my eyes, I cannot tell you the entire history. The first chapter *(sūrat),* the *Lailatul-Qadr,* came down on the twenty-seventh night of the fast, and because today is the twenty-seventh night of our fast, we have been talking briefly about some of the principles of the fast. May we understand these completely, and make our inner hearts pure. May we receive this Light—this perfect completeness— embrace all lives as our own, and bring them peace. This is *Īmān-Islām.* Living our life with inner patience, contentment, trust in God, and total surrender to God is how we praise God. To realize this praise and praising is *Īmān-Islām.* Understanding this essence is an appointed duty of Islam. The fast is one of the five appointed duties.

The *Rasūlullāh* ﷺ stayed on Mount Hira for twenty-seven days,
and on the twenty-seventh day this chapter,
this Light known as *Lailatul-Qadr* descended.
The outer world celebrates this today,
but, in truth,
the inner heart of each individual must celebrate this.
Just as the *Rasūlullāh* ﷺ received the Light,
we too must joyously receive the Qur'an in our inner hearts.
Only when this Light enters our inner hearts
can we receive God's limitless wealth of the three worlds.
We should make this wealth dawn within us.
This is *Īmān-Islām.*
Islam is purity.
When this Light is made complete, that is Islam;
not the killing, hurting, or teasing of other lives.

God gave the *Rasūlullāh* ﷺ the name of *Rahmatul-'ālamīn*—Grace-Wealth of all the Universes. This grace, this *rahmat,* must dawn in our own inner hearts. If we receive this wealth it will be the grace-wealth of all the universes. We must strive diligently to attain this state.

211

Precious children, jeweled lights of my eyes, I have told you a little about this twenty-seventh day of your fast, this day known as *Lailatul-Qadr*. May all of you intend the fast with great determination. Fast for thirty days. Praise and worship God. Glorify Him. Pray to Him with each breath. Meditate upon Him. Try to remember Him with every breath. Worship Him. Pray to Him with a melting heart, and strive to merge your life and death with Him. This will be the state in which to receive grandeur, eminence, and the limitless wealth of God's grace—*rahmat*. This will be *Īmān-Islām*.

Āmīn.

As-salāmu 'alaikum wa rahmatullāhi wa barakātuhu kulluhu.

May all the peace, the beneficence, and the blessings of God

be upon you.

Allah is sufficient for all.

May we praise Him.

Āmīn.

Chapter 15

May Our Inner Hearts Be Pure

August 7, 1980

In the here and in the hereafter,
may we have
an inner heart that does not falter,
that is not deluded by joy or by sorrow,
that is not agitated in illness and in suffering.
May we have this purity—God's rahmat.

May He give us the canopy of clarity,
the canopy of pure īmān,
that we may spread open this canopy
in rain and in sunshine,
that we may not grow weary,
dry out in the sun,
get drenched,
or be perturbed
by the rain of sorrow.

May Our Inner Hearts Be Pure

Bismillāhir-Rahmānir-Rahīm.
In the name of God, most Merciful, most Compassionate.

Children who have received Allah's grace *(rahmat),*
children who have received
Allah's wealth of the three worlds,
children of resolute faith *(īmān),*
may we realize
the benevolence of God
and the benevolence of the prophets,
the love of God
and the love of the prophets.
May we receive God's *rahmat.*
May we receive this wealth
as the prophets did.
May God bestow on us the same wealth of *īmān.*
May He confer this on us today,
and so grace us.
Āmīn.

May He give us an inner heart that is perfection,
wealth that is complete,
and divine knowledge *('ilm)* that is abundant.
May He help us to swim

in the ocean of *rahmat* and divine knowledge,
enabling us to see the shores
of His divine kingdom.
Āmīn.

In the here and in the hereafter,
may we have
an inner heart that does not falter,
that is not deluded by joy or by sorrow,
that is not agitated in illness and in suffering.
May we have this purity—God's *rahmat*.
May God grant us the praiseworthy inner heart
known as
Rahmatul-ʿālamīn—
the grace-wealth of all the universes.
May He grant us this wealth,
and so grace us.
Āmīn.

May He make complete
an inner heart without delusion,
and so grace us.
Āmīn.

May He give our inner hearts
inner patience,
and so grace us.
Āmīn.

May He bestow the divine knowledge
that is His *rahmat,*
and so grace us.
Āmīn.

May He give us an inner heart
that trusts Him completely
and unites with Him,
saying,
"*Tawakkul-'alallāh,* I trust Allah."
May He grant us this,
and so grace us.
Āmīn.

May He grant us the state of praising Him in all situations,
saying, "*Al-hamdu lillāh,* all praise is to God."
May He grant us this state of homage
which enables us to reach Him.
Āmīn.

May He grant us His grace that we may,
at every moment,
in every breath, and in every word,
uphold His *rahmat* saying,
"*In shā' Allāh,* if God wills,"
and
"*Ma shā' Allah,* as God wills."
May we affirm this and praise Him.

In our lives,
may He grant us
tranquillity and peace,
a state of equanimity,
a perfect inner heart,
the Light of the *Nūr,*
His *rahmat,*
the benefits of *rahmat* received by the prophets,
and the inner patience they attained.

May He grant us an exalted life
today and always.
May He give us faith, certitude,
and determination
in Him,
the Singular Ruler who sustains us.
May He give us the conviction
to know that He is the only One worthy of worship,
and the certainty
to pray to Him abidingly.

May He give us the canopy of clarity,
the canopy of pure *īmān,*
that we may spread open this canopy
in rain and in sunshine,
that we may not grow weary,
dry out in the sun,
get drenched,
or be perturbed
by the rain of sorrow.

May we live our lives under the umbrella
of Allah's *rahmat.*
May we obtain this and live a life of freedom.
May we live with His *rahmat*
in the here and in the hereafter
and receive His benevolence—
the grace-wealth of all universes,
the *rahmatul-'ālamīn.*
May God grant us His mercy and His *rahmat*
that we may reach His feet
and His kingdom.
Āmīn.

Each one of you must
foster an inner heart of conviction,
strengthen *īmān,*
purify your inner hearts,
glorify God,
accept unconditionally
that He is the only One worthy of worship,
and offer praise, ritual prayers, and worship to Him alone.
Entrust your hearts to Him.
Keep your inner hearts open for Him
so that He may enter that house and reside there.
Make the house of your inner hearts belong to Him alone
and not to base desires, demons, and cravings.

May we give
the house of our inner hearts
only to God,
may we bow down to Him alone,
may we live as His slaves,
performing our duties,
and may we strive to develop
the dutiful inner hearts
that serve Him.

My precious jeweled lights of my eyes,
live as children of *īmān.*
Have pure hearts—always.
Live as pure beings in
this world, the hereafter,
and the world of souls.
This is the wealth we must acquire,
the fortune we must receive,
and the position we must attain.

My precious jeweled lights of my eyes,
each one of my children,
may you open your hearts
and accomplish this.
When you steadfastly maintain this state,
you will receive its profits and benefits.

To do this,
we must keep our hearts open
unconditionally
and strive courageously to live
trusting God completely.
This, in itself, will be
the wealth of the three worlds.
It will be the joyous treasure of our life.
May we strive for and receive this *rahmat*.
Āmīn.

As-salāmu 'alaikum wa rahmatullāhi wa barakātuhu kulluhu.
May all the peace, the beneficence, and the blessings of God
be upon you.

When faced with any sorrow,
entrust it to Him,
place it in His *tawakkul,*
and offer praise in His name alone.
Āmīn.

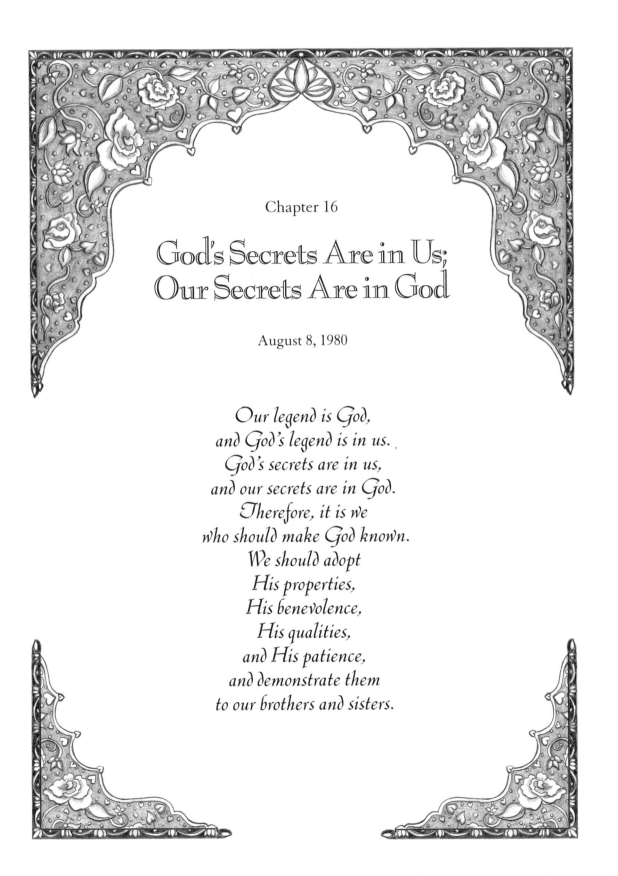

Chapter 16

God's Secrets Are in Us;
Our Secrets Are in God

August 8, 1980

Our legend is God,
and God's legend is in us.
God's secrets are in us,
and our secrets are in God.
Therefore, it is we
who should make God known.
We should adopt
His properties,
His benevolence,
His qualities,
and His patience,
and demonstrate them
to our brothers and sisters.

God's Secrets Are in Us; Our Secrets Are in God

Precious brothers and sisters,
lives of my life,
children born of my body,
bodies intermingled with my body,
precious jeweled lights of my eyes,
we are united in blood, skin, and flesh.

My precious companions,
devotees of God,
companions of God,
lovers of my inner heart,
my precious brothers and sisters,
there is none worthy of worship
except *Allāhu ta'ālā Nāyan,*
the Singular One
who rules and sustains.

This One who is God
has three thousand benevolent qualities.
He has
compassion, love, and patience.
He has no
comparison, parallel, or equal.
May we trust Him.

There is none worthy of prayer other than Him.
May all praise and glory be to Him alone.

My precious jeweled lights of my eyes,
the true God, may we trust Him.
The One who never causes harm, may we trust Him.
The One of eternal purity, may we trust Him.
The Unselfish One, may we trust Him.
The One who serves without forgetting, may we trust Him.
The Mysterious Treasure that exists within us as a secret,
may we realize and know it.

God's secret exists as man,
man's secret exists as God.
My precious jeweled lights of my eyes,
each child,
God's story is in us, and our story is in God.
We must understand this.
Our legend *(purāna)*[1] is God,
and God's legend is in us.
God's secrets are in us,
and our secrets are in God.
Therefore, it is we who should make God known.
We should adopt
His properties,
His benevolence,
His qualities,
and His patience,
and demonstrate them to our brothers and sisters.

---

1. **Purāna:** A Sanskrit word meaning *ancient legend*. The *purānas* are a class of Hindu sacred writings that contain ancient stories. Trans.

If we are children of wisdom,
children who follow Him,
then we must bring to light
His story and His qualities.
We must assimilate His virtues,
adopt His actions,
experience His patience as our patience,
experience His quality of compassion,
experience His code of moral conduct,
adopt these qualities,
live with them,
and guide our brethren.

The noble nature of the Supreme One
and the exaltation of His covenant—
may we attain that state.
May we make those actions our own,
and reveal the Great One
to our brothers and sisters
as the Great One.
We must embrace our brethren in this way.

The Believer in all lives,
the One all lives believe,
the One all lives love,
the Omnipresent One,
il Allāhu,
the Singular One,
the Lone Ruler,
He has no house yet has a home everywhere.
He has no deed of ownership yet owns everything.
He has no palace yet has a palace everywhere.
He has no scepter yet has a scepter everywhere.

He has no nest yet has a nest everywhere.
He has no deeds,
eminence,
or fame,
but wherever His story and Truth are made known,
He has deeds,
eminence,
and fame.

He has no form, yet He dwells everywhere.
He has no birth, yet he is born and lives everywhere.
In their hearts, individuals have given birth to Him.
He has no death, yet is dead in those who do not think of Him.
In those without wisdom, He is dead.
In those with wisdom and faith, He exists
as One born within the inner heart.

To a scholar, He is a scholar.
To those with inner hearts like babies,
He is always young, playing with them.
To a king, He is an exalted King.
To a slave, He is a lowly slave.
To one of fame, He has fame, far greater.
To one of blame, He has blame, far graver.
To one of wealth, He is wealthier.
To one of poverty, He is poorer.

This Power,
intermingled in
food, nourishment, sleep, and body,
is God.
We must understand this Power.
God is intermingled in water,

air, clouds, sun, moon,
body, and life.
We must realize that He is the mystery,
the clarity in wisdom.
He has no eyes but sees through our eyes.
He has no ears but listens through our ears.
He has no nose but smells through our noses.
He has no mouth but speaks through our mouths.
He has no sense of taste but tastes through our tastes.
He has no heart but lives through our heart.
He has no lungs but speaks and breathes through our lungs.
He has no body but lives and bears burdens through our bodies.
He has no hands but gives and receives through our hands.
He has no legs but walks through our legs.
He has no thoughts but understands and knows
through our thoughts.

One like this,
One with such Power,
is God.

He is without parallel or equal.
May we trust Him with conviction.
We should focus intently with our eyes
and realize and accept Him.
We should focus intently with our ears
and realize and accept Him.
We should concentrate with our nose,
focus with wisdom,
realize His fragrance, and accept Him.
We should focus on the good and bad words
that issue from our mouths,
perceive Him in the good words, and know Him.

We should look at our own hearts
and understand and know the Truth within,
realizing that He is in that Truth.
Looking at our two hands
that do good and bad,
we should focus intently within the hand that does good,
and realize and accept His goodness.
We should look at our two legs
that walk on right and wrong paths,
and realize Him as the One
who walks on the right path.

In this way,
within our very selves,
there are instruments,
principles of understanding,
with which to reflect on God—
ways to realize God within us.

His life and scepter are on the right.
If we leave the right path
and walk on the left,
it will be hell.
The true path is on the right;
the evil path is on the left.
On the left
there are differences.
One catches and devours the other,
one attacks another,
one drinks another's blood,
one separates another,
one kills another,
one eats another,

one hits another,
one murders another—
this is the left path.

These acts are caused by
money,
property,
possessions,
pride,
anger,
arrogance,
differences of "I" and "you,"
race,
religion,
and scriptures.
For all these reasons,
one attacks another and separates from another,
causing murders, sins, fights, and enmity.
These belong to the left.
These qualities are from the portion
that belongs to Satan, demons, animals, and snakes.

Patience, compassion, forbearance, equanimity,
truth, life, fullness, wisdom,
good actions, good conduct, morals, service,
and the three thousand gracious qualities,
belong to the right path.
The perception, awareness, intellect,
subtle wisdom, analytic wisdom,
and divine luminous wisdom—*light* wisdom,
(*unarchi, unarvu, pudthi, mathi,
arivu, pahuth arivu,* and *perr arivu*)
that consider other lives as one's own—

these perfect wisdoms,
belong to the right path.
These are the wisdoms that judge and evaluate.
If we adopt their qualities
we will go on the right path,
God's path.
If we adopt the alternate qualities
we will go toward hell
on the left path.

In all things, God has created pairs.
In a seed, He has placed a covering on the outside
and a *point* inside.
In a man, God has placed two eyes,
one on the left and one on the right.
We must understand this—
sun, moon.
Similarly, He has placed two ears,
and there is a difference between them.
He has placed two nostrils,
and there is a difference between them.

In the mouth, there are teeth above and below,
but there is a difference between them,
and different tastes are experienced.
God has also placed two tongues,
a small one and a large one.
The small tongue was given
to discriminate music and truths,
and to distinguish melodies.
It moves constantly
changing good and bad sounds.
There is a different place for taste.

On the good side there is taste,
and on the bad side, the wrong path, there is the *left*.

Your lungs are also fashioned in the same way,
reflect on this.
God has placed the heart in the middle;
we must use it to reflect upon all these things.

We must look at each thing carefully
and search for the good.
Doing this,
traversing the right path,
is called "man."
If one becomes man,
one will know God's secret.
Knowing God's secret,
he will become God's messenger.
He could be God's representative.
God always understands man's secret,
but when man understands God's secret and transforms,
hell is far removed from him.
Ghosts leave him and vanish.
Demons, the monkeys of the mind,
and the dogs of desire
move far away from him.

Then he will be
the man who knows God's secrets in God's kingdom.
He will only find happiness in God's happiness.
He will adopt God's qualities
and conduct,
and love all lives as his own life.

In the kingdom of God,
in the kingdom of hell,
in the kingdom of the world,
and in the kingdom of souls,
he perceives no differences,
no separations from himself.
Hell will move away from him.
He does not concern himself with this.
He does not look back
at all that has died away from him.
Alive in him are
the kingdom of the soul,
the kingdom of the world,
and the kingdom of God.
Man has all three kingdoms.
If he realizes this and makes his heart
pure and whole,
then, when he is in this world,
it will be God's kingdom.
When he is in the kingdom of souls,
it will be God's kingdom,
and when he is in God's kingdom,
it will be God's kingdom.
May we reflect upon this.

Each child,
reflect a little on your own bodies.
Think about your own lives.
Think about your intentions and speech.
One who discovers his own faults can become man.
One who corrects his own actions can become man.
One who perceives his errors,
asks forgiveness from God,

and does not commit them again,
can become man.
If one realizes one's own *right* and *wrong*,
one can become man.

All of us should correct our own faults,
dedicate our lives and bodies to others,
and ask God,
"Please comfort my brothers and sisters,
give them serenity,
give them peace,
give them equanimity."
This is what we must do—this is our secret.

My precious jeweled lights of my eyes,
each child,
let us think about this.
We will not hurt our eyes, will we?
Similarly, we will not hurt other lives
when we perceive them as our own.
We will not sever our own hands, will we?
Similarly, we will not harm others
when we consider them as our brethren.
We will not chop off our own legs, will we?
Similarly, we will not hurt others
or sever their hands and legs
when we perceive the entire human family
as our family.
We will not chop off our own necks, will we?
Similarly, we will not take other lives or mutilate them.

Children who are God's secret,
believers of God,

you must think about this.
Those who have faith in God
must reflect on this,
and act accordingly.
In ourselves,
we must experience these
benefits, qualities,
deeds, conduct,
truth, and justice.

If we arrive at judgment within ourselves,
we will see no differences in the world.
We will experience qualities that comfort others,
a life that brings serenity to others,
and the equanimity that gives others peace.

Each child, realize this.
All the fasting that you do
is only to help you develop these qualities.
This is why the duties were ordained.
They have been given
in order that
arrogance, karma, and maya may be dispelled,
that the pride of the "I" may be banished,
that the arrogance of "mine" may be expelled,
and that harmful intentions of
jealousy, falsehood, theft, and murder
may be extinguished.

It is to attain peace and equanimity
that we observe
the fast, the prayers, and other practices.
We do these, so that we may know

and understand others.
May you realize this.
Precious jeweled lights of my eyes,
each child,
you have trusted God in your hearts.
You are believers of God.
You must understand.
In every situation,
may you ask for God's forgiveness.
Love your neighbor as you love yourself.
Look upon your neighbors as yourselves
and comfort them.
To do this, may God bestow
His help, His grace, and His wisdom.
May He grant us peace, patience, and equanimity.
May He give us
inner patience, contentment, trust in Him,
and total surrender to Him
(*sabūr, shakūr, tawakkul, and al-hamdu lillāh*).
May He grant us this state,
and so grace us.
Āmīn.

As-salāmu 'alaikum wa rahmatullāhi wa barakātuhu kulluhu.
May all the peace, the beneficence, and the blessings of God
be upon you.

Go and fulfill your intentions and your fast.
Āmīn.

235

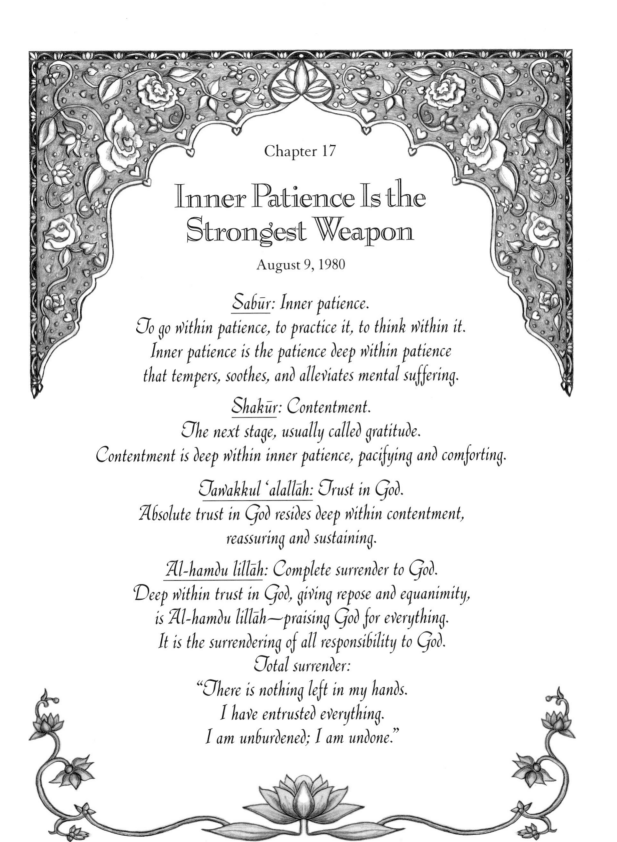

Chapter 17

Inner Patience Is the Strongest Weapon

August 9, 1980

Sabūr: Inner patience.
To go within patience, to practice it, to think within it.
Inner patience is the patience deep within patience
that tempers, soothes, and alleviates mental suffering.

Shakūr: Contentment.
The next stage, usually called gratitude.
Contentment is deep within inner patience, pacifying and comforting.

Tawakkul 'alallāh: Trust in God.
Absolute trust in God resides deep within contentment,
reassuring and sustaining.

Al-hamdu lillāh: Complete surrender to God.
Deep within trust in God, giving repose and equanimity,
is Al-hamdu lillāh—praising God for everything.
It is the surrendering of all responsibility to God.
Total surrender:
"There is nothing left in my hands.
I have entrusted everything.
I am unburdened; I am undone."

Inner Patience Is
the Strongest Weapon

May the peace, the beneficence, and the blessings
of God be with you.
God is the Greatest!

Children with resolute faith *(īmān),*
believers of God,
children devoted to God,
children who attain God's wealth of grace *(rahmat)*
and His qualities,
may *Allāhu ta'ālā Nāyan,*
the Singular One
who rules and sustains,
fulfill your yearnings.
May He fulfill
your ritual prayers,
your melting heart prayers *(ibādat),*
your worship,
your fast,
your charity,
and
your pilgrimage,
according to your intentions,
and so grace you.
Āmīn.

May God, the Singular One who rules and sustains, transform your intentions into the treasures of the three worlds. According to your intentions and faith, may God continue to increase the *rahmat* He showers on you.

May God bestow His grace
according to
the intensity of your *īmān,*
the inquiry and clarity of your wisdom,
your faith, certainty, and determination,
and the conviction of your certitude.
May He bestow His grace
according to
the perseverance of your
inner patience,
contentment,
trust in God,
and surrender to God
(sabūr, shakūr, tawakkul, and al-hamdu lillāh),
which are the grace-wealth of all the universes
(rahmatul-'ālamīn).
According to the intentions that you have strengthened,
may God give you great rewards and benefits,
and so grace you.
Āmīn.

The house of inner patience that you were given, has as its innate quality the most exalted of all strengths. In all the battles you may wage, inner patience is the most magnificent weapon, far surpassing all the other weapons in your possession. It is the mightiest weapon.

Inner patience is the weapon that will bring you victory in life.
It will make you triumphant in

the war of the world,
the war of base desires,
the war of cravings,
and the war of
the senses and sensory enticements.

This will be the weapon of strength in our lives.
It will be the strength and courage in our lives.
This is a weapon that God,
the Lone One who rules and sustains,
possesses in His scepter.
If we who are human
fortify this strength of inner patience,
if we cultivate contentment,
if we trust God
and surrender ourselves
by giving all responsibility to Him,
and if we bear witness to Him,
praising Him with our breath and words,
He will enhance our strength.

In the battles to come, we can be the strongest of them all. In the misfortunes to come, we can stand firm and strong. And when we have this strength, all the sorrow, poverty, debility, disease, satans, ghosts, and demons that attack us and attempt to shake us, will turn around and leave. The most important aspect of our strength is the acknowledgment that God is the Greatest—*Allāhu Akbar.* Inner patience will be a glorious weapon within this acknowledgment. Giving all responsibility to God and adopting inner patience in everything we do is our greatest strength. In war or in life, nothing has as much power. A man who possesses this strength begins to have peace and equanimity. Such a man will determine that tranquillity is the strength in his life.

Each child, think of this and cultivate the strength of inner patience in your inner hearts. In saying, *"Tawwakul 'alallāh*—I place my trust in You, O God," and, *"Al-hamdu lillāh*—All praise is to God," may we give our inner hearts to God, place them in His responsibility, and praise Him. May this praise become a strength in our lives. In all the battles we wage, our might does not come from guns, rifles, knives, and swords. We must therefore, strengthen our inner patience. We must harbor contentment and trust in God within our inner hearts. We must adopt God's qualities according to His intentions. This will be the strength and courage in our lives. This is the mighty weapon. There is no other weapon that is similar or equal to this. No other weapon can oppose it. Anything that attacks it, rebounds and attacks itself. Each child, may you strengthen love, patience, inner patience, contentment, trust in God, and surrender to God. Strengthen this within your inner hearts and experience victory. This will bring peace in your lives.

My precious jeweled lights of my eyes, each child, establish this state. If you do this, you can experience tranquillity in your lives. You can experience peace. You can experience equanimity in your life. When evils come toward us, if we remain steadfast in our conviction, they will butt against us and then go away of their own accord. May you hold on to this as your strength.

This is the seal of īmān.
Inner patience is the stamp of īmān.
The stamp of true prayer is
contentment,
trust in God,
and surrender to God,
saying, "As God wills—ma shā' Allāh,"
and "If God wills—in shā' Allāh."

The goodness
in God's kingdom is
īmān,

purity,

faith,

certitude,

and God's peaceful qualities.

The peaceful qualities of inner patience are the kingdom of God. God's attributes are the means by which we attain the house of God. If we trust God, assimilate His qualities, and establish the praiseworthy state of inner patience, contentment, trust in God, and total surrender to God—that will be paradise, heaven, *firdaus*. This will be the house that we have built. Each child, may you construct this house by maintaining inner patience.

Thinking one thing on the inside and saying something else on the outside—this is the fire of the weapons we perceive in hell. This is poisonous. Slander and the holding of one thought on the inside while expressing another on the outside—these are the weapons that consume us. They consume fire. What we foster and cultivate devours us. This is the stamp of Satan.

Thinking one thing and saying another,

being a false witness,

backbiting,

slander,

inciting another to fight,

ruining another,

bringing another under one's control—

these are the qualities of Satan's kingdom.

Those who possess these traits

are in Satan's house.

They are Satan's children.

However,

if we establish in our inner hearts

truth,
inner patience,
contentment,
trust in God,
total surrender to God,
God's speech,
God's qualities,
God's patience,
God's inner patience,
God's integrity,
and God's Truth,
Satan will not tarry there.

Slander, backbiting, creating dissension, speaking in ignorance, and speaking impulsively are all qualities of Satan. Without our knowledge Satan has tarnished us, and these are the qualities he gathers to his side. Treachery, doubt, and jealousy are qualities of Satan. Saying "I" and "you" or "mine" and "yours" is Satan's work. The traits of divisiveness caused by differences and the traits that break unity apart are qualities of Satan.

Every quality
that does not contain
unconditional
faith, certitude, and determination in God
belongs to Satan.
It is the fire of hell.

Each child should reflect on this. Think about this, understand this, and progress on the path. Progress in *īmān,* inner patience, the good qualities of life, faith, determination, and certitude, entrusting your life to God. This is progress toward God's throne *(dhāhuth)* and God's justice in His kingdom. My children, I pray to God that you will reflect on this and strive to live in this way.

My precious jeweled lights of my eyes,
if each of you establish this state,
it will make your fast the strongest of fasts,
your prayer the strongest of prayers,
and you
the strongest and most upright of all humans.
You will have adopted the qualities of God.
Children, think about this
and live accordingly.

Everything we do without these qualities will be like trying to milk a cow that has no milk. It cannot be done. Similarly, we cannot extract grace from a house devoid of God's qualities. We cannot accomplish this through our intentions alone, but [living with] good virtues will be like milking a cow that has milk. Everything we procure with these qualities will be the milk we receive from God, from His limitless grace-wealth of all the universes. In this way, we will be able to attain the treasure of the three worlds from Him.

However, if you do not have these qualities, it will be like trying to milk a barren cow. What will you get? Only blood. You will not get milk. Think about this. In order to obtain the milk of grace from God, you must strengthen His qualities, His inner patience, His contentment, His belief, and His *īmān*. Only then can you receive from Him the wealth of the three worlds—the milk and honey of grace, as well as His love. This alone will quench your thirst, end your poverty, terminate your karma, and destroy birth and death. You will have the treasured wealth of the three worlds. And in the three worlds—the world of souls, this world, and the next—you will have milk, the milk and honey of God's grace, mixed with His love and given by Him. You can attain this wealth. May you reflect on this. *Āmīn.*

Each of my children,
with certitude, faith, and determination in God,

make your inner hearts clear.
Make your inner hearts perfectly pure.
When you make your hearts resplendent,
God will be the Perfection in it.
If you make your hearts blossom with perfect purity,
He will be the Fragrance.
If you bow down to Him, He will bow down to you.
If you give all responsibility to Him,
He will resolve and end all your karma.
Realize this,
strengthen *īmān,*
make your inner hearts pure,
adopt His qualities,
and conduct yourself with these qualities.
Īmān is Islam—resolute faith is purity.[1]
When faith is strong, that is purity—Islam.
When you clarify faith,
you can receive its benefits,
its advantages,
and God's *rahmat.*
Each child should think of this.
Āmīn.

May the peace, beneficence, and blessings of God be upon you.

Today is the end of the twenty-eighth day of fasting. The twenty-ninth day is about to begin. All praise is to God for this—*Al-hamdu lillāh.* Place your fast and intentions in God's responsibility and complete the fast, but also make your inner hearts perfect and complete

---

1. **Īmān is Islam:** *Īmān* is *resolute faith.* Complete and unshakable faith, certitude, and determination that God alone exists; the complete acceptance by the heart that God is sole and absolute. The author refers to this state of *purity* as *Islam.* Trans.

through *īmān*. Make your wisdom, your inner heart, and God's qualities complete, and may Allah fulfill your fast and your intentions. May He make your inner hearts immaculate. May He make your inner patience complete and protect you. *Āmīn.*

In the world of souls, in this world, and in the hereafter, may He support you, forgive any sins you commit, protect you, accept you as His children, and give you His house of grace, the house of *rahmatul-ʿālamīn.*

Āmīn, Āmīn.
O Lord of all the universes.

May the peace, the beneficence, and the blessings of God
be upon you.
Go and break your fasts.
Āmīn.

As-salāmu ʿalaikum.

Chapter 18

The Mystery Within
(Sirr and Sifāt)

August 10, 1980

He always was.
He still is.
He is the Supreme Primeval One,
the One Power,
the Perfect Light,
the Omnipotent One,
the Infinite One,
the Singular One,
the Absolute,
the Resonance—ill Allāhu,
the Greatest—Allāhu Akbār,
the Lone One—ill Allāh,
unparalleled, matchless,
Leader of messengers,
and Light of prophets.
This Mystery,
the Light within the light
is known as God.
He is the Lord of all the universes.

The Mystery Within
(Sirr and Sifāt)

Bismillāhir-Rahmānir-Rahīm.
In the name of God, most Merciful, most Compassionate.
May the peace, the beneficence, and blessings of God be upon you.

My precious children, jeweled lights of my eyes, today, with faith, you have undertaken one of the five ordained duties. On this, the twenty-ninth day of Ramadan, the yearning and intention within your inner heart has led you to complete another day of fasting. You must realize the value of this fast. *Allāhu ta'ālā Nāyan,* the Singular One, has declared that there are five and six duties[1] and has sent the precept of fasting through each of His prophets.

We came to this world in perfect purity and looked upon God as sufficient [for our lives]. We bowed to Him alone and came here considering Him to be our only support. Allah alone was our wealth, treasure, grace, house, and property. We received this wealth of grace *(rahmat)* and came here in a state of perfect purity. Once we came here, we were influenced by the same Satan who led Adam ☺ astray. Satan, who was flung onto the earth before Adam ☺, inherited earth, opulence,

---

1. **Five and six duties:** The five outer duties in Islam are 1) faith in God and the prophet, 2) prayer, 3) charity, 4) fasting, and 5) the holy pilgrimage of Hajj. The six inner duties are 1) to hear God with the inner ear, 2) to see Him with the inner eye, 3) to smell Him with the inner nose, 4) to speak to Him with the inner tongue, 5) to taste His food and surrender to His essence *(dhāt),* and 6) to commune with God through His essence.

and hell. Praise, honor, titles, and pride are his. The turbulent qualities of deceit, trickery, treachery, envy, jealousy, selfishness, evil tricks, mantras, tantras, magics, mesmerisms, miracles, and miraculous powers arise from his evil properties. Satan was cast onto earth with these qualities.

Later, Adam⊕, succumbing to a grain of wheat,[2] was also cast out, falling onto the same earth as Satan. Because of their mistake, Adam⊕ was flung to the east and Eve⊕ was thrown to the west. They were separated for six hundred years, during which time they cried, praised God, worshipped God, and meditated on God. Finally, God united them in Jiddah where they gave birth to twenty-one pairs of twins—forty-two children in all. From these children, God expanded the human race. We, who are the products of that expansion, must realize the five and six duties in our lives so that we may understand the following.

What should man realize?
What should he do?
What should he attain?
Where should he go?
What benefits should he receive?
Who are we?
Who is our Father?
Who is our Creator?
Who is our Protector?
Who decrees judgment?
Who resurrects us later?

To help us with these questions, God, the Singular One who rules and sustains, has provided us with every variety of good and evil. Both are in His charge; both were created by Him.

---

2. **Grain of wheat:** In Sufi versions of the story, Adam⊕ and Eve⊕ dwell in paradise until Satan tempts them with the fruit of eternal life—a grain of wheat. In those days, as described in the stories, wheat grew to the size of small trees, with each grain being as white as snow and as sweet as honey. Trans.

252

God created
the flower and the fragrance,
the tree and the seed,
the fruit and its taste,
the colors and shades,
darkness and light,
water and salt,
good and evil,
hell and heaven,
the permissible and the impermissible,
the essence of God *(dhāt)* and the attributes of God *(sifāt)*.[3]

We are beings created out of the six kinds of lives.
God created all lives
and placed on earth all lives that live on earth.
He placed in the sky all lives that live in the sky,
on the sun all lives that live on the sun,
on the moon all lives that live on the moon,
in water all lives that live in water,
under the earth all lives that live under the earth,
in the forest all lives that live in the forest,
in God all lives that live in God,
and in hell all lives that live in hell.

God created all these creations, and all of them praise Him. Lives in hell seek God, and lives in heaven seek God. God created the eight heavens, and it was He who created the seven hells. And within all of this, He created a secret—man *(insān)*. He created *sirr* and *sifāt*. God and God's secret are the *sirr*, and the physical bodies are the *sifāt*. Our bodies, as well as everything that is manifested as *sifāt,* are subject to birth.

---

3. **Sifāt:** *Attributes of God*, as distinct from His essence *(dhāt)*. *Dhāt* refers to the nature of the thing itself rather than the qualities *(sifāt)* it possesses. Depending on the context, *sifāt* may also refer to the creations of God. Trans.

Everything that is subject to birth has a visible form. The sun, moon, stars, clouds, winds, water, fire, air, trees, shrubs, plants, flowers, fragrances, worms, insects, beetles, birds, jinns, fairies, angels, archangels, fruits, ocean-lives, land-lives, four-legged beasts, two-legged animals, monkeys, donkeys, dogs, cats, mice, lions, tigers, goats, cows, demons, and ghosts—God created them all.

> God placed a limit on everything that appeared—
> everything that has origin.
> The sun has a limit,
> the moon has a limit,
> the stars have limits,
> the created tree has a limit,
> water has a limit,
> and air has a limit
> set by God.

Similarly, each angel has a limit. Cows, goats, donkeys, and horses all have limits. The body and blood have limits, and we understand this as good and bad, as *sirr* and *sifāt*—the secret and the manifestation. The manifested *sifāt* is our visible body. The *sirr* is that which is within us—the angels, archangels, prophets, enlightened beings, souls, elemental spirits, ghosts, demons, jinns, fairies, the angels—Gabriel☻, Michael☻, *Isrāfil*☻, *Izrā'īl*☻, *Munkar*☻, and *Nakīr*☻—water, fire, air, earth, ether, mind, desire, and base desires. They all have a state of existence. They are the secret within us.

> Within us, therefore,
> without a world, the world exists,
> without ghosts, ghosts exist,
> without Satan, Satan exists,
> without demons, demons exist,
> without the mind, the mind exists,
> without desire, desire exists,

without a monkey, the monkey exists,
without a lion, the lion exists,
without a snake, the snake exists,
without a tiger, the tiger exists,
without an eagle, the eagle exists,
without a vulture, the vulture exists,
without a cow, the cow exists,
without a goat, the goat exists,
without a donkey, the donkey exists,
without a horse, the horse exists,
without an elephant, the elephant of reckless arrogance exists,
without a rat, the rat exists,
without an ocean, the ocean exists,
and without fish, fish exist.

In this way, without the world, the entire world exists within us. Without earth, there is earth, and without salt, there is salt within us. Everything is within our body as the inner secret. *Sirr* is the secret which is inside, and *sifāt* is that which is seen on the outside. Within our bodies, *sirr* takes the form of spirits, various kinds of air, heat, fire, water, and earth. We must understand what exists as the *Sirr* within this *sirr*. *Sirr*, again, is the world within us, and *sifāt* is the world we see on the outside.

Everything that is seen on the outside is *sifāt*, and all these visible things have limits. The *sirr* that is perceived also has a perishability—a limit, an *agreement*. That which is manifest and perceivable as *sifāt* on the outside has a perceivable form, a limit, and an end. Everything that we see within us as *sirr* also has an end. The *Sirr* within the *sirr* is the *dhāt*, the grace of God.

This *dhāt*, this grace,
exists to end everything else.
The *Dhāt* within the *dhāt* is the soul *(rūh)*—

the Grace within grace
is the resplendent soul of man.
The *Rūh* within the *rūh*
is the Grace-Wealth of all the universes,
the *Rahmatul-'ālamīn*—
the *mīm* which is Muhammad.
The Muhammad within Muhammad
is God's grace, His beauty, His light.
The Beauty within that beauty,
the Light within that light,
is God's wisdom, the *qutbiyyat*.
The mystery,
the *Qutbiyyat* within the *qutbiyyat*,
is the stamp of man's resplendent, resolute faith *(īmān)*,
which knows that there is nothing other than God.
The Stamp within the stamp
is the kingdom of the wealth of God's throne,
the *Rūhul-'ālam*.
Within this realm are the lights, the prophets.
The 124,000 prophets encircle this realm.
The lights
Gabriel ☉, Michael ☉, *Isrāfil* ☉, and *Izrā'īl* ☉
are there,
unseen on the outside,
a mysterious secret on the inside.
The Mysterious Secret within the mysterious secret
is God's grace-wealth of all the universes,
the perfect *Nūr*—the Light of God.
The *Nūr* within the *Nūr*
is the mystery of Allah.
Allah exists
as a mystery.

The Mystery within the mystery
are God's qualities, actions, conduct, and wealth *(daulat)*.
Perceived as *Daulat* within His *daulat*
are His actions—the *Asmā'ul-Husnā*.
The ninety-nine actions of the *Asmā'ul-Husnā*,
put into operation as His *wilāyāt*,
cause everything to happen.
God's *rahmat* exists as the *Asmā'ul-Husnā*,
the ninety-nine *wilāyāt* of God.

The *Wilāyat* within the ninety-nine *wilāyāt*
is the mystery known as Allah.
The Mystery within that mystery
is God's judgment—the state of sovereignty.
The Sovereign within the sovereignty
is the One who is Allah
in this world, the world of souls, and everywhere.
He is the Protector.
This One Protector is the Lord,
the Merciful One, the Compassionate One.
This resonant Compassionate One
is the One who creates, protects, and sustains.
One of such qualities
is the All-Pervasive, Complete One.
He is Mystery within the mystery,
Wisdom within wisdom,
Life within life,
and *Īmān* within a life of *īmān*.

The One who fills this world and the world of souls,
this Treasure without parallel or equal
is known as the
Lord of all the universes.

He governs all lives and all bodies.
He governs the sun and the moon.
He governs food and nourishment.
He governs water and fire.
He governs air and ether.
He understands and governs good and evil.
He controls and rules heaven and hell.
God, the Singular One
who governs all lives,
is the Mystery
without form,
without shape,
unconstrained by anything.

He always was.
He still is.
He is the
Supreme Primeval One,
the One Power,
the Perfect Light,
the Omnipotent One,
the Infinite One,
the Singular One,
the Absolute,
the Resonance—*ill Allāhu,*
the Greatest—*Allāhu Akbār,*
the Lone One—*ill Allāh,*
unparalleled,
matchless,
Leader of messengers,
and Light of prophets.
This Mystery,
the Light within the light

is known as God.

He is the Lord of all the universes.

God sent us down in perfect purity that we might worship this incomparable, unequalled One in the right way. He sent our souls in perfect purity, and to everything—earth, gold, trees, leaves, grass, shrubs, fruits, plants, water, fire, air—he made *common* the elements of earth, fire, water, and air. The earth, sky, fruits, grass, and shrubs all have these elements. God made these elements *common* to the six kinds of lives.[4]

Satan's qualities try to possess this *commonwealth*. Satan's intentions, pride, desire, jealousy, treachery, deceit, trickery, mantras, magics, and base desires try to take over what belongs to God. Satan crept into man and habituated him to this state by saying, "This is wealth; it belongs to you. This is gold; it belongs to you. This is earth; it belongs to you. This stone and this fruit belong to you. This garden belongs to you." In this way, through deception and trickery, Satan changed man. Thus man, who had been given perfect purity, was given instead a share of the hell that was Satan's. Satan takes possession of the *commonwealth*, dividing and giving to each man the qualities and hell that had been given to him. He shows man earth, woman, and gold—perishable entities with a defined limit—and seduces him into thinking that they are eternal treasures. Because of this, human beings change into Satan. They turn into animals—into donkeys, horses, snakes, rats, elephants, eagles, vultures, pigs, mice, birds, beetles, and cats. They fall prey to countless such changes.

When man assumed these various forms, God sent down the 124,000 lights (prophets) to help him regain his original self. What we saw in external form were *sifāt*. We believed in these outer forms and called them prophets, but they were only human forms. What resided within

---

4. **Six kinds of lives:** The five kinds of lives are earth-life, fire-life, water-life, air-life, and ether-life. The sixth life is the light-life—the soul. It is a ray of light from the *Nūr* which does not die.

as *sirr,* was the real prophet. The inner form, qualities, and actions are different. On the outside, we perceived them in human form as *sifāt.* Within the *sifāt* were the *sirr,* and in the *sirr* were the prophets. The prophets are within the elements; they are within and beyond the angels. They are the *Sirr* within the *sirr,* in the form of light.

Then and now, they are lights. All the prophets that we saw [with our eyes] were *sifāt,* but if we had looked closely at those *sifāt,* we would have seen the *sirr* within. And if we had carefully examined the *sirr,* we would have perceived a *Sirr* within. A closer scrutiny would have revealed that this *Sirr* within the *sirr* was the *dhāt,* and the *Dhāt* within the *dhāt* was the light, and this light was the mystery, the *Rahmatul-'ālamīn,* the prophets. We should realize this.

Meanwhile, we live as animals, intending to kill other lives.
We worship the cow, but we also chop it up and consume it.
We worship the monkey, but we also make it perform tricks.
We worship rats and then send out cats to catch them.
We worship cats and then let them loose among dogs.
We worship donkeys and then make them carry our burdens.
We worship horses and then send them to the supermarkets.
We worship goats and then send them off to the market.
We worship snakes and then kill them.

Whatever we worship, we first adopt its form within us, and then begin to worship it on the outside. In this way we worship entities that we perceive as being God, and then, since they have a limit, we eat, kill, and destroy them. We must understand this.

The prophets, enlightened beings, *Qutbs,* and friends of God *(auliyā)* were sent as God's mystery to help us realize this. He sent them to correct us, to release us from the animal qualities, the properties, the hell, and the actions of Satan, and thus to transform us. God sent one prophet after another, and finally He sent *Muhammad Mustafar-Rasūl,* may the peace and blessings of God be upon him. The history of all the prophets and their fullness were put together and sent down in completion as 6,666 verses. Through these verses, the five and six duties were ordained so that man, who had become animal, could gradually be transformed. They were sent as the *rahmat* of all the universes, as *Lā ilāha ill Allāh*—there is nothing but God.

> The first of the five duties
> is to believe in God,
> to worship without comparison
> the One who has no comparison;
> to worship without help
> the One who has no help;
> to worship without conformity
> the One who has no conformity.

For those who have wisdom, God is in front of them, and for those who lack wisdom, He is in the unknown realm. God showed us the way to worship. What He showed us through the prophets has no mantras, tricks, magics, mesmerisms, wondrous abilities, or miracles. Every animal—monkey, donkey, horse, elephant—performs miracles. Birds and snakes perform miracles. Displaying their abilities is their miracle. To leave all these aside and perceive the ninety-nine *wilāyāt* of God—His actions, qualities, and ways—is prayer, *'ibādat*. To perceive this, to worship and follow Him, is prayer.

God summoned His believers, established this state of prayer, and sent down His prophets. The five and six duties were additionally given to help man establish this state and change himself. These duties were ordained so that man could pray to the One who has no comparison or likeness, knowing that there is none worthy of worship other than *Allāhu ta'ālā Nāyan,* the Singular One who rules and sustains.

> Man was shown that
> there is only One who accepts prayer,

only One who knows us,
only One who understands our inner heart,
only One who gives and takes life,
and only One who decrees judgment.
He is the only One,
the Giver of food,
the Giver of life,
the Summoner,
the Judge,
the Resurrector.

Those with resolute faith know that everything belongs to God—
the *sirr* and the *sifāt,* the *dhāt,* the good and the evil, the permissible and
the impermissible. "Everything we see belongs to God. Our body and
life are His. Understand this and accept God, the only One worthy of
worship." This is what God has explained. The five and six duties were
established in accordance with His words.

First, believe in God.
Those who accept
that there is none worthy of worship other than God,
that God is their treasure,
their life, their body,
their history, their wealth,
their Lord, and their Father,
will accept no other.
They have received the wealth that is Him.
They will be the ones of resolute faith,
pure spirits,
inhabitants of paradise,
rulers of paradise,
and princes of God.

Those who had lost this wealth were given six inner duties and five outer duties. Man was told, "Accept the five outer duties and, at least through them, gain clarity!" The first duty is faith, the second is worship, the third is charity, the fourth is fasting, and the fifth is the pilgrimage of Hajj. These duties were ordained to help man understand and know himself, thus enabling him to throw away everything given by Satan—his qualities, desires, and hypnotism. In order to know himself, man has to cast away gold, wealth, torpor, and the differences of "I" and "you." The duties were given to help us throw away all the *commonwealth* that we have thievishly hoarded. Anything we have or hold must be cast away.

> If we have a sword, we should get rid of it.
> If we have a gun, we should put it down.
> If we have another's wealth, we should return it.
> If we have jealousy, we should give it up.
> If we have deceit, we should discard it.
> If we have treachery, we should evict it.
> We must abandon everything other than Allah
> and know that He is the Truth.
> The fast was ordained for these purposes.

For two hundred million years, since the creation of Adam⊕, the fast has existed. It is known by different names in different languages, but the same process is referred to as the fast in Christianity, Hinduism, Hanal, Islam, and Judaism. In the Tamil language, the fast is called *nōnbu,* which often turns into a state of no *anbu,* no love.

> If man
> does not have compassion,
> does not see other lives as his own,
> does not consider the hunger of others as his own,
> does not see the sorrow of others as his own

263

and offer comfort,
does not see the illness of others as his own
and offer assistance,
does not see others' need for clothing as his own
and offer clothing,
does not see other lives as his own
and exalt them,
then there is no *anbu,*
no love, [no fast].

To realize this is the fast.
This is the grace-filled fast.
This is the purpose for which it was instituted.
When we understand this
and respect others' lives as our own,
consider others' hunger as our own,
look upon others' happiness as our own,
and regard others' sorrow as our own;
when we attain
the wisdom, abilities, qualities, and actions
to bring peace and comfort to all lives—
that will be the grace and blessings of the fast.

When we acquire these qualities
we will receive the grace,
the wealth of the three worlds,
and the unity of brotherhood.
We will realize that there is
only one family,
one God,
one community.
We will join together and embrace each other
chest to chest,

heart to heart,
body to body,
mind to mind,
and life to life,
without slander, jealousy, or treachery.

Embracing each other,
looking into each other's faces,
eating together,
being joyous in each other's company,
joining together in birth and death,
in good times and bad,
in hunger and illness,
in sorrow and difficulty,
and living in unity—
attaining this state is Islam.
If we comprehend the principles of this state,
we will be *Īmān-Islām*.[5]
If we understand *Īmān-Islām*,
we will be true human beings *(insān)*.
If we realize this state,
we will be perfected beings *(insān kāmil)*.
If we understand *insān kāmil*,
that is *dhāt*.
If we understand *dhāt*,
we will know the lights that resplend,
the prophets.
We will know the form of the prophets.

---

5. **Īmān-Islām:** *Īmān* means resolute faith in God, and *Islām* means purity. *Īmān-Islām* is the state wherein the pure heart, cutting away all evil, takes on the courageous determination called faith and shines in God's resplendence. When the resplendence of God is seen as the completeness within the heart of man, that is *Īmān-Islām*.

If we know the form of the prophets
we will know their mystery.
If we know their mystery
we will know the Light of God, *Nūr.*
If we know the *Nūr*
we will know our soul.
If we know our soul
we will know God and His completeness.

God has instructed us step by step so that we may understand this. My precious jeweled lights of my eyes, may we realize this. In our study, fasting, and learning to discriminate between good and evil are the beginning lessons. We do this according to the practices of *sharī'at*[6] in order to understand right and wrong. The Hindu, or *Zabūr* religion, is the first religion—*sharī'at,* the aspect of creation. Above this is the *Hanal* religion, the aspect of fire— the fire of hunger, illness, old age, death, and hell. The fire, the sun, and the moon are worshipped in this religion. Above this is Christianity. Miracles such as the spirits and the soul are worshipped. Above this is *Furqān*—Islam.

Furqān should be understood through the seven principles.
Look with the inner eye of wisdom,
not with the outer eye that looks at the world.
Within wisdom is another eye, the secret eye.
Within that eye is another eye, the eye of *īmān.*
Within *īmān* is another eye, the eye of light.
Within the eye of light is the eye of the *Nūr.*
Within the *Nūr* is the eye of the Lord.

---

6. **Sharī'at:** The first of four steps of spiritual ascendancy in Islam, its basic tenet being the discrimination of right and wrong. The author also refers to *sharī'at* as Hinduism, the first of four religions, the other three being fire-worship, Christianity, and Islam. The four religions correspond, in ascending order, to four regions in our body. Trans.

With this eye we can see
this world, the world of souls, and everything.

If we look with the outer eyes we will only see the creations of the world, but if we look with the secret inner eye we can see the spirits, ghosts, and demons. If we look with another eye we can see this world *('ālam)* and the world of souls *(arwāh)*. With yet another eye we can see the *Qutbs*. With another we can perceive Allah's *rahmat*. With still another eye, we can see the resplendent, perfect Light, the *Nūr*. And with a final eye we can see God's mystery, the laws of His kingdom. We should attain the wisdom and ability to see with the eyes within the eyes.

Similarly, there are many ears within this ear. There is layer after layer of flesh and skin. When we cut through these layers, God's resonant sound is deep within. We will also hear the sounds of angels, archangels, and prophets. We will hear the sounds of God's revelations. We should hear these sounds with the inner ear and understand.

The outer nose inhales the world and identifies smells as good and bad. Within this nose are seven other noses. We should analyze the seven nodes of flesh in the nose. If we go through each with understanding, the fragrance of Allah, the fragrance of the prophets, and the fragrance of musk *(kasthūrī)* will cascade everywhere. The fragrance of heaven will be pervasive. The fragrance of the heavenly maidens, the fruits of heaven, and the qualities of heaven exist there. Upon perceiving this fragrance we should understand that this is heaven, this is paradise, this is the house of God, this is the fragrance that emanates from Him. We should discover and identify this.

The outer tongue relishes the taste of cows, goats, donkeys, and horses. It also speaks good and evil. There are, however, seven kinds of tongues within this tongue. One by one we should use the different tongues to savor what must be savored—Allah's divine knowledge, *'ilm*, Allah's *rahmat*, Allah's *īmān*, Allah's *sirr*, Allah's *sifāt*, Allah's *Nūr*, Allah's angels, and Allah's archangels. When we proceed in this way, we will finally taste the grace-wealth of all the universes, the *Rahmatul-'ālamīn*. The entire body will relish its sweet taste as it flows through each layer of flesh and skin and through each of the various nerves. The fragrance enters every blood cell, and the taste permeates. Every spoken word and every intention has that sweet taste. You must understand and accept that taste. It is the taste of divine knowledge, the taste of wisdom, the taste of *īmān,* the taste of belief, and the taste of the Lord. We must understand and accept the taste of *Rahmatul-'ālamīn* and extract greater understanding from its sweet taste.

Likewise, the inner heart is made of five elements, and within it are seven kinds of skin and seven kinds of inner hearts. Within them, God has created a mysterious inner heart that contains His secret. God's essence, *dhāt,* exists there as the Secret within the secret. The *Nūr* exists as the *Dhāt* within the *dhāt*—God's Light exists as the Essence within the essence. Lights and perfection exist as the *Nūr* within the *Nūr.* Paradise exists within that, and within paradise is the place where God and His prophets pray—the paradise-place, the prayer-place. In front and back of this place is the throne, the house of prayer, where enlightened beings, *Qutb*s, prophets, friends, and loved ones of God join together and pray. That house of prayer is larger than the eighteen thousand universes, containing over one hundred thousand wonders. It is called a mystery. God has made this a house that we can enter; there we can inhale the fragrance and the qualities, join together, and pray. God has placed all of this within a minute morsel of flesh which is within a tiny dot *(nuqat).* We should open that tiny dot saying, "*Bismillāhir-Rahmānir-Rahīm. Lā ilāha ill Allāhu.* In the name of God, most Merciful, most Compassionate. Other than You there is nothing, You are God." Open it and look within. The *rahmat* within cannot be consumed by anything—by fire, water, air, sun, moon, or earth. It has existed without destruction from day of reckoning to day of reckoning, for aeons and aeons. The mystery known as the soul *(rūh)* is within this.

Thus, the five kinds of lives, the five elements, are in the inner heart. The secret soul is within that. This is where the light and perfection are. This is the mystery. The other heart consists of the five elements. When fever strikes, illness assails, or blood boils, doctors locate this heart and calculate the decrease in blood or air. They can do that because this heart is made up of earth, fire, water, air, and ether. However, since these five elements cannot be seen in the soul, the soul cannot be detected through research or through any kind of instrument. Allah alone can find this place. He alone comprehends the soul.

The prophets were sent down one after another to reveal different principles of understanding that will enable us to realize this. In everything we do, we must understand that there are four scriptures, four religions—*sharī'at, tarīqat, haqīqat,* and *ma'rifat.* They are not miraculous powers, mantras, or miracles. We should think about this. My precious jeweled lights of my eyes, may we reflect on this. May we climb up one step after another, understand more and more, and gain realization. It is for this purpose that the fast, charity, pilgrimage of Hajj, prayer, ritual prayer, and melting-heart prayers were instituted for us by God. He has given us one principle after another. Each prophet was handed the principles, one after another, and sent down to us. We should understand this in truth. *Lā ilāha ill Allāhu*—Other than You there is nothing, You alone are God.

May the peace, beneficence, and blessings of God be upon you.
May we realize this. All praise is to God. He is the Greatest.
(The author offers greetings to all the angels and recites
the *Sūratul-Fātihah*)

My precious jeweled lights of my eyes, it is quite late.
Go and break your fasts.
May Allah fulfill your intentions and so grace you.
May He fulfill your yearnings and so bless you.
May He fulfill your certainty and grant His grace.
May He guide your search and lead you to success.
May He give you resolute faith, wealth,

divine knowledge,
wisdom, the wealth of the soul-world,
and the wealth of the three worlds—
the grace-wealth of all the universes,
and so grace you.
Āmīn, Āmīn,
O Lord of the universes.
As-salāmu ʿalaikum wa rahmatullāhi wa barakātuhu kulluhu.
May the peace, beneficence, and blessings of God
be upon you.
Go and fulfill your fasts.
Āmīn.

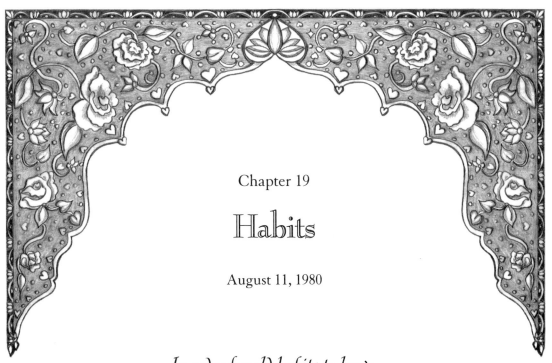

Chapter 19

Habits

August 11, 1980

In order for old habits to leave,
you have to control them.
When you govern them and they leave,
you will have peace.
You will hear nothing.
There will be no sounds,
no messages, no revelations,
no mesmerisms, no miraculous powers,
no witchcraft, no spells,
no mantras, no tricks, no deceit.
When it is all over,
there is a quiet tranquillity.

Habits

Question: My question is about the additional ten days of fasting. Is that something we can do, should do, or not do?

Bawa Muhaiyaddeen: First, do the thirty days of fasting properly. You will not do the extra ten. Have you finished fasting for thirty days? No, you have not. Finish that first, and when that Great Day arrives we can look ahead to the Divine Day. Complete the thirty days first. I have not seen you fast for thirty days, you have not completed this part. Do this first.

Whatever you do, do it properly. Whatever you set out to do, correct yourself and do it well. Whatever needs medicine, give it the right medicine; then the illness will be cured. Know the remedy, know what needs to be joined with what, and do it properly.

[A baby begins to cry aloud. Bawa Muhaiyaddeen talks to the child very lovingly, "Oh no, no, no. My love you, my love you. *Anbu*. You should not cry; there is love here." The baby stops crying immediately, and Bawa asks, "Did your father pinch you?" The father replies, "No, it is twenty minutes past her bedtime."]

Bawa Muhaiyaddeen: That is all right, if you have habituated the child day after day in this way, that is how it is.

If you habituate a child to eat at a certain time, the child will say, "I'm hungry, I'm hungry." The intellect will search for food, asking, "Where is the food, where is the food?" A certain energy is present. Perception and awareness (*unarvu* and *unarchi,* two of the seven wis-

273

doms in man) remind the child, and the child begins to search. Intellect (*pudthi*) says, "There is food here," and the child experiences hunger immediately.

> Perception, awareness, and intellect
> operate like this in every part of the body.
> As soon as perception stirs something up,
> awareness picks up on it,
> and the different organs start to function.
> Perception ignites everything:
> sleep, memory, intention, attachment, and passion.
> It is an energy in the skin.
> Then awareness stirs,
> causing the intellect to cry out immediately,
> "O my daughter, my wife, my child,"
> and begin its search.
> Everything is initiated by perception and awareness.

Therefore, if one has acquired the habit of sleeping at a particular time, then as that time approaches, the kindling begins. Sleep, love, lust—everything functions in this manner. As soon as perception and awareness stir things up, the intellect starts to operate, the search begins, and the person is mesmerized. If a man acquires the habit of sleeping during the day, he will have to fall asleep at the scheduled time. The kindling begins without his knowledge, but if he refuses to sleep, drives it away, and says, "Go away," he will not fall asleep. You must push away the perception, chase it away.

It is the same with every illness, demon, ghost, and satan. There is a magnet, an energy, in the five elements, and every habit is kindled at the appropriate time. As soon as it is aroused, the one who will be mesmerized gets mesmerized, the one who will sleep grows sleepy, and the one who will get hungry heads off to eat. Perception, awareness, and intellect operate, causing these things to happen. Through their agency, the mind of man governs his body and the world.

Habits formed in the cradle are taken to the grave. Just as parents foster habits in the cradle, man continues to foster habits until he reaches the cemetery. He develops habits for every aspect [of his life]. For each habit, a certain energy is activated at the appropriate time, intellect operates, and man sets out to do the task. The intellect acts on everything it sees. This intellect, this monkey-mind, will do whatever it sees, repeating what it has done before. This is the activity of the intellect.

Wisdom, on the other hand, analyzes and researches. It will delve deeper. The height of intellect is religion and philosophy. The boundaries of religion and philosophy are the boundaries of the intellect. The intellect operates on and stores everything it perceives—scriptures, ancient legends, histories. But what is its limit? Its limit is religion and philosophy. It will go up to the level it perceives. It absorbs and takes for itself what it has seen. That is the level it can attain. But the path of God is far beyond the scriptures and philosophies; it is the path of Wisdom within wisdom. It is far, far beyond all the energies, cells, and viruses. Intellect, however, ends with the scriptures.

The five elements function to arouse the connections to earth, maya, arrogance, lust, anger, pride, desire, torpor, self-interest, and cravings. This is the monkey-mind, the five elements which make man act upon whatever he sees. Intellect is the state that associates with the monkey-mind and the five elements, acting upon whatever it sees. The result is the *purānas*.[1] [The first six *purānas*] are arrogance, karma, maya, and the three children of maya—*tārahan*, *singhan*, and *sūran*. *Tārahan* is the energy, the focused entry into the sexual organ, *singhan* is the quality, the *force* behind the entry, and *sūran* is the sixty-four sexual arts. The sixty-four sexual games that are played out in a dark room are enacted

---

1. **Purānas:** *Ancient legends,* a class of Hindu writings containing ancient stories. Each of the seventeen *purānic* stories highlights a particular quality in the hero and the role it plays in his life. The author speaks of the seventeen *purānas,* the *ancient legends,* within man: arrogance, karma, and maya; the three sons of maya—*tārahan, singhan, and sūran*; and lust, anger, miserliness, attachment, fanaticism, envy, intoxicants, desire, theft, murder, and falsehood. Trans.

in the daylight as the sixty-four arts and sciences. This is *sūran*. Together with desire, anger, miserliness, attachment, fanaticism, envy, intoxicants, lust, theft, murder, and falsehood—these seventeen are the ancient stories of mankind, the *vedic purānas*. They are the seventeen worlds. The intellect operates and functions within them. Beyond this are judgment, subtle wisdom, analytic wisdom, and divine luminous wisdom *(mathi, arivu, pahuth arivu, and perr arivu),* operating at a much higher level. Only when man transcends these seventeen realms will he be able to investigate and answer the questions that lead to God's Kingdom: Where was he before? What is he doing now? Where should he go next? What exists there? What is his kingdom? What is his soul?

The *purānas* are energies. They dwell in the body and operate through the energies, cells, and viruses. Perception, awareness, and intellect extract these *purānas,* drawing man's attention to them. They show him what the *purānas* have done, and as soon as man sees these things, he falls prey to them and is hypnotized. We must transcend this state. To go beyond this and study is wisdom. Go beyond to your "birth-path." Then your perception will be Divine Perception, enabling you to cross the limits of the five elements.

> Everything limits man—
> he sleeps, he eats,
> he has attachments, he has affections,
> he has blood-disorders, he has blood-ties,
> he has a house, and he has property.
> All these things operate in him,
> causing him to get entangled in different places.
> At various times they take him and rivet him to different things.
> At a particular time they push him in a specific direction
> and say, "Look, this is yours!"
> Man goes and gets buried in these places.
> He will lie down, sleep, drink, get intoxicated,
> grab, bite, and do all the work that a monkey does.

This is the mind—the monkey-mind
that imitates everything it sees.
Whatever it thinks, it does.
Each thing it possesses
causes it to get stuck at a different place,
and man becomes lethargic.

Whether you habitually smoke cigars, smoke opium, visit bars, drink brandy, fall asleep, feel hungry, have attachments, or feel passionate— when a habit comes around at its specified time, you will succumb to it. Man calls this the world, hell, base desires, elements, and life. We have to transcend this; we have to conquer it and go beyond to attain wisdom and fortitude.

Everything mentioned earlier is an energy in the body. They are all energies of the five elements present in the blood, skin, flesh, bones, and marrow. They are energies of the five kinds of lives: earth-life, fire-life, water-life, air-life, and ether-life. Man's life, however, is connected to God. It is Light. Earth-lives live on earth, and water-lives live in water, or they would die. Air-lives die if there is no air. Fire-lives die if there is no fire, and ether-lives die if there is no ether. Ether lives are light-lives connected to the sun and the moon. They live with the spirits, the angel-lives, and the jinns and the fairies who are created out of fire. This is the magic, the mesmerism—forms that change continually. They are ether-lives.

Man's life, man's soul, is a *light-form* of perfect purity, connected to God. The other five lives are connected to the earth's energy. Man's soul, as Wisdom within wisdom, is connected to God, to His grace and His essence *(dhāt)*.

Man's soul is with God,
but the five energies flutter
between the connections to earth and ether.
They fly around, make noise, tremble, laugh, cry,

277

rejoice, praise, blame, rise, and descend.
This is what the five elements do.
They are five of the six kinds of lives.
They run about and bring messages to man.
But the life which is the soul-light,
this purity merged in wisdom,
this wisdom-soul light, is always stable.
It has no comings and goings.
It is firmly established,
and it is very strong.
This light stays in one place,
while the other energies bring messages.

The messages come and go while we are here in one place. The soul stays, but the five elements move about. As soon as a person sits down, an element flits around, asking, "I wonder how my wife is? I went there, my wife was like this, my children were like that." Then another one comes along, saying, "Oo, look there, look at what your wife and child are doing. They are calling out to you. They want you to come. It is dark now. They want you to come."

The person is right here, but the elements come and deliver these messages. Then another element arrives, saying, "Look, you have some work to do. There is a lawsuit you have to deal with in regard to your income-tax. What have you done about it? Your lawyer is looking for you." Another element says, "You should go to Atlantic City; all the children are crying. You said that they could go. You should go there. Why are you sitting here? Come on, let's go." When this element leaves, another comes running, saying, "What foolishness is this? What is the use of talking like this? You should study this philosophy, you should meditate, you should write what you have to write, you should study what you have to study. People are looking for you there, so why are you here? There is a meeting there." Then another element hurries over to advise, "Let it all be. Don't worry. Go ahead and sleep. You need to rest. Rest awhile; then you can do everything."

[Bawa asks the man with the child, "Do they tell you this? Do you hear these messages?" The man laughs and says, "All the time."]

So the person stays in one place, but the five kinds of lives scurry around. The life that is the soul-light remains silent. When the messages come one after another, just brush them aside, saying, "Go over there, I know all about it." The elements will clamor, "These are the messages we have brought. Look at them." Just say, "Be gone. I know everything. Come only when I call you." When another element comes, say, "Get over there." Yet another comes and you say, "Go far away." It says, "I'm hungry." You reply, "I can give you food, but this is not the right time. There is plenty of time. Go and wait awhile." Another one presents itself, crying, "You did not give me a fruit today. Well, I don't want a fruit now; I want a beer. I want brandy. You did not give me any books to read. I have to go to school; I have to do so many things." The next one rushes in, saying, "I have to sleep. I don't have a bed to sleep on." Yet another one says, "I have a bed, but the bed hurts my body. Besides, it has no sheets."

When all these messages come, man's job is to control them, saying, "Go there and wait!" Wisdom has to control and deal with all the messages, telling each to go and stay where they should. Some messages will even say, "I am bringing you God's sound! Look, God is speaking here! He is calling you!" But these are just energies of the five kinds of lives. Wisdom must govern them. The state of the soul is as it is, pure. Wisdom—sun—God. Wisdom is the sun, the light. It must keep each of the five lives where they belong and control them, saying, "Go where you belong, and stay there."

While a man stays in one place,
the mind flies about through the agency of the five elements.
Each element brings its own relationships and ties:
the connections of earth,
connections of fire,

connections of water,
connections of air,
and connections of ether.
This is all that they bring.
And through this, the messages,
miraculous powers *(sidhis)*,
and miracles are delivered to man.
But these are not real messages.
Each element only brings its own state of being—
its intentions, its desires, and its hunger.
This is their work.

Man has six kinds of lives within him. They are often called spirits. They could take the form of demons, ghosts, jinns, fairies, maya, delusion, and angels. They could come in different ways, but this is all that they are—elements, flying and wandering. We must realize this. We must control all of them, saying, "You stay there. You stay there. Go!" Focus on them and tell them to leave.

A wise man will know
that the only beneficial thing is one's true state.
Everything else has to be scrutinized and controlled.

When he regulates them, they will cry out, "O I am so hungry; you did not give me any food. I am really hungry, and I feel faint. Give me something to drink!" The next one weeps, "Look, I have not attained divine wisdom. I have no one to teach me divine wisdom." You ask it, "What is this divine wisdom?" and it replies, "I want miracles. I don't have anything." They will repeatedly cry, bring messages, and make noise. You have to drive them away. They will continue to babble and wail, "I stayed with him for so long but I have nothing to show for it. He is crazy. He wants me to leave. Well, I am going. I will not stay with him." They will try to cry their way back, but the wise man just watches them leave and says, "All right, thank you." In this way, say, "Thank you," and let each depart. Each desire, each aspect must leave on its own. Control them and let them leave on their own. So too, control your sleep and let it leave on its own.

There are four hundred trillion, ten thousand spiritual energies, miracles, and messages. Control them and let them flee of their own accord. When they leave, they will say, "Thank you. I am leaving. I cannot stay here." Say, "Thanks a lot. Go ahead." The four hundred trillion, ten thousand miracles, forces, energies, beliefs, and messages must leave. To that degree must you control each of them, forcing their departure. They must stay and depart of their own accord. When they don't get what they want, they will leave. Some will inform you of their departure and others will not. "I cannot stay here. You did not give me this, and you did not give me that. I'm getting out of here," some will say. You should respond, "Thank you!"and watch them go.

But in order for them to leave,
you have to control them.
When you govern them and they leave,
you will have peace.
You will hear nothing.
There will be no sounds,
no messages, no revelations,
no mesmerisms, no miraculous powers,
no witchcraft, no spells,
no mantras, no tricks, no deceit.
When it is all over, there is a quiet tranquillity.
A period of speaking without speaking dawns.
It is a period of sleeping without sleeping,
laughing without laughing,
eating without eating,
and dying without dying—
a time of peace, equanimity, and tranquillity.

There is silence.
Everything is finished!

Prior to this, we keep four hundred trillion, ten thousand people with us and try to find peace, but we are unable to do any of the work we attempt. If there is no control, everything is a message, everything is a miracle, everything is magic, and there is noise, noise, noise! When seventy thousand donkeys, seventy thousand foxes, seventy thousand elephants, seventy thousand cats, and seventy thousand snakes are howling, how are you going to sing? It is like trying to sing in the messy midst of preparing a meal. How can you focus on the melody? When all the foxes, cats, rats, and donkeys sing their songs and dance around, you can't do anything. "Woof, woof, woof," goes one. "Hoo, hoo, hoo," goes another. "Roar," goes the lion. "Aheehaah," trumpets the elephant. Amidst all this noise, what is man's writing, what is his speech, what is his perception, what is his meditation, what is his prayer? He cannot do anything. Not for a single day can he pray, speak, or meditate. He can never do it. He might say, "I am meditating," but he will feel an itch somewhere on his body; a voice will call out, "Father, you did not give me this, and I did not get that," and he will scratch himself and squirm. Everything will scratch him, bite him, torment him, pinch him, and poke him. So what meditation does he have? He cannot meditate, not even for a day. There are endless sounds, disturbances, pinches, tears, itches, and probes. He cannot do anything in this state. On the day when all these annoyances leave, he will be in peace. Only then will he meditate. Only then will he pray to God. Until then, he cannot do anything; he is not still for even a second.

The five elements scurry about and the five kinds of lives mingle with man, rolling him around and causing him to undergo frightful difficulties. When four hundred trillion, ten thousand ghosts, demons, thoughts, desires, attachments, blood-ties, religions, races, scriptures, miraculous powers, miracles, mesmerisms, magics, mantras, and tricks are tormenting him, when they are killing him without killing him, when can he attain peace and tranquillity? When can he pray? When can he worship? When will he live in equality, peace, and equanimity? Not even for a day, not even for a second.

Meanwhile man thinks, "I am praying." But all he has done is taken a lot of [the hallucinogenic drug] LSD. There are two kinds of LSD—the chemical LSD, and the maya LSD, which is mind, desire, illusion, and thoughts. When you take the chemical, you are in a drugged state and you think you are watching a show. But when you take this other LSD, it is very powerful, and the mind will show you every single thing. Therefore, man cries, laughs, babbles, trembles, shakes, praises, reveres, falls, rises, rolls, and does all manner of things. This LSD is powerful; this LSD of the five elements is remarkably potent. Four hundred trillion, ten thousand kinds of LSD are within man. His mind, body, and desire drug him with every kind of LSD and degrade him. They tell him they will raise him, and they tell him they will lower him; they praise him, they make him laugh, they make him cry, and they torment him.

When man overcomes this LSD,
when he stops it,
when he controls it—freedom dawns.
He will find the fortitude to be still.

But as long as this LSD is in him, this forceful LSD works with the energies, with perception, with awareness, with the blood, with karma, with arrogance, and with maya. These are the forces of desire, the ghosts and demons that continue to operate. Man will be free only when he alters this LSD. He can then reach the right state wherein his mind is tranquil and serene. But as long as this LSD exists, he cannot be tranquil for a day or even a second. He has no peace. There is never a moment when his energies and cells are still, and not in constant motion. Think about this. Reflect on this and control all these things. They must depart. The more you control them, the more they will choose to leave. They will leave on their own, one after another, and you can just stand there waving good-bye. Then everything comes to a close and there is tranquillity. Only then can you meditate and pray. Only then can you experience peace and equanimity. You cannot retain all these distractions and expect to do anything.

The inner LSD is the most potent one of all. It is within us, killing without killing, deluding without deluding, distracting us, and proclaiming its four hundred trillion, ten thousand miracles. What we have within us now are ghosts, demons, qualities, actions, behaviors, energies, viruses, cells, and spirits. We must overcome them in order to attain peace. We must control them. If you listen to their sounds, you will never have peace. If, after laboring with these things, you still consider them to be your strength, and you believe their sounds to be the truth, then that is hell.

Thank you, children.
Anbu—love.

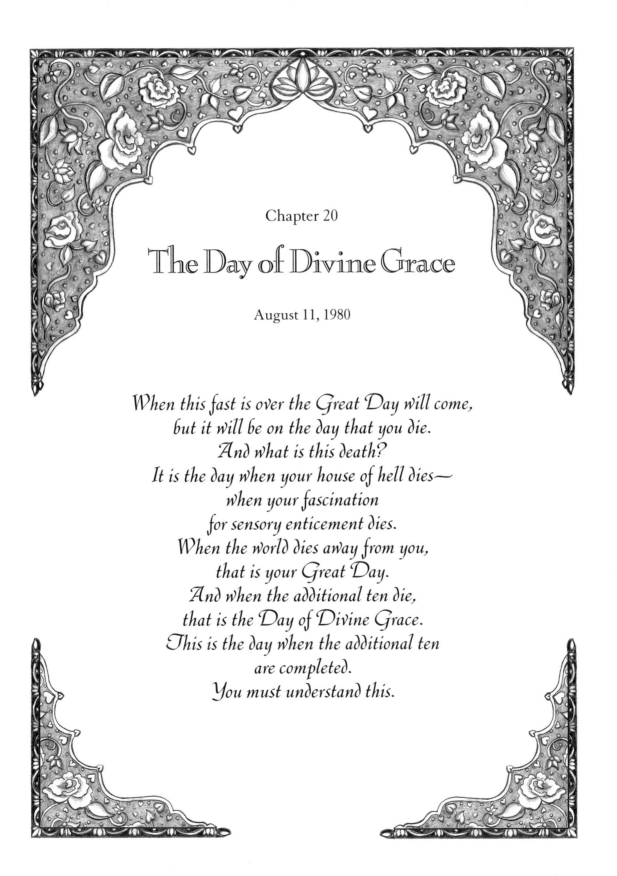

Chapter 20

The Day of Divine Grace

August 11, 1980

When this fast is over the Great Day will come,
but it will be on the day that you die.
And what is this death?
It is the day when your house of hell dies—
when your fascination
for sensory enticement dies.
When the world dies away from you,
that is your Great Day.
And when the additional ten die,
that is the Day of Divine Grace.
This is the day when the additional ten
are completed.
You must understand this.

The Day of Divine Grace

Bismillāhir-Rahmānir-Rahīm.
In the name of God, most Merciful, most Compassionate.
A'ūdhu billāhi minash-shaitānir-rajīm.
I seek refuge in Allah from the accursed Satan.
In the name of God, most Merciful, most Compassionate.

One of unfathomable grace,
One of incomparable love,
Allāhu ta'ālā Nāyan,
the Singular One who rules and sustains,
may all praise and praising belong to Him alone.
Āmīn.
His grace has no comparison, no end.
His love has no parallel, no equal.
May this One of grace bestow on us
His blessings and His unequalled love.
Āmīn.

One who has affection for all lives,
One who loves all lives,
the Mighty One who is the Life in all lives,
it is He whom we worship.
It is to Him that we devote
our ritual prayers *(tholuhai),*

our worship,
our prayers with a melting heart *('ibādat),*
our meditation,
our remembrance *(dhikr),*
and our focused contemplation *(fikr).*

May we offer
the joyous love of the soul
that unites with God,
the love that causes the Soul within the soul
to merge with Him,
the grace *(rahmat)* of that love
which is the wealth of the three worlds,
the love of that grace,
our remembrance,
and our melting-heart prayers
to God alone.
When we offer to Him what is rightfully His,
He will accept our bodies, wealth, and spirit
as His responsibility,
and so grace us.
Āmīn.

For those who observe this fast
and for those who do not,
for those who intend God
and for those who do not,
according to your
yearning, focusing, and searching,
may God fulfill your intentions,
and so grace you.
Āmīn.

The One who understands your inner heart
and knows you through that inner heart,
the One who understands your prayer
and knows you through that prayer,
the One who understands your speech
and knows you through that speech,
the One who looks through your eyes
and understands you through those eyes,
the One who is intermingled in your
breath, speech, body, wounds, and blood
and knows every aspect of you—
may He give you the full benefits of your intentions,
and so grace you.
Āmīn.

May He dispel from you
bad intentions, evil aspirations,
the pride of "I,"
the arrogance of "mine,"
jealousy, deceit, and trickery,
and so grace you.
Āmīn.

For those who have observed this fast,
today brings to completion thirty days of fasting.
May God bestow
the benefits and merits of the fast
to all those who have so intended.
Āmīn.

To those who have fasted,
may the peace, beneficence,
and blessings of God be upon you.

May God fulfill the love
and devotion you have for Him.
May He fulfill the completion of your fast
and the worth of your intentions,
and so grace you.
Āmīn.

In the name of God, most Merciful, most Compassionate.
May our prayers, intentions, praise, and glorifications
always acknowledge Him as the Greatest.

(Bawa Muhaiyaddeen☺ does the Call to Prayer
followed by four *sūrats:Sūratul-Fātihah, Sūratul-Ikhlās,
Sūratul-Falaq, and Sūratun-Nās.)*

To those who have observed the fast,
may God, the Singular One who rules and sustains,
bestow His wealth of the three worlds,
and so grace you.
Āmīn.

May He fulfill your intentions,
and so grace you,
Āmīn.

May He fulfill your aspirations,
and so grace you,
Āmīn.

In this world and in the hereafter,
may God grant you His grace.
Āmīn.

Precious jeweled lights of my eyes,
may God fulfill your melting-heart prayers
and the search within your prayers,
and so grace you.
Āmīn.

The thirty days of fasting is the period when the light known as *Lailatul-Qadr* descended to God's messenger *(Rasūlullāh)*⊖, and his intention was fulfilled. Let us think about this. The first Qur'anic chapter that was sent down at this time was the *Sūratul-Iqrā* or *Sūratul-'alaq*. This ray of light which descended with the *Bismin* (the sacred word—God, most Merciful, most Compassionate) is known as the Qur'an. The Qur'an is not an ordinary thing; neither is its inherent meaning. May we reflect on this. The Qur'an is complete. It is all rays, all light—complete. The fast is a part of the practices we derive from the Qur'an. In this ordained duty *(fard),* one part of the fast is the state of *'ibādat,* praying with a melting heart. Other parts of the fast include intention, yearning, and wisdom's understanding.

It is a part of our step by step understanding of *sharī'at, tarīqat, haqīqat,* and *ma'rifat* (the steps of spiritual ascendancy in Islam). This fast is to help us understand and realize ourselves. Charity, fasting, and the pilgrimage of Hajj—these duties were ordained so that we may understand ourselves and die [before death].

Those with clear wisdom and resolute faith *(īmān)*
will accept that there is nothing other than God,
and believe in Him.
If they realize that there is none worthy
of worship other than Allah,
hand all responsibility to Him,
and die in Him,
then Allah and the hereafter
are all that remain.

When they die in *'ibādat*
and love for God,
that is prayer.
This fulfills the first two ordained duties—
faith and prayer.
When these two duties are accomplished,
man should understand the purpose of the duties.
Otherwise, he has to die within charity
or die within fasting.
Man must put to death
his base desires and his attraction for sensory enticements.
If he does not, he must then die
within the pilgrimage of Hajj.

This world and the *section* of the world, praise and the *section* of praise, pride and the *section* of pride, desire and the *section* of desire, mind and the *section* of the mind, craving and the *section* of craving, death and the *section* of death, earth and the *section* of earth—putting all these to death within us is the purpose of the Hajj.

Charity, fasting, and the pilgrimage of Hajj are three of Islam's five and six duties[1] through which we can understand ourselves. If we do understand, then we will put to death everything we have within us.

We will put to death
everything we have sought and gathered,
everything we have intentionally collected.
We will put to death

---

1 **Five and six duties:** The five outer duties in Islam are 1) faith in God, 2) prayer, 3) charity, 4) fasting, and 5) the pilgrimage of Hajj. The six inner duties are 1) to hear God with the inner ear, 2) to see Him with the inner eye, 3) to smell Him with the inner nose, 4) to speak to Him with the inner tongue, 5) to taste His food and surrender to His essence (*dhāt*), and 6) to commune with God through His essence.

292

anything we continually praise.
We will put to death
anything we believe to be advantageous to us.
We will put to death anything we hold on to as ours.
We will terminate anything we look upon as a blood-tie,
as something that will always accompany us.
We should cast away from us anything
we love with abandon.
We must realize these states
through the ordained duties.
This is the wealth, the essence, the meaning, and the wisdom
that can be realized
through the five ordained duties.

If we understand this, we will die before death. If we understand the duties, complete our actions, put everything to death, and die within *Allāhu,* within His wealth, intention, and purpose, then we will die before death. Attaining this state is the benefit and worth of the thirty days of fasting. There is more to the meaning of this fast. As wisdom develops, the explanations, understandings, and meanings will increase. May we realize this.

These are the first thirty days of the fast, but after this, there are ten more days. The meaning of these additional days is much more difficult to understand. If we do not understand the purpose of the first thirty days and die before death, we have to fast for ten more days. These ten days are to eradicate the ten evils, the ten sins: earth, fire, water, air, ether, mind, desire, arrogance, karma, and maya. They must be destroyed. We must eliminate the five elements, arrogance, karma, maya, the sexual games that shake us, and the arts and sciences that intoxicate us.

If we kill all ten,
we will die before death.
When we fulfill this, we will have died in Allah.

We will have merged with the Treasure
of Him who created that Treasure.
Two halves will merge as One.
One Light absorbs another light.
The perfect, mysterious Light of God,
the Singular One who rules and sustains,
absorbs the ray of light which He created.
We attain that Perfection.
We contract into that Perfection.
Since Allah's Treasure contracts into Allah,
it appears as though it has disappeared.
It is not two;
it is One.
This is the final sound.
There is no sound after this—
this sound neither comes nor goes.

What happens when a copper wire is strung on a violin and strummed? The notes of the violin reverberate in the string. Similarly, when we contract into Allah, only Allah's sounds reverberate in us. Only Allah's sounds will be voiced. None of our sounds exist here; nor do we have any work to do.

When iron is placed in fire, there is only fire, no iron. We must realize this; we must die in Allah in the same manner. When a piece of firewood is placed in the fire, it can be inched forward as long as a part of it is outside the fire. It can still be touched and pushed, but when the entire piece becomes fire, it cannot be touched.

Similarly, as long as the "I" remains,
as long as the "mine" remains,
as long as the attachments remain,
as long as the world is in us,
as long as praise and status are in us,

as long as pride and glory are there,
as long as we have these connections
to earth, ether, maya, torpor, lust, anger, gold,
desire, and high esteem—Satan will touch us.
He can touch us.
Desire can touch us,
lust can touch us,
attachment can touch us,
blood-ties can touch us,
race can touch us,
religion can touch us,
ghosts can touch us,
spells can touch us,
black-magic can touch us,
the five elements can touch us,
monkeys can touch us,
evil qualities can touch us—
everything can touch us.
They can grab us, push us, and pull us.
When we lose all these connections
and turn into the firewood that has become fire,
nothing can touch us.

Satan will be able to influence you through everything you keep within you. If you have desire, you give him room to touch you. If you want praise, he will come. He will enter through wealth, attachments, wife, child, religion, race, color, poverty, hunger, disease, illness, fasci-

---

2   **Purānas:** *Ancient legends*, a class of Hindu writings containing seventeen ancient stories. Each *purānic* story highlights a particular quality in the hero and
the role it plays in ruining his life. The author speaks of the seventeen *purānas*,
the ancient legends within man: arrogance, karma, and maya; the three sons of
maya—*tārahan, singhan, and sūran*; lust, anger, miserliness, attachment, fanaticism, envy, intoxicants, desire, theft, murder, and falsehood. Trans.

nations, lust, *purānas,*[2] jealousy, pride, and titles. He will come through the self-importance of "I." He will come as any one of the four hundred trillion, ten thousand energies. He will come through miraculous powers, through the intellect, or through miracles. He will come and touch you, and once he does he will enter instantly. This is black magic. When we possess spaces that he can seize, that is black magic. When this state comes to an end, when the firewood becomes fire, Satan will not touch us. When the iron becomes fire, he will not hold us. When we die within the Light in Allah, he will not touch us. However, as long as we have any connections, he can connect with and influence us. Satan will raise and lower us by exalting us and then pulling us down.

There is such a thing as destiny *(nasīb),* and according to this destiny, man dies. God allocated a certain amount of nourishment *(rizq)* and water for each individual—this is known as destiny. When the nourishment and water allocated by Allah come to an end, that is death; everything is subdued. In this way, there is an appointed time for us. What should we search for before this time arrives? In whom should we die? We should die within God before our nourishment and water come to an end. We should seek the benefits before that time arrives.

> My precious jeweled lights of my eyes,
> may we establish this state.
> May we have this trust.
> Only after we die
> in the Treasure that is Allah,
> will we escape.
> Until then, Satan will touch us
> through anything we foster in our keeping.

When the prophet Job [peace be upon him] had nothing left to touch, Satan tried to touch his inner heart. Satan has attempted to touch many prophets in this manner. We must reflect on this. If we do, we will understand the purpose of the forty days of fasting—thirty days, and then ten more.

Anyone who fasts for the additional ten days and dies, receives the wealth of Allah. God speaks to him. But as long as man has even a splinter of the four quadrillion, ten thousand connections, God will not speak. Everything that speaks until then are man's base desires, his cravings, his satans, his ghosts, and his demons. They will speak in words. They will speak as energies of the mind and as energies of maya. Jinns and fairies will speak. Jinns created from fire and led astray by Satan will come forth and speak; so too will others of his group. It is their sound that is heard.

After Adam ⊙ was cast onto the earth, and before the 124,000 prophets were sent down, Satan stood on rocks, trees, thorns, and other plants, delivering his speeches. He also positioned himself on the head and the body and spoke from these locations. In the form of bird, rooster, and cow, Satan spoke as though his words were revelations from God saying, "I will protect you. I will give you what you need. I will invite you to my heaven. Do this, do that." This occurred frequently in the Asian continent, in Greece, Jerusalem, Egypt, Iran, India, Mecca, and Medina. With the arrival of each prophet, the speech of various animal forms was brought to an end. Finally, with the arrival of *Muhammadur-Rasūl,* may the peace and blessings of God be upon him, all the animal forms were extinguished.

When certain prophets arrived, Satan was still climbing up as far as the fourth heaven. He could hear the secrets of the angels, the secrets of God, and the secrets of Gabriel ⊙ and Michael ⊙. He could hear God's sounds, but when he came down, he would distort the messages to deliver the opposite meaning. This is how he altered people's minds. "Allah told me this," he would say convincingly. At first, he could climb up to the seventh heaven, but after the arrival of certain prophets, he was sent down to the fourth heaven. Finally, he could not climb up there at all.

As long as Satan could climb the four heavens, he would listen to God's sounds and then come down saying, "God told me this, God told me that. I am your God." He spoke from within cows, skulls, rocks, trees, snakes, scorpions, demonic forms, vultures, and eagles. He made human sounds and even spoke from within birds. In this way, he spoke from within four hundred trillion, ten thousand spiritual gods, disseminating false knowledge and false wisdom.

Then *Allāhu ta'ālā Nāyan*, the Singular One who rules and sustains, sent down His divine messenger *Muhammad Mustafar-Rasūl* ☺ and terminated the speech of the animal forms. Satan could no longer speak from within these forms. The Prophet's arrival silenced Satan and brought his evil, animal-form miracles to an end.

> As he tried with Prophet Job ☺ earlier,
> Satan now tries to attach himself to us
> by speaking
> through the qualities we retain.

Satan was prohibited from ascending to the four heavens by angels placed there to prevent him. Instead, Satan climbed into the four religions, the four heavens on the left. In these four heavens, he climbed earth, fire, water, and air. In man, these four are *sharī'at, tarīqat, haqīqat, and ma'rifat* (the four regions of the human body; also the four steps of spiritual ascendancy). They are also known as the four heavens of *Zabūr, Jabrāt, Injīl,* and *Furqān* (the four religions: Hinduism, Fire-worship, Christianity, and Islam). Satan, accustomed to speaking through animal forms and statues, now began to speak through the beautiful forms of man that God had created. He started to speak through these statues. He entered these *plastic bags*, these human forms. Within these *plastic bags*—filled with things that belong in a trash truck—Satan found an entrance and began to speak through desire, through thoughts, and through the monkey-mind. He started to say, "God has told you this. God is telling you that. I am God. Do this. Go and do that!" He began to change mankind. He would speak through the mind, saying, "I am telling you this. Do it. I will give you heaven. Do this!"

298

> Satan began to merge with man's mind and speak.
> He mingled with man's thoughts and began to speak.
> He flowed into man's blood and began to speak.
> He merged with man's desire and began to speak.
> He entered man's intentions and began to speak.
> He meshed with man's ideas and began to speak.
> He crept into man's prayer and began to speak—
> thus speaking through every available *section*.

Satan speaks in everyone. The only exception is one who, accepting Allah as the only Lord, has died in Him. Satan is currently speaking everywhere else. He is speaking to each individual. He makes sounds, he speaks, and he shows many images. He makes everything appear as a hallucinogenic (LSD) vision. He shows man the heavens, the sky, the earth, the stars, and many miracles. Having shown and spoken such things, he provides explanations that are contradictory to God and wisdom, while declaring, "I am God. Believe in me. Trust me. Do what I say."

Satan speaks in many ways. To some it will appear as though the mind is talking, and to others it will seem as though the words are spoken in their ears. Satan will make people see things with their eyes or make them think that the sound is coming from beyond themselves. To some he will speak from within their minds; to others he will speak through their rising spirits; and to some he will ascend from the energy center at the base of the spine (*mūlādhāra chakrā*), claiming that he is light.

Since Satan has room to climb into [the four regions of the body, the four religions] *Zabūr, Jabrāt, Injīl,* and *Furqān,* he will enter.

> The eye has filth,
> the mouth has filth,
> the nose has filth,
> the ear has filth,

the heart has filth,
the entire skin has filth,
the blood has filth,
all the tissues have filth,
the marrow has filth—
hell is present in the entire body.

The entire body is filled with *sections* that belong to hell, ghosts, animals, Satan, base desires, cravings, arrogance, karma, maya, forces of desire, forces of seduction, lust, attachment, arts, sciences, "I," "you," religions, and scriptures. Since all these are intermingled in the body, this body is hell. Hell is Satan's home, and all these attachments are his energies. The energies, cells, and viruses of this hell are the tools through which he speaks in *Zabūr, Jabrāt, Injīl,* and *Furqān*—earth, fire, water, and air.

As long as the connections to the five elements exist, Satan will climb up the body through these elements and speak through the ear, eye, mouth, and blood. He will also speak within the mind. Satan will make many speeches, but they will be his words, not the words of Allah. When man dies within Allah, then Satan can neither speak nor breathe. He is dead. We must realize this.

These are God's words. According to His words, the additional ten days of fasting are to help us attain this state. The first thirty days, together with ten more days, make forty days of fasting. Before we die, before speech and breath end, we must fulfill this.

When man dies,
when he curbs his speech,
when he controls his breath,
when he reins in his base desires,
when he resists his cravings,
when he restrains his attachments,
when he crosses over the four religion steps—

Zabūr, Jabrāt, Injīl, and *Furqān*—
when he prays with a melting heart,
speaking without speaking,
sleeping without sleeping,
and dying without dying,
when he annihilates
hunger, illness, old age, and death,
and when he stops praying
in order to attain either the world or heaven—
he will realize God.

Anything we desire and pray for gives Satan room to enter. He will creep in through our desires as a sound or as a new form of learning. Only after we put an end to this state can we realize God. Then God, the Singular One who rules and sustains, calls out to man, "My son, My representative, My messenger! I now show you how I will send you [forth]." And thus, God makes the light resplend as Light.

It is only when one dies [in Allah] that one transcends the four regions of the body. Until then, Satan can climb up because the body is hell. The mouth is hell, the backside is hell, the body is hell, the stomach is hell, the nose is hell, the eyes, ears, mind—everything is hell. And since the body is a house of hell, it belongs to Satan. Hell was given to Satan by God as his property. All the connections to hell are his, and he will speak from these places. Earlier he spoke through animal forms and statues; later he entered these hell-forms—the statues of man.

This is why some people are crazy.
Some are crazy for titles,
some are crazy for money,
some are crazy for women,
some are crazy for earth,
some are crazy for education,
some have the craziness of the bile,

some are crazy for passion,
some are crazy for status,
some are crazy for praise,
some are crazy for sex,
some are crazy for drugs,
some are crazy for liquor,
some have the craziness of "I,"
some are crazy for gold and possessions,
some are crazy for the sciences,
some are crazy for the arts,
some are crazy about themselves,
some are crazy for divine wisdom,
some are crazy for yoga,
some are crazy about miraculous powers,
and some are crazy about miracles.

There are many types of craziness, and Satan will speak through each of them. Man has the craziness for children, the craziness of blood, the craziness of the body, the craziness for beauty, and the craziness for cosmetics. Satan enters, speaking through each craziness in the body, the house of hell.

When all this craziness dies, when man dies and completes forty years, he is God's representative. Each day of the fast represents one year; forty days represent forty years. When these forty days are completed, God, the Singular One who rules and sustains, bestows on the light the title of representative, messenger, *nabī*. God keeps this light in Him. It is only after forty days—which represent forty years—that man realizes true prayer *(vanakkam)*, prayer with a melting heart *('ibādat)*, and God. Before this, he is a statue filled with four hundred trillion, ten thousand crazy forms. He prays in a state of duality, worshipping something as equal or parallel to God. He prays desiring something other than God, wanting to satisfy his cravings. This is craziness. Each child must understand and think about this. Everything one does at this time is Satan's speech, Satan's intention, Satan's miracle, Satan's light, his brilliance, his glittering, his blacks, and his whites. He will show you all of this.

Within man's various crazinesses of mind, desire, attachments, and cravings, Satan will show him the sky, earth, and heaven. Because of this, man experiences pain and pleasure, and then dies. Satan ascends the four heavens in the body: the four religions, the four steps, the four scriptures. Through the eyes, ears, speech, and breath, he climbs *Zabūr, Jabrāt, Injīl,* and *Furqān.* The benefits he gives us in return trick us, confuse us, entangle us in maya, and cause us to fall from the fourth heaven. Ruined and tottering, we fall down to the place of birth.

We have to end this state. When, within forty, these connections die, that is when we speak to God and God speaks to us. There is no duality—the speech is One. Speech and breath are Him. A state without [our] speech and breath dawns. My precious jeweled lights of my eyes, we must contemplate the fact that the forty days of fasting reflect our age. When the forty are complete, we must die. This is known as the fast. This is its meaning. This is the explanation.

Since the statues and hell-house of the body belong to Satan, everything he speaks is contrary to God's words. Everything he does is the opposite of God: his miracles, his energies, the craziness, the changes he brings about, the praise, and the wealth. He enters us through anything we desire and anything we search for. If we seek heaven, he will enter. If we search for divine wisdom, he will enter. If we desire praise, he will enter. If we chase after wealth, he will join the chase. If we pursue desire, he will come in through that pursuit. These are the doorways for his entry, places from which he can ascend. They must be put to death. This is the true path. From my experience, these are the true paths. This is *sirr,* secret. I had to reveal this today because you have unwaveringly completed thirty days of the fast, and tomorrow you will celebrate a joyous occasion that you call the Great Day, the sacred day. But this is not the Great Day; the real Great Day dawns when you make yourself die.

When this fast is over the Great Day will come,
but it will be on the day that you die.
And what is this death?
It is the day when your house of hell dies—
when your fascination for sensory enticement dies.
When the world dies away from you,
that is your Great Day.
And when the additional ten die,
that is the Day of Divine Grace.
This is the day when the additional ten
are completed.
You must understand this.

Until you reach this day, everything you do is done with statues, with craziness, with desire for wealth, with maya, with arrogance, and with karma. We stay in this state with these intoxicants. Some are intoxicated by drinking alcohol, but we are intoxicated by imbibing mind-desires and lust-energies. Some of us are drunk on attachments, some are intoxicated by lust, some by the liquor of desire, and others by praise. One man's drunkenness is caused by the liquor store and another man's intoxication is caused by his own mind. Both are inebriated, one by real alcohol, and the other by the alcohol of lust, earth, and attachments. In this way, each one will leave God and go away. Why? Because if people have these *sections*, they will leave God's Treasure and turn to the earth-section, toward blood-ties, wife-ties, and child-ties. And when God calls out, saying, "Come, come, come," they will say, "My child is crying. I will attend to it and come in a little while. Please wait! I will attend to this first, and to that next, and then I will come." They will offer excuses to God and move away. This is the path that takes them to hell. This is what brings them down.

Only when all these things die, will a man go toward God and speak to Him as soon as He calls. Such a man is very rare. A perfected man (*insān kāmil*) is one in ten million. Two hundred million years ago, in the days of Adam ☺, there were eighty such men in every hundred. From an eighty percent population of perfected men, the numbers have decreased to thirty percent, eighteen percent, and now, two hundred million years later, it is difficult to find even one who is *insān kāmil*. It is very rare to find such a man today. There is only one—the *Qutb*.[3] God, the Singular One who rules and sustains, has sent a light into the world known as the *Qutbiyyat*.[4] It is because of this light that the world endures; otherwise the world would be destroyed—it would end. It exists because of the one.

Today everyone claims to be a man of divine wisdom. "I am a sheikh. You are a sheikh. I am a big man. You are a big man. I am Allah. You are Allah," they announce. Everyone is Allah. Everyone is great. This is the hell that currently exists. However, if the one *Qutb* did not exist, everything would be destroyed. You and I must think about this. Until we die in Allah, we must realize what is worthy of our search, know the benefits, and seek them. Everything else must die. Otherwise, Satan will continue to climb within us through anything we keep alive.

Each child must think about this. When you fulfill this, your Great Day will come, and then your Day of Divine Grace will dawn. When you complete the ten days, it will be your Day of Divine Grace—the day you are crowned by God. You will receive the crown of God's kingdom. This is the day *you* die.

---

3   **Qutb:** The literal meaning of the Arabic word is *axis, pole, pivot*. Sufis define *Qutb* as a conjoining of the magnetic axis of the cosmos and the spiritual axis of human consciousness. The idea of *Qutb* acknowledges that the function of *spiritual center* can reside in a human being. The author defines *Qutb* as the divine analytic wisdom *(pahuth arivu)* in man, which explains and awakens all truths that have been destroyed and buried in the ocean of maya. It awakens true *īmān* and the twelve gifts or weapons of the *Qutb*. It explains the state of purity as it existed in the beginning of creation. As the inner sheikh, the inner guide, the grace of God's essence, it awakens the purity of life, transforming it into the divine vibration. Trans.

4   **Qutbiyyat:** The wisdom of the *Qutb*, the sixth wisdom—divine analytic wisdom, which explains the Truth of God.

Each child must reflect on this.
What is the fast?
What is its worth?
From where does Satan speak?
What does he speak?
What does he say?

When you believe in all those other things, you will be following Satan. Satan used to speak from rocks and stones, but now he speaks from within your body, which is made of rocks, earth, fire, water, and air. He has entered your body. You should understand this through wisdom, through the True Light, through the Sheikh. Understand this and put everything to death.

The *Rasūl* ☺ went on *Mi'rāj*[5] accompanied by the angel Gabriel ☺. When they crossed the third heaven and entered the fourth heaven, a sound, like a revelation, was heard. A woman on their left shouted, "O *Rasūl* of Allah, stop, stop, stop! May the peace of God be upon you. Please stop! Look at me, look at me! Look at me for just a little while. You are going to God on *Mi'rāj,* but please look at me. I have something to tell you, something you can ask God on my behalf."

Angel Gabriel ☺ looked around and saw a very old woman who had adorned herself like a young maiden. She was adorned with all the riches of the world which glittered as her ornaments, but she was very, very old. When Muhammad ☺ turned around slightly, Gabriel ☺ said, "O Muhammad, do not respond to that voice. Do not think that the voice is coming from the sky. Do not reply. It is not God's voice. Do not

---

5   **Mi'rāj:** The night journey or *ascent (al-Mi'rāj)* of the Prophet Muhammad ☺ through the heavens. It is said to have taken place in the twelfth year of the Prophet's ☺ mission, on the twenty-seventh day of the month of *Rajab.* During *Mi'rāj,* wisdom, the purity of resolute faith *(īmān),* the beauty of the face *(Muhammad),* and the beauty of the heart *(Ahamad)* meet Allah and commune with Him.

even turn around and look. Do not reply and do not look!"

The sound had come from the left of the heavens. These heavens were *Zabūr, Jabrāt, Injīl,* and *Furqān.* He was crossing over the body, over the four religions, when he heard another sound. It was someone calling out, "O *Rasūl* of Allah, you are going to Allah on *Mi'rāj.* May the peace of God be with you. Please look at me. Listen to what I say; ask God a question on my behalf." Gabriel ⊕ immediately instructed, "O Muhammad, do not reply to those greetings. That is not the sound of God, it is not the sound of angels, but it is the sound of Satan. Do not reply to that sound. Come. Come directly!" And without responding, they moved on.

When they had reached the seventh heaven, Muhammad ⊕ asked, "Who made that sound?" Gabriel ⊕ responded, "She is Maya. She is the world. The one who was standing there calling out to you is the world. All of hell was on her head. All the snakes in the world were on her head. All the venom was there. It is that same venom that is in each person's mind. If maya has touched a person, that person is filled with poison. Each hair on Maya's head is a poisonous snake. Her blood was snakes, her body was snakes. Hell and snakes covered her. She is Maya. She is hell. If you had returned her greetings she would have pulled you down, and you would not have reached this place. She is Maya, and the sound that came from the left was Satan. He called out to you from the left to try to change you. If you had returned his greetings, you would never have come to Allah's side. We have encountered Satan and Maya."

Similarly, the sounds, speech, and words that come to us in our [present] state, come through Satan, jinns, fairies, ghosts, the mind, the bile, and torpor. Satan provides the words according to our desires, the way we search, and the way we think. Only Gabriel ⊕ and God knew that the *Rasūl* ⊕ was going toward God, but Satan also discovered this, because he climbed up into the four regions. We must realize that Satan is within the body, making sounds and trying to ruin us. Angel Gabriel ⊕ was able to warn the *Rasūl* ⊕ immediately and prevent him from turning around. In the same way, we should not pay any attention to these [inner] sounds. For some the talking is in the mind, and for others it is in the ear, the head, the blood, or in the *gas*. These are the activities of Satan's hell, his speech, and his intentions. We should get away from these words. We must escape!

You should cut away these things, one after another and go on the straight path. You must have complete surrender *(thānam)*, concentration *(nīthānam)*, judgment and balance *(avathānam)*, and divine wisdom *(gnānam)*. First dedicate yourself; get rid of all sounds—that is surrender. Then the path you walk on is very sharp, sharper than the edge of a sword, and more direct than wisdom. You will have to walk on this sharp path. The world will rise up to meet you. On one side there is maya, on the other side there is hell, and if you look behind you there is karma. You should look ahead—at God, *Āndavan*. You must have balance. This is a path that goes into the sky. It is very sharp, so be very attentive. First, offer yourself to God—that is *thānam*. Then, when you place each foot on the sharp, narrow path, use your judgment and be extremely cautious—that is *nīthānam*. You have to focus on the *point*. If you look here and there, you will fall. Next, you need balance— *avathānam*. As you proceed, there are sounds everywhere, with maya, hell, and karma hovering around. Everything will pull at you—wife and children tug at you, maya lures you, hell pulls you, desire entices you, karma draws you, and blood ties yank at you. You need to maintain your balance. Behind you is the karma of your birth. You need *thānam, nīthānam, avathānam,* balance, God, and wisdom. If you waver here, maya will pull you; if you waver there, hell will pull you; if you look behind, your birth, your karma, will grab at you. You need perfect balance. If you waver ever so slightly, you will fall. Gales and storms come to knock you down. Magics, miracles, words, sounds, desire, attachments, wife, child, blood-ties, praise, honor, gifts, "I," "you," religion, and race will come on all sides, whirling turbulently around you. You must look ahead, maintain your balance, and focus on the *point*. You cannot stop, or listen to these sounds, or look around. Most people make an excuse to God and leave. "Please wait awhile, I have to attend to other things first," they reason. These are the sounds that hold them back in the world, bewildered, confused, and disheartened.

These sounds will pull you back. They have attacked you in many ways through praise, honor, books, wealth, and lust. These are all paths through which Satan climbs up and pulls you down. When all these things are put to death, you attain a state of balance, and because of that balance Satan cannot pull you down. With this balance you see only the *point,* nothing else; you experience the balance, nothing else; you see the *point* straight ahead.

When the thirty and the ten are done, we will be forty—forty years old. It does not mean growing to be forty years old. It is not the physical age of your body and actions. Attaining the above-mentioned state is reaching the fortieth year. That is the *point.* When you reach that state, you will be the representative of God—His son. *You* will have died, and the kingdom of God will be yours. Only then does God hold you and accept you. When *you* have died, and God is all that is left, His kingdom is attained.

May you reflect on this, my precious jeweled lights of my eyes. When you realize the value of this path and put everything else to death, then you can see your Father. On that day you will become His sons and representatives in His kingdom. May you realize this. You have finished the thirty days of fasting. There are ten more, are there not? I do not perceive that you have fulfilled these thirty as yet. You did fast, but I do not see that you have reached thirty years as yet. You must fast with greater understanding now. There are ten more days of the fast. Do these also. Then you will understand. That will be very good.

May God, the Singular One who rules and sustains, give you the grace and the wisdom to understand the eminence and value of this fast. May He provide the explanations that help you understand. May He bestow increasing benefits on you, make you exalted, give you the wealth of the forty [days], and thus grant you eternal life. May He give you eternal life in the kingdom of souls and keep you with Him. May God bestow this *rahmat* and so grace you. If you try, you will achieve! Please understand what I am saying. Please strive, make every effort, and keep on trying! When you take one step forward, do not look back, but go forth. As you move forward and see new sights, let them go by, leave them behind, and don't hang on to them. When you place one foot forward and perceive new *reels,* leave them behind as you take the next step. Take the *point* and move on. You will see further wonders as you walk forward, but leave them behind and go forth. Cast everything behind you. Do not embrace or hold fast to anything. You cannot carry it. Hurl it behind you and go forward.

In this way, let go of everything you have seen and everything you have sought. Go beyond—to the open path! Leave everything behind. Until you reach Allah, everything is *business*. This is death. This is creation. These things have a limit. Abandon everything that has a limit and go to the limitless place. You must get there. Therefore, do not carry these things with you. Throw them away and walk on. Only then can you proceed on the path. If you carry these things with you, you will not progress on your journey. If you carry anything at all, you will not proceed on this journey. It will be very burdensome. There is wonder after wonder after wonder, but if you choose to carry these things, they will be very heavy, and you will fall as a donkey falls. At each step, cast behind everything you see there. Do not stop in awe, gaping at everything. Go forward in this way. Only then will you experience victory. Precious jeweled lights of my eyes, may God, the Singular One who rules and sustains, give you wisdom, explanations, Truth, as well as the value, benefits, and clarity [of the fast] and so grace you. *Āmīn.*

Precious jeweled lights of my eyes, according to your intentions, you have finished thirty days of fasting. Tomorrow is the celebration, the Great Day, but this is not your Great Day. When you truly complete thirty—that is your Great Day. When the world dies in you—that is your Great Day. And when all the inner, base desires die—that is the Day of Divine Grace, the day you attain God's kingdom. That is the day you complete forty days of fasting, the day you are forty years old. Please reflect on this. May God, the Singular One who rules and sustains, grant you this, and so grace you. *Āmīn, Āmīn,* O Lord of the universes. All praise is to You alone. May the peace, the beneficence, and the blessings of God be upon you.

(Bawa Muhaiyaddeen☺ recites the *Sūratul-Fātihah*)

The breaking of the fast has been delayed for one hour and nine minutes, but you waited with great patience and listened as we spoke about God. That is very good. Now go and break your fast. Today is the last day of the fast for this year. In the future do it in the way I have explained.

Al-hamdu lillāh.
All praise is to God.

Chapter 21

The Inner Form of Man

August 12, 1980

We have been given an
inner form (sūratul-insān),
the Chapter that Opens (Sūratul-Fātihah).

If we, who come in the form of sūratul-insān,
research and investigate this form,
we will perceive it to be
the sūratul-insān, the Sūratul-Fātihah,
Al-hamdu lillāh—God's praise.

The Inner Form of Man

When we observe the fast of Ramadan in the proper manner,
when we fast for thirty days (ten less than forty) and see the One,
when we fulfill the fast in this way,
we will perceive Allah alone to be sufficient.
We have been given an
inner form *(sūratul-insān)*,
the Chapter that Opens *(Sūratul-Fātihah)*.[1]
If we, who come in the form of *sūratul-insān*,
research and investigate this form,
we will perceive it to be
the *sūratul-insān,* the *Sūratul-Fātihah*,
Al-hamdu lillāh—God's praise.

We will realize the Praiseworthy One and understand our form to
be the *sūratul- Qur'ān,* the form of the Qur'an. The Qur'an, consisting

---

1. **Sūratul-insān:** In Arabic, *sūrat* is a word used exclusively for *chapters in the Qur'an*, of which there are one hundred and fourteen. In Hindi, *sūrat* means *form, shape, face, state, or condition*, and the author often interprets the word in this manner. Hence, *sūratul-insān* means the form of man, or the true state of man. The first chapter of the Qur'an, *the chapter of praise*, is called the *Sūratul-Hamd* because its first word is *al-hamd—praise*. This chapter is also called the *Sūratul Fātihah, the opening chapter*. In Tamil, the word *pātiyah* means *have you seen*. The author, interpreting through several languages, combines *sūratul-insān* and *Sūratul Fātihah* to instruct man to *open* up his *form (sūrat)* and *see* his true inner *state* of *praise (al-hamd)*. His question to us is, *Sūraté Pātiyah—Have you perceived your true self?* Trans.

of 6,666 verses was conceived from twenty-eight letters. God revealed His grace-wealth *(rahmat)* within this *sūrat*. The twenty-eight letters are represented by the twenty-eight days of the fast. To understand the origin of man, the origin of this world *(dunyā)*, and the origin of the soul-world *(awwal)*, to comprehend the *rahmat* of the soul-world, and to be victorious in this world, one must understand the mystery that is man—*insān, sūratul-insān*. When this *sūrat* is understood, it will be *Sūratul-Fātihah*. Then man is the Qur'an, the *sūratul-Qur'ān*.

Man must understand the twenty-eight letters well,[2] and then understand two more letters—death and birth [origin]—by studying this *Sūratul-Fātihah* and this Qur'an. Then he will be *Īmān-Islām*—resolute faith and spotless purity. He will have attained Allah and *īmān*.

To whom was the Qur'an revealed? Who is the Qur'an? It is Allah and Allah's *Rasūl* ☻. When we understand the two, we are thirty. The inner heart *(qalb)* blossoms. If, understanding all thirty [letters], we have resolute *īmān*, then [we will realize] *Sūratul-Rahmān, Sūratul-Rahīm*—the state of God, Lord of all the universes, most Merciful, most Compassionate. When we unite with and understand this Lord of all the universes, His wealth of the three worlds will be our *īmān*.

At this time, there is none worthy of worship except God, *Allāhu ta'ālā Nāyan*, the Singular One who rules and sustains. His wealth is our wealth. When we understand this, the form of man becomes perfected man, *sūratul-insān* becomes *insān-kāmil*. We must reflect on this carefully and understand the ordained duty of the fast and the five and

---

2. **Twenty-eight letters:** The inner form *(sūrat)* of man, composed of twenty-eight inter-linked letters, is the actual inner Qu'ran. This is where revelations occur. Everything has been placed here as a secret: the sounds of the Qu'ran that resonate through wisdom, the prophet Muhammad ☻, the angels, and the heavenly beings. Man's heart is composed of five of these letters, *alif, lām, mīm, hā',* and *dāl. Alif* represents God, *lām* represents the Light of God *(Nūr), mīm* represents the eternal messenger of God (Muhammad)☻, *hā'* represents the physical body, and *dāl* represents the world. In the heart of a true human being these letters are transformed to *alhmd,* which is the praise of God—All praise is to You, O God; You are the Glory and Greatness that deserves all praise.

six tasks within this Qur'an. There are six inner tasks and five outer tasks. We have to realize what is outside the form and what is inside. What is within this *sūrat?* The Qur'an, the *sūratul-Qur'ān* is within. What is inside the Qur'an? The *Fātihah* is inside. And what is inside the *Fātihah?* We should understand this, and understand the six and five tasks.

Of the five tasks, the first is faith in God. The second is to worship Him—worship the One worthy of worship. Worship Him alone.

He is the One who gave us our soul.
He gave us our body.
He gave us light.
He gave us eyes, ears, and nose;
He gave us sound, hands, legs, body,
inner heart, blood, strength,
food, and true nourishment *(rizq).*

The One who gave us everything, the One who protects us, is God, most Merciful, most Compassionate. He alone can create, protect, and sustain. Everything belongs to this Ruler—earth, sky, and all forms. Our body, wealth, and spirit belong to Him. We have to understand His wealth. All of everything is His. Our soul and our body are His. The light in our eye, the sound in our ear, the scent in our nose, and the speech in our mouth are His.

When we understand this, we realize that God's *rahmat,* His grace-wealth of all the universes, was created equally for all. We must understand this. Everything is His *rahmat.* Allah alone is our support, our wealth. He created the sun, moon, and stars in order to reveal this to us. To help us understand this and attain *Īmān-Islām,* He further provided the five and six tasks.

God made earth common to all. He made water common to all. In the earth, He placed the secret and the manifestations *(sirr* and *sifāt),* the good and the bad, the permissible and the impermissible, the essence *(dhāt)* and the manifestations *(sifāt)*. If we understand this, we will know that God made the sun, moon, stars, earth, oceans, land, fire, water, air, and ether common to all. All lives have a right to them. They are to be shared by all. This is His *rahmat*.

Allah has shown us that His wealth is common property. It is meant for all—cows, goats, lions, tigers, bears, reptiles, and birds. Every creature has a place in this world; His *rahmat* has been given to all. Even the crawling ant has been given a place on this earth. Snakes have been given a place. Satan has also been given a place. This is common ground for everyone.

"This is My *rahmat*,
understand it!
Understand the good and the bad,
the permissible and the impermissible,
the right and the wrong,
the essence and the manifestations.
Understand this.
I have made everything common to all.
Realize this.
All of everything is My wealth.
I have provided My *rahmat* to be shared by all lives,
and within this commonwealth
each one of you
has been allotted a place to live.
The ant, the fly,
the beetle, and the honeybee
take from this what they need.
The honeybee takes the honey that it needs
without hurting the flower.
The cow eats the grass but leaves the earth intact.
I have created the grass as its nourishment,
and it nibbles the grass, taking only what it needs.
I created fruit-bearing trees for the birds

318

and they eat what they need,
leaving the rest behind.
Some animals consume the leaves,
leaving the fruits untouched.
In this way, all lives created by Me
partake of the sustenance
I have spread out for them.
To each I have apportioned light, air, and a dwelling place.
When a cow drinks water,
it takes what it requires and leaves the rest behind.
Even the ants do the same.
They are My *arts,* My *creations.*
My common wealth
is to be shared by all.
You cannot take it for yourself, saying,
'It is for me! It is for me!'
Understand this,"
God declared.

To understand this, *Allāhu taʿālā Nāyan,* the Singular One who rules and sustains, has shown us the cause (*kāranam*) and the effect (*kāriyam*) [the principle and the manifest examples],[3] saying, "This is the world." The leaf-eater eats leaves, the grass-eater eats grass, the fruit-eater eats fruits, the mud-eater eats mud, the air-drinker drinks air, and the water-dweller drinks and lives in water. God has placed the nourishment, the *rizq,* for each life within its own habitat. The animals in the forest have been given caves and trees. Snakes, scorpions, and beetles have

---

3. **Kāranam and kāriyam:** In Tamil, *kāranam* means cause, origin, source, principle, foundation, reason, purpose. *Kāriyam* means effect, result, product, issue—as opposed to *kāranam. Kāranam* and *kāriyam* are usually interpreted as *cause* and *effect.* The author, however, explains *kāranam* to be the principle or foundation that has been extracted from the examples. The two words will, therefore, be translated as the *principle* and the *exemplifications.* Trans.

been given holes in the ground. Ants, termites, and worms that perforate the soil have been given soil as a dwelling-place. Each living creature has been given what is appropriate for its life. Understand this. "The wealth that belongs to One has been given to all. Understand this," Allah declared.

In order to understand this, God the Supreme Creator has shown us the principle and the examples in this world, saying, "This is the principle, this is the exemplification." He reveals the principle through the exemplifications within the principle.

He shows us the *sūrat*
as a principle
by placing the exemplar within it.
He shows us the Qur'an
as a principle
by placing the exemplar within it.
The stories or observations *(ahādith)* related by the Prophet ☺
have been shown as principles
through the principle within them.
The word, Allah, has been shown as a principle
because Allah is within.
Prayer has been shown
as a principle,
and the principle is within.
Divine knowledge has been shown as a principle
and the principle has been placed within it.

Realizing this is *Īmān-Islām—brotherhood.* This is equanimity and forbearance—equanimity on earth, equanimity in heaven, equanimity in life—patience, inner patience, contentment, and surrender to God *(sabūr, shakūr, tawakkul,* and *al-hamdu lillāh).* "Practice these as principles," God has said. With *Īmān-Islām* as the objective, He has asked us, Adam's ☺ children, to understand the principles and their examples.

Meanwhile, we have made every item of God's commonwealth into individual possessions. Saying, "Mine, mine," we have grabbed portions of land, water, and air for ourselves. This is why God sent the 124,000 prophets, enlightened beings, friends of God *(auliyā')*, messengers *(ambiyā')*, angels, and archangels. Among the 124,000 prophets, God refined twenty-five prophets and then clarified eight of them to a higher degree. Finally, He sent *Muhammad Mustafā Rasūl*, may the peace and blessings of God be upon him, with the 6,666 verses.

Through each word
Muhammad⊕ revealed the principles and the exemplifications:
the equanimity and unity of *Īmān-Islām*,
inner patience—*sabūr,*
the affirmation of faith—the *Kalimah,*
trust in God—*tawwakul 'alallāh,*
and the acceptance of God's will—*in shā'Allāh, mā shā'Allāh.*
The principle was revealed
and the exemplifications were explained in terms of the principle.

Understanding this and accepting Allah as our only support is *Īmān-Islām*. Islam is perfectly pure light. It is completeness. To realize this, God placed the Light of *Nūr Muhammad* in Adam's ⊕ forehead, while creating him out of earth. At that time, this Light had not been accepted by anything else. The mountains, oceans, and land had been asked to accept the Light, but they had refused. All the lights, souls, and spirits had been absorbed by this Light. This Light of *Nūr Muhammad* engulfed all other lights. It is the completeness of God—the ninety-nine attributes of God *(Asmā'ul-Husnā),* and the actions of those attributes *(wilāyāt).* When the oceans, lands, mountains, and trees refused to accept the *Nūr,* God assembled all the lights once more, showed them the perfect Light of *Nūr Muhammad,* which contained everything that was His—His words, His actions, and His attributes—and asked them, "Who will accept this Light?" But this Light had absorbed all the lights that were present, all the souls, and all the worlds. Therefore, when God asked, "Which one of you will be able to accept My Intrinsic Treasure," all the lights said, "O Allah, our Creator, Merciful One, we cannot accept this Light. This Light absorbed all of our light. This Light, which is Your *rahmat,* engulfed all the souls and all the worlds, making them disappear. It is the only Light now. It swallowed everything else. We cannot accept it. We are not capable of accepting it."

Then the earth rose up and said,
"O my Allah, I will accept the Light."

God replied,
"O Earth, this is My purity and perfection.
It is My Intrinsic Treasure.
You say that you will accept it,
but know that it has no flaw or blemish.
It is faultless.
It is from within Me.
It is My *rahmat.*
You say you will accept it,
but if you do, you will have to bring it back
in the same state
as when you accepted it.
It should not be returned to Me with any fault or blemish.
It is fine that you accept it,
but protect it vigilantly.
It has My 3,000 benevolent qualities,
My *rahmat,*
and My ninety-nine qualities and actions.
Everything has been brought together
to form the *Nūr.*
This is My *wilāyāt*—
compassion,

love,
forbearance,
equanimity,
patience,
inner patience,
My actions, conduct, and qualities.
I am giving you this Light
which is My Treasure.
Take it!
You have accepted it!
But if you do not bring it back to Me in the right state,
you will have sought your own ruin.
O Earth, you will have sought your own downfall.
Return it to Me very carefully.
My Treasures—the soul, *īmān,* the Light,
My actions, conduct, and qualities—
are in the *Nūr.*
The effects of everything I say
fill the *Nūr.*
It is My Light Resonance.
You must return this Treasure to Me."

This is the Light that was placed in Adam⊙ when he was created out of the earth that was taken from the four directions. When the angels Gabriel⊙, Michael⊙, and *Isrāfīl*⊙ were sent to collect that earth, it cried out, "I beseech you, in God's name, to not take any earth, because there are many colors [many differences] in me." Through [saying] these words, the earth attained divine knowledge, and it called out once more, "I beseech you, in God's name, do not take any earth from me."

After the other angels returned unsuccessfully, God sent angel *'Izrā'īl*⊙ on the same mission. When *'Izrā'īl*⊙ was collecting earth from the four directions, the earth spoke up once more, "I beseech you, in God's name, do not take any earth from me." *'Izrā'īl*⊙, replied, "The One in whose name you beseech me, is the same One who sent me here to gather earth. Speak to Him yourself; I am only following His commands." And collecting earth from the east, the north, the south, and the west, he carried it away.

Then the earth called out to Allah, and Allah spoke to the earth, "O Earth, you called out My name." "My God, You placed many colors in me. There is a lot of filth in me, many colors, many hues, gold, gems, dirt, stench, filth, water, sludge, fertilizer—everything is in me. O God, if You create my people out of me, they will adopt these very qualities. They will acquire filth, they will attain everything that is bad in me, and therefore, go to hell. O Father, my inner heart cannot accept that all the children created out of me will go to hell. This is why I used Your name. If the children created out of me go to hell, and if I am the cause of that, I cannot bear it. O Lord, this is why I called out Your name."

Then God said,
"O Earth, for as many colors as I placed in you,
as many valuables as I placed in you,
as many lowly things as I placed in you,
and as much dirt and filth as I placed in you,
I will allot the appropriate stations
for the lives I will create from you.
That will be their destiny.
Depending upon what they adopt,
what they create, and where they live,
I will allot a place for them.
For those who take the valuables in you and develop,
I will grant excellence.
For those who take the hell in you and develop,
I will grant hell.
I am the One who apportions
the appropriate place for each being created out of you.

>   That is My work—
>   creation, protection, sustenance."
>   Then God said,
>   "For this purpose, I will be Me,
>   and I will create you as Adam ⊙,
>   a being more exalted than all other creations."

God then asked *'Izrā'īl* ⊙ to take the Light [encased] in its earthen form [earth taken from the four directions] and place it, as Adam, in a central location of the earth, called *Karbalā'*. This place is a battlefield. In the world, this central spot is in the area near Jerusalem and Jiddah. But the true center of this world, the world of souls, and all of everything is the inner heart—the *qalb*. It is the center of the 18,000 universes—this *qalb,* this one handful of earth.

Kalballa means black dog.[4] The inner heart can be a black dog, it can be the Light known as the *Rahmatul-'ālamīn,* and it can also be Allah—*Qalb-Allah.* When Adam ⊙ was being created, the "dog" came into being, as well. This dog is the poison, the saliva, that entered man when Satan spat on Adam ⊙. It is the power of desire, Satan's jealousy and thoughts, arising from jinns. This poison became the dog. When Gabriel ⊙ was asked to lift and throw away the spittle that had fallen on Adam's ⊙ abdomen, he also threw away one of the twenty-eight letters of the body, and that spot became the navel. That one letter fell on the crown of the dog; the rest of the dog is spittle. This is why the dog lives on spit, lapping every filth and licking its entire body, while its tongue drips with saliva. Why does this happen? It happens because the one who spit on Adam ⊙ was Satan, the leader of the *jinns,* and this spittle drips from him at all times. This is the reason why a dog is filthy. Other than the one letter on the crown of its head, everything else is unclean. It is because of that one letter that the dog has gratitude. Every other part is

---

4. **Kalballa:** In Singhalese, *kalu* is *black* and *balla* is *dog*. In Arabic, *kalb* means *dog*. The author uses the word *Kalballa* to mean *black dog*, the dog of desire. Trans.

unclean and cannot be touched. When Adam⊙ came into being, so did this dog. It has been called Satan.

Meanwhile, God placed the Light of *Nūr Muhammad* in the forehead of man. I do not have time to tell you the entire story in detail, but having received this Light, we are all called Adam. We are all man, *insān*. God, the Singular One who rules and sustains, called this [Light] the *kursī*, the gnostic eye. The one letter—Allah—known as the *alif* is in the crown of the head, the *'arsh*.

The inner heart, the center, the *qalb*, is known as *Karbalā'*. This is man's battlefield; this inner heart is where his battles are fought. In this battlefield, filled with the 18,000 universes, man battles against Satan, base desires, animals, demons, angels, jinns, fairies, and the five elements: earth, fire, water, air, and ether. This bloody *Karbalā'* is a place of war. This is where blood is spilled, where sacrifices are offered, where quarrels and differences exist. Everything comes to destroy the inner heart, this *('arshul-mu'min)*—this throne of one of pure faith. They come to destroy that purity. They come to destroy Allah's qualities, His actions, His patience, and His inner patience. Everything comes here; this is where the battle occurs. This is *Karbalā'*.

In this place called *Karbalā'*, we should use the swords known as *Allāh, Muhammad,* and *Muhaiyaddeen,* and the weapons of belief, certitude, and resolute faith. We should employ the strength of inner patience, God's *rahmat* known as contentment, and the might that is derived from trusting God completely, having Him as the Helper, and giving all responsibility to Him. Then we can wage war, holding these weapons in the hand of *īmān*. When we complete the war successfully, we praise God, saying, "All praise is to God—*al-hamdu lillāh*. There is none worthy of worship except *Allāhu ta'ālā Nāyan,* the Singular One who rules and sustains. There is no other Helper. All praise is to Him."

Qul: Huwallāhu ahad —Say: God the One and Only.
Allāhus-samad—God, the Eternal Absolute.
Lam yalid, Wa lam yūlad—He begetteth not, nor is He begotten.

(He dwells on the right).

Wa lam yakul-lahu—And there is none like Him.

Kufuwan ahad—This is the One, the Absolute, the *Ahad*.

When we complete the war we will understand this. When we understand this story, we are *Īmān-Islām*. The war must end. In this state, we will praise God every moment for the *rizq* we receive. Even if we receive only water, we will say, "All praise is to God—*al-hamdu lillāh*." We will be content, possessing inner patience. When difficult situations arise, we will hold on to contentment. When things are hard, we will trust in God completely—*tawakkul-'alallāh,* and when things worsen, we will surrender completely to God, saying, "All praise is to God—*al-hamdu lillāh*."

God has placed man's nourishment *(rizq)* within a seed, within a drop of water, within a tiny fruit, within a blade of grass, or within a single leaf. God's *rahmat* is present when man has resolute faith and total surrender to God; therein is his nourishment. Man should sit down and partake of his nourishment saying, "All praise is to God." To perceive the given food as plentiful is *īmān*. This is *Islām*. There is no point in complaining. First, say the *Bismin*—"*Bismillāhir-Rahmānir-Rahīm,* in the name of God, most Merciful, most Compassionate." Say this when you receive food, before you eat it, and while you eat it. Then that food will be sufficient, your fatigue will clear, and you will feel refreshed. This is *īmān*. You have the Light, the *kursī,* that enables you to see everything in this world and in the world of souls. All sufficiency is within you.

God, the Singular One who rules and sustains, created this most exalted man and showed him this *rahmat*. God made *insān* most exalted by showing him His examples, and revealing the principles governing those examples. God gave *insān* seven wisdoms. All other creations were given only three—perception, awareness, and intellect *(unarchi, unarvu,* and *pudthi)*. All creations have death; they have fear, soul-fear. They give birth to their young, raise them, live with them, and embrace them,

327

but they do not differentiate between right and wrong, and they do not know what is permissible and impermissible. In the realm of souls, the Light of *Nūr Muhammad* is embedded in man's forehead. Because of this, he has judgment *(mathi)*, subtle wisdom *(arivu)*, analytic wisdom *(pahuth arivu)*—*Qutbiyyat*-wisdom, and *Nūr*-wisdom *(perr arivu)*—Divine Luminous Wisdom, the wisdom known as Muhammad. God gave man this additional beauty and wisdom—Ahamad and Muhammad. When the inner heart *(aham)* of man resplends, it is Ahamad, and the resulting resplendent beauty of the face *(muham)* is Muhammad. The beauty of the heart is reflected in the face, making it beautiful.

If our inner hearts become resplendent, our faces will be radiant. If there is darkness in our inner hearts, our faces will be dark. If there is anger in the inner heart, there will be anger in the face. If jealousy stirs in the heart, it will be reflected in the face. If envy resides in the heart, it will be seen in the face. If there is happiness in the heart, it will be perceived in the face. If there is wealth in the heart, there is wealth in the face. If there is bliss in the heart, it is reflected in a blissful face. If Allah is in the heart, Allah is in the face. God has given us this *rahmat*. He has provided examples from which we can abstract the Truth.

To understand, realize, and extract this [Truth] is *Īmān-Islām*. We should look at this body, this *sūrat*. It also appears as a heifer—*Suratul-Baqarāh*.[5] The world is being carried by a heifer. The two horns of the heifer hold up the earth. This body, *baqarāh*, is carrying the world and the 18,000 universes. The *Suratul-Baqarāh*, the chapter of the heifer, has many verses which describe the entire world. The *Suratul-Baqarāh*, this heifer, pulls everything: the world, the hereafter, heaven, and the world of souls. We must understand this. The heifer carries the world on its two horns—mind and desire—and it tosses and turns. If instead, we support the world on the horns of *Īmān-Islām*, the earth will not move, it will not shake, it will not roll. We should imbed the horns of *Īmān-Islām* in the world and hold it still.

---

5. **Suratul-Baqarāh:** The second chapter in the Qur'an, the chapter of the heifer.

If we imbed the two horns
of *Lā ilāha ill Allāh*—
Other than You, there is nothing,
Only You are God—
the world will be still.
If we *point* with
the completeness of *You are God,*
īmān will be established.
Say,
"Other than You, there is nothing, You alone are God."
Focus the Light of the *Nūr* on the world,
and point the repleteness of "You alone are God" at the world.
Then *īmān* will be established.
When the strength of *īmān* is established, we will understand.
When we attain this state,
we will see God as the only One, the only Thing we need.
He will be our All-Sufficient Treasure,
and we will realize the *kalimah, īmān,* and *Islām.*

All children of Adam☺ are created out of earth, and all lives are within that. All lives exist within each human being. Everything that lives on the earth is within the one handful of earth—worms, insects, base desires, cravings, water, fire, air, ether, sun, moon, stars, lions, snakes, scorpions, spiders, pigs, dogs, foxes, cats, rats, and fish. Satan exists within the bile. The *mīm,* the *alif,* the *Nūr,* the *Qutbiyyat,* the *Qutb,* the prophets, and enlightened beings are all there. We should understand this. We must understand this! This, my brother, is Islam. It should be understood through the examples, through the five and six examples. There is prayer—realizing God in the place where He should be realized. And there is the fast.

It is said,
"See the moon, and begin the fast.
See the moon, and end the fast."

Prayer, *'ibādat,* should be done in the same way.
See Allah, and worship.
See Allah, and end:
Lose yourself! Let go! Die!
You commence your fast by looking at the moon
and end your fast by looking at the moon.
[These two lines can also be interpreted as:
find the moon and hold fast; perceive the moon and let go.]
Worship in the same way.
Find Allah, and hold fast.
Find Allah, and let go.
Immerse yourself in Him, and let go.
This is *'ibādat.*
When this day dawns in us,
we are Muhammad.
We are Muhammad and Ahamad.
As soon as we attain this state
we attain *Qutbiyyat,* divine analytic wisdom,
and Allah alone becomes sufficient.
He is *Rahmat.*
We must understand this.
This is prayer.
When this state is established
it is the prayer of *'ibādat.*
When this state exists,
Allah is all that one needs.
Nothing in the world is desirable.

Because we did not realize this, the *Rasūl* ☝ said, "Go even unto China and acquire *'ilm*—divine knowledge." The *Rasūl* ☝ did not say, "Keep praying. Hold on to this. Stay here." "Go and acquire *'ilm!*" he instructed. There is no greater *'ilm* than the Qur'an, but there is another way to understand the Qur'an. The entirety of this world and the world of the souls is within the Qur'an, but the *Rasūl* ☺ said, "Go even unto China to acquire *'ilm*." He said this because that *'ilm* is a mystery. To understand the Qur'an, you should understand *'ilm,* and you can only learn *'ilm* from a wise man. When you acquire *'ilm* from a wise man, you will understand the Qur'an. You will understand yourself, because the Qur'an is you. Within you is the *Ummul Qur'an,* the silent Qur'an, and to understand that Qur'an, you need wisdom. To understand this *'ilm* [in the silent Qur'an] you must learn the other *'ilm* first. This is the meaning.

When viewed in this way,
Allah is Sufficient!
That is wealth!
That is heaven!
That is the soul!
That is all!
Al-hamdu lillāh—All praise is to God!
Tawakkul- 'alallāh—Trust in God Alone!

For what happens at each moment, we say, "*Al-hamdu lillāh*—All praise is to God," and for what may happen at the next moment, we say, "*Tawakkul-'alallāh*—I trust in Him alone." When we speak of something [that might happen], we say, "*In shā'Allāh*—if God wills," and when we hear of something [that has happened], we say, *Mā shā'Allāh*—as God wills. Then we are *Īmān-Islām*. To be Islam, we must understand this.

When we understand this, the war is within ourselves; the battle is within ourselves, not in the world. On the outside there is no fight, no enmity, no hatred, no envy, no jealousy—nothing. The only place of battle is at the center of man, at the (*'arshul-mu'min*), the throne of one of pure faith. Once we complete the war in this inner place, the only One worthy of worship will be Allah, the Singular One who rules and sustains. He will be the Treasure. For those of resolute faith, God is

Abundance. He is wealth, *rahmat,* and the riches of the three worlds. May we realize this. *Āmīn.*

However, because we did not acquire this understanding, this *'ilm* of *Īmān-Islām,* and since we were stuck in the "I," the five and six duties were revealed. Because we did not perceive Allah as sufficient, we were given the duty of charity. Since we did not gain the necessary understanding through charity, the duty of the fast was given. And since the fast did not convince us that God alone is sufficient, the pilgrimage of Hajj was instituted. The instructions were, "Die! Wear death garb, give your wife her dowry, give money to your relatives, give money to the poor, and go in the state of death. This is Hajj. Wear your shroud; you are dead. When you travel to Mecca and Medina on this pilgrimage, you should have terminated the world, your cravings, and base desires. This is what you must do."

However, since we still have not accomplished this, we are left with nothing—there are no more ordained duties. There are the five and six duties, and we have completed the five. But even though we went on the pilgrimage, we did not die. The world within us did not die, cravings did not die, base desires did not die, and all that we brought back was a title—*Hajjiar,* one who has been on the pilgrimage of Hajj. Instead of returning with Allah, we return with a *label.* It is for such people that there is a Judgment Day and a Day of Reckoning—*Qiyammah.* God has allotted a day of questioning, and this is why He told us to believe in the angels, the archangels, the prophets, the Day of Judgment, and the Day of Reckoning. He has explained these *sections* to us, told us to believe in them, and live our lives accordingly.

Well, my brother, if we understand all thirty [letters] of this Qur'an, it will be thirty years. When we understand the thirty meanings and reach the state of praising God in all situations (*al-hamdu lillāh),* we will be thirty years old. When we understand, perceive, pray, and acquire *'ilm,* we will end with *al-hamdu lillāh,* and *tawakkul-'alallāh.* Thirty years will have passed. The thirty days of the fast will end as thirty years. You will be thirty years old. Then, there are ten additional days of fasting. Earth, fire, water, air, and ether are five; with arrogance, karma, maya, mind, and desire we have ten. This body [containing the ten] has to die.

When this body dies
and Allah alone is in the *sūrat,*
when Allah and the *Rasūl* ⊛
exist as two breaths—as Allah-*Rasūl,*
and when these two breaths operate,
God, the Singular One who rules and sustains, will speak,
saying, "O Muhammad!"

Then the explanations of *'ilm,* the Light known as *Lailatul-Qadr,* will be sent down. The Qur'an descends—*Alif, Lām, Mīm.* God will say, "O Muhammad," and send down the *Sūratul-Iqrā.* The *'ilm* that will operate at this time is that of an *ummi*—a silent one replete in Allah. Gabriel ⊛ holds onto such a one three times, crushing the earth, fire, water, air, mind, and desire out of him. When Gabriel ⊛ holds tight with *Alif, Lām,* and *Mīm,* everything within dies and is brought under control. Then God sends down the Light of the *Nūr,* the *Lailatul-Qadr,* and as soon as that Light descends, one becomes *ummi,* silent. That which speaks without speech is the Qur'an. Everything that was subsequently sent down [to the prophet] will be sent down [to the *ummi*]. This is the Qur'an, the *Ummul Qur'ān.* We must study this [silent, inner] Qur'an and its illustrations *(ahādith).*

This Qur'an cannot be touched without performing ablutions. In this inner-heart, God has placed a minute morsel of flesh. He has created it as paradise, as the *rahmat* of all the universes, and as the throne of one of pure faith.

Within this minute morsel,
God has placed His Essence *(dhāt)*
as a tiny *point.*

333

Within this point are the 124,000 prophets, God's angels, His archangels, their places of worship, their ritual prayers *(tholuhai)*, their melted-heart prayers *('ibādat)*, their remembrances of God *(dhikr)*, their constant contemplation of Him *(fikr)*, the resonances of God and His angels, and the understandings He understands. This *rahmat* resonates within that *point.* That place is a mystery—*dhāt*. It is a place that earth will not consume, fire will not consume, water will not consume, air will not consume, ether will not consume, and Satan will not touch. Nothing can consume this *point.* God has placed this as the realm of the souls, as His paradise, as His seat of judgment, His place of worship. This is His sovereignty. Realizing this *point,* pray with a melting heart, and live with the prophets. The *rasūls,* angels, jinns, fairies, and those of resolute faith will gather here. This place is larger than the 18,000 universes. Its depth, length, and *rahmat* cannot be described. *In shā' Allāh,* we cannot say any more. As wisdom develops, deeper explanations will dawn within.

When we attain this state,
the title of prophet will be given to Muhammad,
to the *sūrat* of *mīm*.
When the *Lailatul-Qadr* descends,
we will have "died,"
and the *rahmat* that is the Qur'an will be understood.

In order to receive this *rahmat,* we have to understand everything, step by step. Then we are thirty plus ten, forty. When we complete the forty [days] properly, the *Lailatul-Qadr* descends. If within the thirty days of the fast, within these thirty years, we attain this *seed,* understand its benefits, and complete the ten, then the *rahmat* will descend.

This is the title that the *Rasūl,* may the peace of God be upon him, received at the age of forty. Through the fast, we should attain the benefits of thirty years. Then, in the last ten days, we should understand the secret of the mystery and the manifestations of Allah *(sirr* and *sifāt)*. If we understand this, we will be *Īmān-Islām* and Allah alone will be sufficient. It is this *sirr,* this mystery, that must be understood. This is the *rahmat*.

May the peace, the beneficence, and the blessings of God
be upon you.
Āmīn.

May God give us this *rahmat,*
and so grace us.
May God, the Singular One who rules and sustains,
give us these treasures of the three worlds,
and so grace us.
May He give us this *īmān,*
and this eminent gift of purity, *Islām.*
Now and in the future,
in this world and in the hereafter,
may He give us the triumphant wealth
known as the grace-wealth of all the universes—
the *Rahmatul-'ālamīn.*
May He grant each child this *rahmat,*
making inner hearts resplend,
and so grace us.
May He give us His Light,
His Completeness, and His Perfection,
and so grace us.
Āmīn

This undiminishing *rahmat,*
this *rahmat* that never disappears,
this everlasting *rahmat*—
may He grant us this *Rahmatul-'ālamīn.*
Āmīn.

May the Peace of God be with you.
Āmīn.

My precious brother, I cooked for thirty days. Today is the "Great Day," and I cooked some food. There is some buriyani (a rice dish) for you and your children. Please go and eat it. We kept it in the second floor kitchen for you. Please go and eat. *Āmīn.*

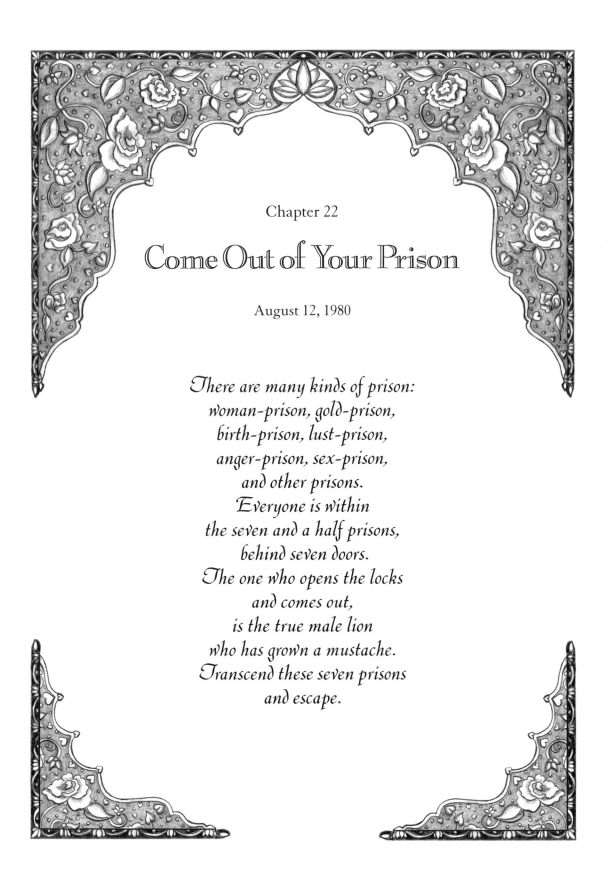

Chapter 22

Come Out of Your Prison

August 12, 1980

There are many kinds of prison:
woman-prison, gold-prison,
birth-prison, lust-prison,
anger-prison, sex-prison,
and other prisons.
Everyone is within
the seven and a half prisons,
behind seven doors.
The one who opens the locks
and comes out,
is the true male lion
who has grown a mustache.
Transcend these seven prisons
and escape.

Come Out of Your Prison

False wisdom races in.
It is the mind.
It is a sign of defeat.
Gently flowing water wears away the stone gradually,
but false wisdom rushes in rapidly.

I have explained this in a song I sang about fate called, *What will fate do to me?*[1] Many are in this state [wherein false wisdom enters]. The first line in the song asks, *What will it do, this fate of mine? What else will it do to me?* Do not entangle yourself in fate-games. All that you harness and garner from these fate-games will be energies *(saktis)*.

Some of you say that you would like to fast for ten more days, but you have not understood the substance of what I have said so far. The weight and gravity of my explanations about the first thirty days have not yet been understood by you. Buy the audio-tapes of my explanations and listen to them before you fast. You must understand the importance, the weightiness of the first thirty days of fasting. When you are able to bear its weight and substance and control your base-desires and cravings, you can fast for ten more days. These ten days are meant to be undertaken after you have "died." The base desires and the world in you should have died. This could be a time when you converse with

---

1. **What will fate do to me:** This song is published in the book *Maya Veeram: The Forces of Illusion,* by the same author. Trans.

God; a time of merging with Him. You do not yet understand the weight of this.

Everyone fasts, everyone meditates, everyone prays—but you do not really understand. Begin by listening to everything I explained during the first thirty days of the fast. Listen carefully to the detailed explanations I have given in the last three days, as the fast draws to an end. Buy the audio-tapes and listen to them on your own. You must understand the weight, substance, and power of the fast. Without understanding the magnitude of my explanations, you should not say, "It should be done like this, it should be done like that."

One hundred and forty-five years ago, I explained much of this in a song. Later, some verses were published in a book. In it I describe the conditions under which I was tossed about by various *sections*, how different wisdoms emerged, and how [true] wisdom ultimately dawns. The song consists of explanations from my own experience.

It is a very lengthy song, and I have forgotten some of it. It has been one hundred and forty-five years since I first sang it. I remember a few verses.

This fate of mine, what will it do to me?
What else will it do?
Will it fill me with earth-desire and change my course?
Will it make me bow down to the braggarts I see?
Will it cause me to pick up remnant scraps of food?
Will it enable me to see my Supreme Creator?
This fate of mine, what will it do to me?
What else will it do?

Will it make me search for Cupid and become entranced?
Will it ruin my living days and leave me worthless?
Will false wisdom enter and make me lament?
Will fate turn me into a vagabond?
This fate of mine, what will it do to me?
What else will it do?

Will it send me in search of drugs and alcohol?
Will it make me stray like a wild buffalo?
Will it lead me to believe that destiny plays itself out?
Will it help me see my Supreme Creator?
This fate of mine, what will it do to me?
What else will it do?

Will it trick me into perceiving alcohol as milk?
Will it lead me to join a band of sinners?
Will it have me bury the Treasure I seek?
Will it help me attain divine grace-wisdom?
This fate of mine, what will it do to me?
What else will it do?

Will it impel me to pursue prostitutes?
Will it help me attain the gift of deathlessness
and keep me from dying?
Will it drive me to seek wealth in the world continually?
Will it make me realize the mantra of silence?
This fate of mine, what will it do to me?
What else will it do?

Will it return me to my mother's womb, only to be born again?
Will it give me the gift of deathlessness
and keep me from dying?
Will it run me around like a city-wandering dog?
Will it destroy me in the pit of filth and stench?
This fate of mine, what will it do to me?
What else will it do?

Will it keep me agitated, chasing after prosperity?
Will it make others drive me away as the dog of desire?
Will it find me hoarding tarnished money?

341

Will it help me attain the divine grace of the One God?
This fate of mine, what will it do to me?
What else will it do?

Will it make me tarry amidst prostitutes?
Will it embed me in the womb of a whore?
Will it make me join these women of maya?
Will it make me boastful?
This fate of mine, what will it do to me?
What else will it do?

Will it make me think unthinkable thoughts?
Will it cause me to be bewitched by
the maya-demon that produced me?
Will it leave me wandering as a ghost
because of my desire for wife and child?
Will it take me back to the place of birth?
This fate of mine, what will it do to me?
What else will it do?

Will it compel me to run into five and six openings?
Will it help me to receive the Lord's divine grace?
Will it enable me to scorn everything as false?
Will it deliver me finally into the hands of *Yaman*?[2]
This fate of mine, what will it do to me?
What else will it do?

Will it make me toil to appease hunger and illness?
Will it leave me wandering like an outsider in a strange land?
Will it help me to receive wealth from the Noble One?
Will it have the world chase me away like a disgusting dog?

---

2. **Yaman:** The *angel of death*.

This fate of mine, what will it do to me?
What else will it do?

Will it have me contract into myself upon seeing
all the maya of the world?
Will it make me wander and roam—run without running?
Will it bury my life in boastful mayic-knowledge?
Will it gather the mind-demons to seize and drag me?
This fate of mine, what will it do to me?
What else will it do?

Will it cause the desire-monkey to beat me?
Will it induce me to act on everything I see
and so agitate my heart?
Will it make me forget the One Supreme God,
or will it make me humble, knowing that He is everything?
This fate of mine, what will it do to me?
What else will it do?

I have sung these words of wisdom earlier. This song about fate has three hundred and fifty verses. This is just a small portion.

False wisdom will make you feel important; it will invigorate and alter you. Conversely, just as an ant creeps slowly and finds what it needs, true wisdom should creep gently and discover the Truth. Everything the mind speaks comes from the sky, from ether, as it continually flies around. Let me sing you another song that I have sung earlier about returning to the birth-place.

O, you male lions who grow your mustaches,
come out and look!
Come out and look!
O, you male lions who grow your mustaches,
come out and look!
Come out and look!

343

That song is from the following story. Once upon a time a king fell ill, and no treatment was of any avail. The so-called wise men *(gnanis)* and religious scholars were summoned, but nothing worked. All the physicians and doctors were held captive, but no one could cure the king. Finally, all those who claimed to be men of wisdom were captured and locked in prison. Because these *gnanis* could not heal the king, he angrily declared, "No wise man, no *gnani*, can stay in my kingdom. Leave! You run the world by deceiving the people." One thousand *gnanis* were rounded up and imprisoned. Each one was locked in an individual cell in the royal prison.

In the process of locking everyone up, they also imprisoned the one true man of wisdom, the one true *gnani,* named Gunam Kudi Mastaan— the one who has imbibed good qualities. Though they bolted the locks, he managed to free himself. He was one of my children. He came out of captivity and sang to all the other *gnanis* who had grown long hair, mustaches, beards, and braids as part of their quackery. He walked by their prison cells singing this song.

O, you male lions who have grown your mustaches,
come out! Come out!
All you have is
a bundle of hair on your head,
a small basket of hair in your arm pit,
and a basket of hair on your face.
Only a bushel of hair will grow in your groin;
only a bushel of hair will grow.
O, you male lions who lengthen your mustaches,
come out!
Come out and look!

Why the mustache on your face?
Why this basket of hair?
Why the bundle of hair on the head?

344

You have a small basket of hair in the arm pit
and seven baskets of hair in the groin.
All you have done is grow your hair. What is the use?
Come on, come out!
O you male lions who grow your mustaches,
come out!

"Come out and look! Come, let us go out," called Mastaan, but no one emerged. They could not open the locks. Only Gunam Kudi Mastaan walked out. He had never attempted to cure the king, but when they rounded everyone up, they imprisoned him as well. All the others had arrived claiming lofty titles and lineage but were unable to cure the king's illness.

Mastaan had not attempted to do so but had been captured while walking on the street. Curing illness was not his work. Now, as he sang his song to the other prisoners, it was reported to the king that one of the prisoners had freed himself. "One man is free, and he is singing a song," they told the king. The king exclaimed, "He is the *gnani*. Bring him here!" The king welcomed Mastaan and fell at his feet. Mastaan asked him, "O king, what is it you need?" and proceeded to sing a song.

May everyone worship the One God!
Worship this Marvel!
Everyone worship the One Allah!
Worship this Miracle!
Worship this Miraculous One, O king!
Worship this Miracle!
You took all the animals into your possession
and fell into this illness.
You [then] worshipped as gods of the earth
all the ghosts, demons, dogs, and foxes
that were instantly born.
The herds of dogs and foxes that thrive

all over the earth,
you worshipped and called your "Lord."
You claimed as "God"
all the lions, tigers, bears, elephants, and cats.
Entangling your thoughts in the mantras of maya,
you began to perish.
Stuck in mayic-mantras
you started to wither.
Land and city, house and property,
and the four corners of the globe—
you claimed them all as yours.
The deity you perceived at birth,
you labeled as divine bliss.
(In the Hindu religion it is known as *Shīva* and *Shakti*.)
Do you not recognize the base action
that Adam⁀ and Eve⁀ united to create?
Do you not understand this, O king?
Trusting this mysterious body which arose out of maya,
you do not strive to see and realize the One
before death arrives.
Without realizing the One before death arrives,
why do you become a corpse, O king?
This is your illness.
A desire-filled mind
and attachment-laden thoughts are ruining you.
Wealth, property, wife, children, house, goats, and cows
are your mammoth illness, O king.
They are your mammoth illness, O king.
Your wife, with all her monkey-acts, is your enemy.
But you accept this wife-relationship and link your mouth to hers.

[Bawa Muhaiyaddeen explains that man's wife is his enemy. He
claims as his own, the wife and children who are his foes.]

346

You acknowledge this wife,
who joins a band of monkeys,
as one who was born with you.
You uphold as supreme—
earth, women, and gold—
things uncontrollable by you.
These wicked monkeys
have joined together
and made you worthless.
They have made you into
a demon, a ghost, and a sick man.
Understand your birth, O man, O king!
If you analyze, you will know
that nothing was born with you.
Only herds of dogs, foxes,
braggarts, demons, and ghosts
live here.
But you call them "God"
and worship them day and night.
Instead, place within your heart
the One who serves all equally—
Allah,
the Precious Supreme Light.
If you place Him in your inner heart
your illness will be cured instantly.
Realize this, O king!
The entire world is an actor's stage, O man!
The entire world is an actor's stage,
and if you live believing in it,
it will be your loss.
If you live believing in it,
it will be your loss.

There is a Light known as the Primal One.
When you realize this, benefits follow.
Saturn's influence of seven and a half years
has taken hold of you, tormenting your heart.

[Bawa Muhaiyaddeen explains that the planet Saturn is a satan that
torments man for periods of seven and a half years during his lifetime.]

Day after day, serve God,
and worship in this world.
That One who fills the earth
will carry you with love, embrace you,
and feed you with milk.
Realize this, O king!
You extol as great
the sinners who seduce you with their eyes,
with a wink here and a wink there;
they purse their lips, display their teeth,
and hypnotize you.
You extol these sinners as great beings.
Your inner entrancement
brings you the dreadful illness
that emaciates your body, O man.
With your organs darkened
and your body shrunken,
you cry, forgetting God.
You cry in the world.

First,
speak the truth,
and search for the Good One.
Worship the One
who will be with you day and night.

There is a good mantra
which is the most exalted in the land.
It is the most exalted in the world of souls,
this world, and the hereafter.
This mantra is
Allāhu,
Lā ilāha ill-Allāhū.[3]
Say this, O king.
Say this.

Stay alone and recite this mantra.
It will end your death.
Look, this is the medicine for all ills.
It is the grace-medicine
that will end your death.
This is the banquet provided by God.
Eat the food from this banquet, O man,
this banquet that God has provided.
The darkness, illusion, illness, and disease
will be dispelled.
Look, O man!
Lights will dawn within you.
Yes, O man,
if you understand this intrinsic meaning,
your illness will vanish.

The *gnani* sang this song and then spat on the king. The king was cured immediately. He arose and told the *gnani,* "I will go with you. Please accept me."

In the same way, many kinds of false wisdoms come, roll us around,

---

3. **Allāhū, Lā ilāha ill-Allāhū:** O God, other than You there is nothing; You alone are God.

and turn us into dogs and foxes. The mind speaks to us from above, from the sky, or from wherever it is as it flies around. This mind will say numerous things, it will make many sounds, and it will show you a multitude of sights. It will show you lights, it will resonate, it will speak, it will hypnotize you, it will make noise, it will cry, it will pray, it will laugh, and it will take many forms. It will arouse desire, it will show you everything it conceives, and it will make all of them appear to be instantly available. It does these things to alter us and make us lose our way. It will makes us forget God. You must completely uproot this state.

This is why the *gnani* tells the king that the "male lions" who grow their [physical] mustaches are all imprisoned within the birth-cave. Not one has emerged from this prison-cell. They have not yet left the cave where they were born. They are still in the cave seeking shelter. They cannot open the locks and come out. There are many kinds of prison: woman-prison, gold-prison, birth-prison, lust-prison, anger-prison, sex-prison, and other prisons. They are within the seven and a half prisons, behind seven doors. The one who opens these locks and comes out is the true male lion who has grown a mustache.[4] He is the one who can cure diseases. "O king, transcend these seven prisons and escape. Go outside," the *gnani* instructed.

> Similarly, all of you say you are fasting,
> but what is this fast called *nōnbu*?[5]
> It is just *no anbu*, no love.
> The real fast, *nōnbu*, is the blossoming of the inner heart.
> Fragrance must emanate.

---

4. **Mustache:** The reference here is to *the mustache of resolute faith*. It is described as the fortitude of God, the Singular One who rules and sustains, the divine beauty of the Absolute Lord. It is one of the three thousand attributes of God, who has neither male nor female form. This fortitude, shining as the Divine Emperor's male lion, is the mustache of *īmān*.

5. **Nōnbu:** The Tamil word *nōnbu* means *fasting*. It is divided in two by the author as *no anbu,* to mean *no love.*

The qualities, conduct, behavior, and disposition
that accompany this blossoming make no sound.
Light and fragrance must dawn in the inner heart.
The one *point* which is God must resplend.
Do fast, but make sure the heart blossoms;
make it fragrant.
The flowering scent must emanate,
and when that *space* is perceived,
the One who inhales that perfume will come.
The One who perceives that fragrance will come.
He is the Lord.
When that Fragrant One comes,
hold on to Him and destroy all ten [sins].
Die within Him.
This is the benefit.
This is being forty.
God will show you the benefits.
Once you disappear in Him, there is nothing more to be done.
Your only task is to disappear in Him.
Die within Him.
Surrender to Him.
Then you have no work here.
Realize this state.
Thank you.

Nōnbu!
That's all right, everything is all right.
We must realize the fast.
All right, thank you.

Chapter 23

Beloved One

August 14, 1980

O Beloved One,
God of my love,
in my ignorant days,
I undergo so much suffering
as I search for You.
The difficulties I undergo
searching for You in my ignorance
are many.
O my Father, O God,
if You give me wisdom,
if You give me the light of my heart,
if You give me spotless purity
as my protection,
I will realize You, O Lord.
I will serve You;
I will not find fault
with anyone in the world.

Beloved One

Bismillāhir-Rahmānir-Rahīm.
In the name of God, most Merciful, most Compassionate.

Beloved One who ends my sorrow,
Beloved One, O Beloved One!
One who ends my sorrow,
Beloved One, my Beloved One!
One who knows my intention
and understands,
Beloved One, my Beloved One!

Beloved
who dispels the darkness of the mind,
my Beloved!
Beloved who dwells in my heart,
my Beloved!
O dweller in my heart,
where have you gone, my Beloved?
Beloved One, O Light,
O Jewel that pervades intention,
Father who has created and protected me,
where have you gone,
where have you gone?

My eye does not see You;
You are not visible to my eye.
I wander searching and searching for You.
I came with earnest desire, seeking only You.
Searching and searching,
contemplating and contemplating,
I came running to Your abode.

One who knows me,
One who understands me,
I run and wander, not understanding You.
You understand me,
You know my heart;
please show
this poor soul who runs and wanders
without knowing You,
please show me an abode.

I searched for You,
I sang to You in many different ways,
I looked for You,
I sang songs contemplating You,
I made this my quest
and looked for You in many places.
I searched for You in many places,
in the street, in the jungle,
in the hills, and everywhere.
I searched for You, O my God.

To the degraded eye, You are invisible,
and to my eye of physical desire you are incomprehensible.
Have You disappeared
or do You remain hidden?

You stay hidden as though You have vanished.
At this time, when my mind wavers,
come, end my suffering!
Come, end my suffering,
and show me a progression in my living days.
Open up the path to reach You.
Show me the way to reach You with certitude,
so I may serve You properly.
O Father, please come and grant Your grace
that I may serve You in a good way
and attain goodness.
My Mighty One, Valiant One,
show me the way.
Show me the way,
show me victory in my living days.

To sever the karma of my birth,
to discard the ninety-six obsessions of the bile,
to dispel mind, desire, and thoughts,
to expel maya, its mantras, and its trickery,
O Primal One, to realize Your path,
to open the eye of my heart and sing to You,
to realize You,
to realize divine analytic wisdom,
to attain the right state and serve You,
to walk on the path with good conduct, in the right way,
to destroy arrogance, karma, and maya
in the past and in the future,
You have to come!
You must come and end my suffering!

As Wisdom within wisdom,
as the state of bliss,

as Life within life,
You are merged within us,
O God, my God!
Not knowing where You are,
I think every kind of thought.
Where are You?
Wherever You are, please resonate
and help me to understand You with wisdom.
Clear my heart,
help me see the value of wisdom,
make my wisdom resplend so I may see You.
Please grant Your grace that I may accomplish this;
please grant me Your grace.

To dispel the darkness of birth,
to destroy karma,
to make sins flee,
to help me reach Your feet,
grant me Your grace.
Grant me Your grace
that I may reach Your feet and serve You
O God of perfection,
All-pervading, Complete One.

The mind as a monkey,
maya as illusion,
and desire as a dog
have ruined my heart and changed my disposition.
They have spoiled my heart and changed my qualities.
I am a corpse seeing only corpses.
They have turned me into a walking corpse now;
I am now nothing but a walking corpse.
Please come and save me,

teach me the good way,
and merge me in Your love.
In this world, the world of souls, and everywhere,
You are God, Wisdom within wisdom.
O God, Wisdom within wisdom,
before the angel of death arrives,
before my inherent wealth is lost,
before I join a band of sinners,
before I join those who are vengeful and treacherous,
help me!

Help me
to live with human beings,
to abide by my conscience,
to live in a community of mankind,
to know my mind, and to do my duty.
Please give me Your honorable qualities,
Your grace, and Your wisdom.
Please grant me this, and save me.

Before the angel of death arrives,
may I do my duty and improve.
May I receive the divine grace of the Creator
and worship under Your divine feet.
I need Your grace.
I need You to embrace me,
love me, and protect me.
I need this!

Whatever wrong I may have done
please forgive my mistakes.
Gather me into Your care and protect me,
O Father, O True One!

Gather me under You and protect me.
O Father, O True One,
Lord of all universes,
Allāhu!

There is none greater in this world than You.
You are Father, You are Mother.
You gave birth to me,
You raised me,
You are the only One.
You gave me life, You gave me body,
You gave me everything from my food
to the light in my eye.
You gave sound to my tongue,
You gave hearing to my ears,
You gave great understanding
to my speech and breath,
One who is my Father—it is You!

To realize You,
to know Your inner being,
to transcend all my thievish qualities,
to understand the Truth,
to merge with You,
to perform Your duties of grace in the proper way,
Mighty One, come and protect me.
Accept me into Your order,
and grant me Your grace
that I may do Your loving service.
Grant me Your grace and protect me.

O Primal Lord,
God of my love,

in my ignorant days,
I undergo so much suffering
as I search for You.
The difficulties I undergo
searching for You in my ignorance
are many.
O my Father, O God,
if You give me wisdom,
if You give me the light of my heart,
if You give me spotless purity as my protection,
I will realize You, O Lord.
I will serve You;
I will not find fault with anyone in the world.
I will not blame anyone, O Lord;
I will not blame anyone.
I will correct my own faults.
I will understand myself.
My Leader, my Father,
I will understand You.
I will know You,
I will live controlling my mind,
I will do Your duty and service without wavering,
and I will act according to the words of the Creator.
O Ocean of compassion, please come!
Intended One, Ocean of compassion,
please come!
Provide me with
the principles of understanding,
make me complete,
and so grace me, my Father!
O Primal Lord,
One who rules the heart,
Allāhu, Allāhu, Allāhu!

Lord of all universes,
so be it— *Āmīn,*
O Lord of the universes.
Mighty One, Ruler of all lives,
so be it—*Āmīn, Āmīn,*
O Lord of the universes.

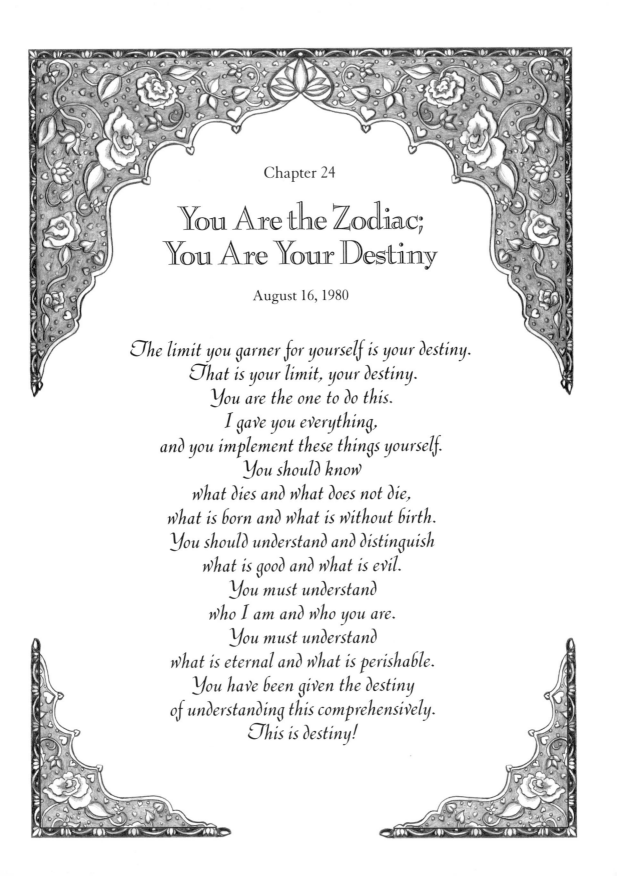

Chapter 24

You Are the Zodiac; You Are Your Destiny

August 16, 1980

The limit you garner for yourself is your destiny.
That is your limit, your destiny.
You are the one to do this.
I gave you everything,
and you implement these things yourself.
You should know
what dies and what does not die,
what is born and what is without birth.
You should understand and distinguish
what is good and what is evil.
You must understand
who I am and who you are.
You must understand
what is eternal and what is perishable.
You have been given the destiny
of understanding this comprehensively.
This is destiny!

You Are the Zodiac;
You Are Your Destiny

[The following is a response to a recently widowed woman who explains all of her "learning" but says, "I have lost all desire to live. I have many anxieties."]

Bawa Muhaiyaddeen: Is this what you have discovered in life? When your husband left, your life left, and you said, "I don't want to live anymore." This is an erroneous *point* in your life. Whom did you trust? Did you trust your husband, or did you trust God? Did you live your life believing in God, or believing in your husband—in creation?
[The woman replies, "God cheated me."]

Bawa Muhaiyaddeen: No, you cheated God. You lived your life trusting a tree. You lived believing in earth, fire, water, air, and ether. You believed in the clouds, but clouds roll on. Colors, rain, storms, darkness, light, sun, moon, and stars, all move on. You cannot depend on such things.

You plant a seed in the garden, believe it to be yours, and then live your life trusting that seed. But it will not last. You bring a jug of water from the ocean and think, "This is my water. This is my life." This is how you have lived your life. But water carried in a single pot will dry out, will it not? It will come to an end. You may drink the water, but it will run out. This is ignorance. This is maya.

Who gave you life? Who created you? Who feeds you? Who gave you everything you have? Who gave your husband everything he had? Who gave you eyes? Who gave you ears? Who gave you a nose? Who gave you a tongue? Who gave you a mouth? Who gave you taste? Who gave you all these things? You must understand this.

Thinking your eyes are yours, you say, "O my eyes! Look they are my eyes, my ears, my mouth, my hands." You have lived your life believing in these hands, eyes, ears, nose, tongue, and taste. This is the ignorance of your life. You should live your life believing in the One who gave you all of this. Everything else has a *limit*. The eye is an organ that is consumed by earth. The ears, the flesh, and the body—everything will be consumed by earth. Why did you live your life believing in these things? If you consider these things to be the strength in your life, then, when their life and *limit* come to an end, so will your *limit*. This is your mistake.

The One who is infinite,
without destruction,
without birth or death,
without beginning or end,
without wife or child,
without relationships or attachments,
without race or religion,
without scriptures,
without house, property, or deed,
without anything—
is everywhere.

This All-Pervasive Power is your Father, the Father of your soul and the Father of your life. If you had lived believing in Him, you would not have spoken the words you just uttered. Everything you have studied so far is like words written on water. When you write words on water and look back, they will no longer be there. Even as you wrote them, they were not there. Words written on water cannot be called wisdom. You cannot claim to have studied them, heard them, or lived by them, because this type of learning perishes very quickly. You thought everything written by the mind was a written letter, but those letters quickly wash away, disappearing, one after another.

You should have faith, certainty, and conviction in your Father, the One who gave you life. He is the One who raised you in the dark room for ten months. With no earth-connection, He gave you food, water, warmth, fire, and air. For ten months, God raised you in this way in the dark room [of the womb]. Then He showed you the *school* and said, "This is the world that you have to comprehend. Look at it. You now understand what is inside, and just as I raised you here on the inside, I will raise you in the world. Without anyone knowing, I fed you here, and I will continue to do so. Look! Look at My creations, My *arts-work*. None of My creations can nourish you as I do. I am the secret. I gave you food when you were inside, and I will be the One to feed you when you are outside. The One who gave you life will feed you; He will not forget. Understand Me through this *show,* through this story. Believe in the One who gave you your soul; believe in your Father." Upon telling you this, God displayed the world to you as a *show*. But did you believe Him? No! You believed what you saw in the world. That was merely God's art. You believed in the tree of God's art, saying, "It will give me fruit. This is my life." This is what you trusted. You invested your belief in this, acknowledging this as your wealth. You considered this to be God. You believed this to be heaven. You thought this was the world. This is the state you described—this wisdom, these things you heard and studied. But they are only words written on water.

You should have trusted the One who placed you in the dark room, the One who placed and fed you in the world of souls earlier, and the One who sent you into the world saying, "Understand the world and understand Me." This same One will invite you back, saying, "Come, it is over, your *limit* has been reached, come." Had you trusted Him, none of these things would have happened to you. If you had studied that wisdom, these things would not have occurred." If that had entered, these words would not have emerged from you. If that had been uncovered, you would not have believed in this. You would not undergo this suffering.

367

You have been raising a cow and depending on it for its milk, but its milk has a *limit*. When the milk stops, what can it do? Nothing! Then your faith is destroyed. You raised a cow and believed its milk to be yours. But the milk is depleted, its limit has been reached, and there is no more milk. Then you suffer. Now the only place left for the cow is the supermarket. The butcher shop takes the cow, everyone gets a pound of its flesh, and it goes to hell. Its remains enter the earth as fertilizer. Trusting in this was your mistake. You thought this was your life; that was a mistake. Had you believed in the One who is not subject to these changes, you would not have reached this state, and you would not say that your life is finished.

When fire and iron merge, there is only fire. When the iron is in the fire, it is fire. It is no longer iron, and if you touch it, it will burn you. However, if the iron stays outside the fire but says, "I am fire," it is not fire, just iron. As iron, it can be hammered many times, it can be broken, it can be cut, and it can be bent in many different ways, but it will not burn. Nevertheless, there is fire within the iron. You must understand this. You should either be in the fire, or you should realize the fire within. If iron is rubbed correctly, heat is generated and it will burn when touched. In the same way, if you had at least rubbed and polished what is within you, the heat would have emerged. The heat in the iron would have emerged, and you could have touched it and felt the heat. Even a piece of wood will burn after being rubbed vigorously. When you do this, you will realize that there is heat within the wood. Similarly, if you had scoured and polished yourself, you would have perceived the warmth of God. If you had fallen into the fire with faith, you could have been the fire. A little rubbing and polishing of yourself would have, at the very least, made you realize, "O, this is the Power. This is God. I feel the heat."

You have neither polished nor examined yourself. If you had examined yourself, the fire would have blazed. If you had examined your mind, you would have understood. But you have not done any of these things. You are not in the fire, you did not polish yourself, and you did not examine yourself. You continue to be iron and think, "This is life!" But iron can be bent in many different ways, and it can be attached to many things. It can be put into cement and into the ground. It will also grow rusty and be destroyed by the corrosion. If it is not in the right state, it will be corroded by rust and consumed by earth. You trusted the iron that can be consumed by earth, experienced what it had to offer, and thought it was your life. Is this wisdom? Did you study this? Did you hear this? Did you understand this? Think about this. It is wrong.

This is parrot-learning. The parrot repeats the same thing over and over. This learning does not differentiate right and wrong. The parrot can be taught to say, "Here comes a thief, here comes a thief," and it will screech, "Here comes a thief!" even when a good man arrives. When a man enters, the parrot will say, "A woman is here, a woman is here, a woman is here!" When a woman enters, it will say, "A man is here, a man is here, a man is here!" When a thief enters, it will say, "A good man is here!" Why does it do this? Because it lacks analytic wisdom (*pahuth-arivu*). This is similar to the parrot-learning and *book-knowledge* that you have acquired. You understood that kind of knowledge but did not discriminate between right and wrong or good and evil, and so you speak of what you have heard and what you have learned. These are letters written on water, not real learning. Two things are dangerous: if a good man is called a thief, and if a thief is called a good man. If a man is called a woman, that is dangerous, and if a woman is called a man, that is also dangerous. This is what the parrot says. In the same way, your current perception of life is wrong and dangerous. Think about this, think about true learning.

You have a *limit*. There are various things in you—faith, soul, stomach, body, vision—each one separate from the other. And what your husband has is different from what you have. He has a different eye, and you have a different eye. He has a different stomach, just as you have a different stomach. He has a different *section,* and you have a different *section.* As he has different judgment, you have different judg-

369

ment. He has different ears, and you have different ears. He has one nose, and you have another nose. He has a certain mind, but you have a different mind. This is how it is. The two are not one. But you have lived your life believing in those eyes. That is astonishing! You lived your life believing in those ears, nose, body, stomach, hands, and legs. This is wrong.

[The woman interjects that she still does not have the will to live.]

Bawa Muhaiyaddeen: Even a beautiful apple tree has a *limit*, does it not? Think about this. If you look at an apple tree you will understand. An apple tree bears fruit, and from a single seed come many branches, leaves, flowers, and fruit. As the tree grows and is laden with more fruit, its burden increases. The branches bend down, but it continues to bear the weight of the fruit. The tree neither eats its own fruit nor blames the fruit for its burden. Birds come to eat the fruit, cows and goats relish the fallen apples, and finally the farmer comes and picks the apples. If the farmer has guarded the tree, he may pick the apples. Otherwise a thief, a "satan," comes and takes them away. Therefore, the farmer must guard the tree. Then he can pick the fruits and distribute them to others. The tree bore the weight of all the apples and yet does not eat even a single fruit.

Reflect a little about what an apple tree does. If you live your life in that manner, if you do your duty like that, it will be very good.

I never married. I have no children, yet I have many thousands of children. I have many brothers and sisters, younger and older. I did not give birth to any children, but I have so many children. I did not get married, but God gave me many, many children. God is One. I married Him. I married this one God, and He gave me so many children and so much work. I have to feed a child on one side, give milk to another on the other side, carry one child on my back, and lift another onto my shoulder. One kicks my back, one kicks my chest, one bites my hand, and one bites my nose. But what does it matter? It does not hurt at all. I am not distressed, troubled, or saddened. When their teeth grow, children bite, but I just brush that aside and carry them again.

[The woman asks, "Is there any hope for me in the future?"]

Bawa Muhaiyaddeen: Once I asked God (my own Father, Husband, Brother, and Soul), "You have placed a *limit* on everything. Everything in creation has a *limit*. Everything comes to an end, and people call it fate, destiny. What is this destiny *(nasīb)*? What is its conclusion?" I asked this question one hundred and fourteen years ago. To this He replied,

"I have given you My kingdom,
My purity, My light, and
My wealth.
I have given you the kingdom of God,
the kingdom of hell, and the kingdom of the world.
I have given you My soul.
I have given you everything.
I have given you death and birth,
that which is deathless
and that which is birthless.
I have given you every wealth.
I have given you wisdom.
I have given you grace.
I have given you darkness.
There is good and evil, and I have given you everything.
You have to understand these things.
If you do understand, it will be good.
You are the cause of death,
and you are the cause of birth.
You are the cause of grief,
and you are the cause of joy.
You are the cause of deathlessness
and the cause of birthlessness.

"The *limit* you garner for yourself is your destiny.
That is your *limit,* your destiny.
You are the one to do this.
I gave you everything,
and you implement these things yourself.
You should know what dies and what does not die,
what is born and what is without birth.
You should understand and distinguish what is good and what is evil.
You must understand who I am and who you are.
You must understand what is eternal and what is perishable.
You have been given the destiny of understanding this comprehensively.
This is destiny!
You understand it, and you tally up the accounts!
When you discover your profit,
when you know what is productive for you,
you will attain the benefits.
But if you do not discover this, it will be your loss.
Calculate this *limit* and these accounts.
This is your destiny!

"When I gave birth to the body, I did not give you anything. When I formed your body, I did not show you this world, the Divine world, or the world of hell. I sent you in perfect purity. You were My baby, My prince, My princess. I carried you then, and when you return, I will carry you in the same way. If you come back in the same state, I will carry you, and you will be My baby once more. In the same way that I carried you before, I will carry you on your return. Know and realize this state. The way in which you went and the way in which you return determine whether I can carry you or not. If you come in a carry-able state, I will carry you. But if you change and deviate from this state, I cannot carry you. Your knowing this is your destiny. You create this.

"I created this *show* and formed you out of twenty-seven letters. There is one dark letter, and the other twenty-seven are light. This is your form. It is the zodiac. The twenty-seven letters are the twenty-seven stars that constitute the 12 signs of the zodiac. There is a six-pointed star with six wisdoms inside. Within this is the almanac of five letters *(panjāngam)*. This inner heart created of five letters[1] has six points and six wisdoms.[2] The five letters are the almanac. Think about this. Earth, fire, water, air, and ether are the five letters. This is your form. Understand it! The sixth letter is the six wisdoms. Together they constitute the six-pointed star.

"There are twelve signs of the zodiac *(rāsi),* and nine planets *(navagraham)* that cause agitation: two nostrils, two eyes, two ears, one mouth, and two openings below. The eyes, nose, mouth, ears, and the openings below will all churn you around. They are the nine planets. Thus, you are the nine planets. Of the twelve zodiacal signs, I am in the *'arsh* [God's throne in the crown of the head], and the *Nūr,* My light, is here [in the center of the forehead, the *kursī*]. One sign is in the navel. It was cut away and sealed because of its poison. Ten of the twelve signs are sinful; they are the ten sins.[3] You must understand them. If you open the gnostic eye, the *kursī,* and see Me, you will know that I am in the *'arsh.* There is a connection between the *'arsh* and the *kursī.* Avoid the ten signs and understand the two—you and I. You are the light and I am the Resplendence. Understand this. These are the twelve signs, the zodiac.

---

1. **Five letters:** Man's heart is composed of five letters, *alif, lām, mīm, hā',* and *dāl. Alif* represents God, *lām* represents the light of God *(Nūr), mīm* represents the eternal messenger of God (Muhammad)☺, *hā'* represents the physical body, and *dāl* represents the world. In the heart of a true human being these letters are transformed to *alhmd* which is the praise of God—All praise is to You, O God; You are the glory and greatness that deserves all praise.

2. **Six wisdoms:** The six wisdoms are perception *(unarchi),* awareness *(unarvu),* intellect *(pudthi),* judgment *(mathi),* wisdom *(arivu),* and divine analytic wisdom *(pahuth arivu).* The seventh wisdom is divine luminous wisdom *(perr arivu).*

3. **Ten sins:** The ten sins are those wrought by the five elements—earth, fire, water, air, and ether—and by mind, desire, arrogance, karma, and maya.

"If you look at the twelve signs, you see animals and even reptiles: a crab, a lion, a bull, a goat, a fish. You will not see a [true] human being, just animals. Ten [signs] are like this. When you become a human being, you become a light. Then you will see Me. When you become Me, you will be complete. Until then, there are twelve zodiacal signs and twenty-seven stars. I created you out of twenty-seven letters—you are the zodiac, and you are your destiny. Calculate and analyze this. This is the *nujūm*-calculation[4]—the analysis and calculation of your destiny. When you understand this, you will be a *Nujūmi*. When you understand and analyze this, you are the *son*, and I am God."

This is what God said. These are the twelve signs of the zodiac. The nine planets that churn you are the eyes, ears, nostrils, mouth, and two openings below. One has been cut away and sealed [the navel], and two have to be opened [the *'arsh* and the *kursī*]. When you see God, you will be the *son*. When you reach this state you will be God. This is what He said. This is the zodiac. These are the planets. Understand this!

---

4. **Nujūm:** The Arabic word *'ilmun-nujūm* refers to the knowledge of ancient astronomical calculations through which astrological horoscopes were charted. In this context, the author uses the word to mean *man's own analysis of the zodiac within his body to calculate and chart his destiny.* Trans.

Chapter 25

Divine Wisdom
is Very Subtle

August 18, 1980

Understanding sound, understanding speech,
understanding the reels,
understanding history, understanding the mystery,
understanding the resonance,
understanding the explanation, understanding Truth,
understanding grace, understanding wisdom,
understanding the Father, understanding yourself,
and speaking from that knowing—
that is divine wisdom.

Divine Wisdom Is Very Subtle

Divine wisdom *(gnānam)* is very, very subtle.
To realize it one has to go inside—
deep, deep, deep, deep within.
A gem attains its power and brilliance
only after it has been repeatedly cut and facetted.
Only after it has been carefully cut and crafted
does it achieve its value and significance.
In the same way, everything in us
should be cut and facetted with wisdom.

The mind, the four hundred trillion ten thousand spiritual energies, the miracles, the mesmerisms, the miraculous powers, the cravings, the sixty-four arts and sciences, the sixty-four sexual games, the desires of the mind, and the five elements must be severed. Blood-ties, religions, races, scriptures, philosophies, "I," and "You" should be cut away. All these things enshroud the gem. Only when you sever them and go beyond is there any value. To do this you need wisdom. Then you can reveal the calibre of the gem and say, "My God, it is of great value." Only then can its worth be assessed. But as long as you do not sever the rest, the gem has no worth. Cut everything away!

Everything else is *self-business*. Divine wisdom is very difficult; it is very subtle. A very big building is anchored by a very small *point* in the foundation. Similarly, the eighteen thousand universes must be anchored in this very subtle *point* within wisdom. Everything—life, the world, heaven, and hell—must be arrested at this tiny point, saying, "Stop! Stay!" This is divine wisdom. Study it. It takes a lot of work.

A picture of a vegetable is not real. It cannot be used to cook a meal. Similarly, what we study now is not real learning. We cannot cook a meal with what we have, for we have only pictures. Everything we have studied thus far is not learning, just pictures. Pictures of carrots, pumpkins, and guavas have been drawn, and that is what you have studied. These illustrations are acclaimed to be "this" and "that," but studying them is not real learning.

The important point is knowing that you have to go beyond all of this. What you have now is merely art work that is shown to infants— pictures shown to young children who cannot understand the written word. Children are shown these picture books as someone explains the meaning or tells the story. But this is not wisdom.

Knowledge must come directly.

Those *reels* should be perceived firsthand. That *television,* that knowledge, must be accessed directly. When everything else is known, that will be known directly. That is true learning.

Understanding sound, understanding speech,
understanding the *reels,*
understanding history, understanding the mystery,
understanding the resonance,
understanding the explanation, understanding Truth,
understanding grace, understanding wisdom,
understanding the Father, understanding yourself,
and speaking from that knowing—
that is divine wisdom.

Everything I show you now is a picture, picture books.
I show you pictures and name all the vegetables
depicted in the pictures.
But this is not it.
Realize this!

Chapter 26

O Mind,
Be Not Disturbed

August 18, 1980

Why do you fear, O mind?
Why are you afraid?
What is your sorrow?
What is your fear, O mind?
What troubles you?
God, the One, exists.
Realize this!
He is the One
who creates, rules,
protects, and nourishes all lives.
When this One King exists,
why do you fear, O mind?
Why do you fear?

O Mind, Be Not Disturbed

O mind!
Come what may,
be not disturbed, O mind.
Be not disturbed.
Come what may, O mind,
come what may,
be not disheartened.

Even if the world
comes rolling toward you;
even if the ocean
comes rolling here,
be not disturbed.
O mind, be not disturbed,
be not disheartened.

When the One
who created you is within you,
why do you fear?
When your Creator is in you,
why are you afraid?
When the Almighty One
who protects you and keeps you safe
is intermingled with your life,

why do you fear?
When this Supreme God
intermingles with your life
and speaks to you,
why do you fear?
Why do you fear, O mind?
Why are you afraid?

The One who creates grass
also nourishes it.
Don't you realize this, O mind?
The One who creates grass
provides its nourishment,
giving it water, air, and earth,
helping it to grow.
Don't you know
this Original Treasure, O mind?
O mind,
do you not know?

Why do you fear, O mind?
Why are you afraid?
What is your sorrow?
What is your fear, O mind?
What troubles you?
God, the One, exists,
realize this!
He is the One
who creates, rules,
protects, and nourishes all lives.
When this One King exists,
why do you fear, O mind?
Why do you fear?

The One who created the trees
also created its leaves.
He created its branches
and flowers.
He also created its fruits
which produced more seeds.
Thus
the seed
that perished to become the tree,
God created once again.

God is the One
who raised the tree
and gave it
fruits, taste, and color.
He gave it
fruits, taste, color, and fragrance.
He nurtured the tree
and provided its fruits
as food for all mankind.
He made it nourish all lives,
bringing peace to all.

When this All-Pervasive,
Omnipotent One exists,
why do you fear, O mind?
What do you fear?
What is your distress?
What is your fear?
What is your sorrow?

Live with confidence!

Live with wisdom!

Believe in God,
the One without the six evils.
Believe only in Him
and live.

May you live in this way, O mind.
What is your fear?
What is your distress?
What is your sorrow?

O mind,
dispel your ignorance
and control your desires.
Push away rage and hastiness.
Avoid anger, hastiness,
and the impulsiveness born of fury.
O mind,
hastiness born of anger is wisdom's enemy.
Impulsiveness devours your wisdom,
and anger will bring you sin.
Angry haste,
impulsiveness, and fury
will bring you
raging difficulties.

Lust is vaster that the ocean.
Duty,
duty to God,
is the greatest victory in your life.
O mind,
duty is the victory in your life.

But what distresses you?
What frightens you?
What saddens you?

O ignorant mind,
you ignorant mind!
Understand yourself
and realize that
God, the One, exists.
Know Him and search for Him.
Trust
the One
who is eternal,
who is within everyone,
who protects all lives,
who rules
within the heart
and without.
Trust Him, O mind.

If you attain this state
you will have no sorrow in the world.
In this state
what sorrow is there in the world?
What sadness?
What distress?
What fear?
What can you fear in this world,
O mind?

O mind,
God is One without form.
He is the One without anything:

without shape,
without color,
without wife,
without child,
without birth,
without end,
without house,
without property.
He is One who is always free.
He stays single,
yet intermingles in all lives.
He is the Blissful Power
that has transcended
beginning and end.

This is a Power
without form,
without color,
without race,
without religion,
without selfishness,
without anger,
and without sin.
This One Power
is God.

Trust the One of such calibre.
Trust Him with love.
Believe Him.
Trust Him.
Trust Him with love.
Search with wisdom.
Search!

Search!
Search within you,
and look at the world—
this One Treasure
will resplend
in all lives.

Understand this, O mind.
May you understand this,
O mind.
What do you fear?
What is your fear?
What is your distress?
What is your sorrow?
What is your sorrow, O mind?
What ails you?

May you realize yourself, O mind.
May you know yourself today.
Then all sorrow will leave you.
All sorrow, grief, evil actions,
karma, and sin
will run away.
Know this.
Realize this, O mind.
Why should you fear?

Try to control the pleasure-seeking monkey.
Beat and drive away the bestial dog of desire.
Chase it away.
The monkey of attachments,
the monkey-mind,
acts on everything it sees.

It will ask for everything it sees
and hold on to everything it touches.
May you control
this monkey-mind with wisdom.
O mind,
may you control it
with wisdom.
Catch the dog of desire
and tie it up with wisdom.
Catch the dog of desire and
restrain it with wisdom.
You will then reach
the Loving God and His grace.
You will reach Him
through your love.
O mind,
you will reach Him
through love.

O mind, what worries you?
What troubles you?
What makes you sad?
What ails you, O mind?
When the One God exists,
why should you fear?
Why should you be afraid,
O mind?

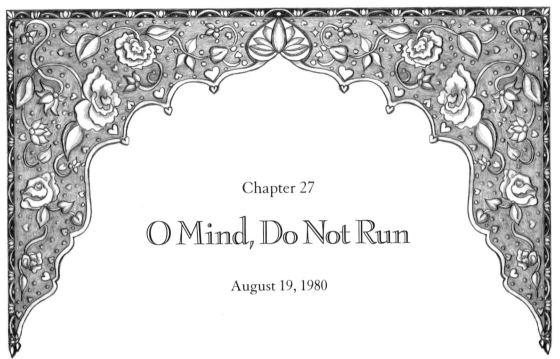

Chapter 27

O Mind, Do Not Run

August 19, 1980

The One who created you on that day,
the One who rules you today,
the One who is everywhere,
the Singular One,
that Lord—
seek and know Him, O mind.
Intend and worship Him always.
Search for Him
with love and resolute faith.
Search!
O mind, you must search.

O Mind, Do Not Run

O mind, O mind!
Do not run about, O mind,
do not run anywhere.
Look at God, look at the One!
Do not dance and roam around, O mind.
Intend Him—
the Supreme One,
the Supreme Primal One,
the Light,
the Mighty One.
Intend Him, O mind!
O mind, seek to attain the Supreme Primal Treasure,
the Resplendent Lord.

Do not run about like the animals, O mind.
Do not run around as a dog,
a fox, a cat, a snake, or a scorpion.
Do not become a pig, a donkey, or a horse
and roam around.
Do not run, do not run, O mind.

He who is forever is One.
Look, He exists!
He is the One of perfection.

He is the Eternal One.
He exists as absolute perfection.
Look, O mind!
O mind, look!

Do not run in search of earth.
Do not live seeking the woman of maya.
Do not wander in pursuit of wealth.
Do not run after sensual pleasures.
Do not seek out sexual games.
Do not dance holding on to the sixty-four arts.
Do not enact the sixty-four sexual acts like a dog.
Do not consume hell and live like the animals of hell.

O mind, O mind!
Take stock!
Look at yourself.
Reflect upon your life.
Analyze your birth—
your becoming an embryo
and your coming here.
Comprehend this!
O mind, do reflect and understand.

Do not intend the place of birth.
Do not chase after the place of birth with your thoughts.
Do not lust for the breasts you once suckled.
Do not dance at the doorway of your birth,
perceiving it to be a pleasurable game.
O mind, O mind, O mind!
Where you were born, and what you suckled,
are the hell of karma and maya.

Open your eyes and look;
Truth will be known.
Open your eye of wisdom;
you will know the Truth.
Do not hang on to the demons that torment you—
your eyes, ears, nose, mouth, and the two openings below.
They are the nine planets[1] that torment you.
They are nine planets.
Realize this, O mind!
Analyze with wisdom everything you believe.
Do this, O mind.

Do not roam around without understanding.
Do not trust this expansive world.
Do not take on the karma of bygone births.
Do not desire the cravings of the monkey-mind
and enact its actions.
Do not live with this thievish mind.
O mind,
do not dwell with the deceitful monkey-mind.
It will change you,
drive you off the path,
and ruin you.
Do not join that dog of desire, O mind!
Do not join that dog.

The One who created you on that day,
the One who rules you today,

---

1. **Nine planets:** The planets in the Hindu system are nine—the sun, the moon, Mars, Mercury, Jupiter, Venus, Saturn, Caput draconis, and Cauda draconis. The last two are considered visible in eclipses of the sun and moon, being black and red. The positions of the planets are considered to exert an influence on man's life. Trans.

the One who is everywhere,
the Singular One,
that Lord—
seek and know Him, O mind.
Intend and worship Him always.
Search for Him with love and resolute faith.
Search!
O mind, you must search.

Do not consume one thing after another and perish.
Do not live believing in worldly desires.
Do not join arrogance, karma, and maya.
Do not merge with the darkness of ignorance.
Do not live with the monkey-mind of desire.
With wisdom, seek the one God
who dwells as Love within love.
Search for Him with wisdom, O mind.

O mind, O mind!
No matter how long you live
you end up as food for the earth.
No matter how you live
you end up as bait for maya's line.
You will be bait
for wealth, gold, lust, desire,
blood-attachments, and bodily pleasures.
You will be degraded into bodily pleasures,
made into fodder,
and led to hell.

Do not associate with these ghosts and mind-desires.
O mind, O mind, know yourself and evaluate!
Know your life and understand.

Know the victory in your life,
and realize, study, understand!
Realize this with wisdom, O mind.

There is one Creator.
He is the Eternal Leader who protects.
This Leader is the Ruler who watches over you.
O mind, may you bow down
to this God who showers compassion.
May you always bow down and worship Him.
O mind, may you bow down to Him.
O mind, may you understand.

The divine grace
of the Creator who is filled with compassionate love,
the One in whom excellence resides,
the One of true wisdom and grace—
may you believe Him, O mind.
May you intend His divine grace.
May you seek His divine feet.
O mind,
May you seek His divine feet.
Āmīn.

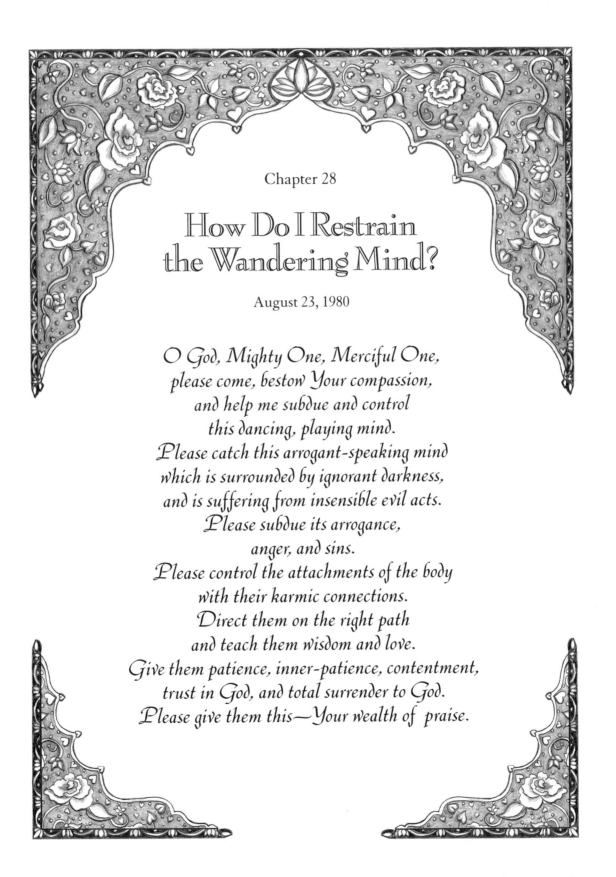

Chapter 28

How Do I Restrain the Wandering Mind?

August 23, 1980

O God, Mighty One, Merciful One,
please come, bestow Your compassion,
and help me subdue and control
this dancing, playing mind.
Please catch this arrogant-speaking mind
which is surrounded by ignorant darkness,
and is suffering from insensible evil acts.
Please subdue its arrogance,
anger, and sins.
Please control the attachments of the body
with their karmic connections.
Direct them on the right path
and teach them wisdom and love.
Give them patience, inner-patience, contentment,
trust in God, and total surrender to God.
Please give them this—Your wealth of praise.

How Do I Restrain
the Wandering Mind?

What can I do to restrain my uncontrollable mind?
What can I do, what can I do?
Is there a method to harness this running mind?
This mind
which laments without understanding;
how do I control it?
What can I do?
What can I do to control my cantering mind?
What can I do, O God?
Is there a way to control my uncontrollable mind?
What is the way?
How do I accomplish this, O God?

This mind runs without informing me
and wanders around with its sensibilities blunted.
Without notifying me, it runs around.
O God, what can I do to a mind that lacks honor?

What can I do to
a mind without compassion,
a mind that does not care about others,
a mind that does not attend to others as it attends to itself?
What can I do to this mind
that wanders and labors for its selfish needs?

What can I do?
O God, what can I do?

What can I do
when it keeps me in disharmony,
and when it entraps me in old habits?
What can I do to
a mind devoid of devotion and sensibility
that begets only sorrow?
What can I do, what can I do, O God?
What is the way?
What is the method?
What must I do to control the mind, O God?

A mind without wisdom,
a mind that plays with the five elements,
a mind that seeks sensory enticements,
a mind that loses its wisdom and hurts others—
what can I do for such a mind?
What can I do, O God?

This mind will not be controlled.
What can I do to this unbridled mind
that wanders without wisdom?
What can I do?

It wanders like a dog.
It roams around like a four-legged animal—
frightened, agitated, running.
It runs around capturing lives like a lion, bear, and tiger.
It lumbers like an elephant all over the jungle,
and jumps everywhere like a monkey,
performing many monkey-acts.

What can I do to
a mind that does not understand the house of the inner heart,
a mind that does not know the Supreme Creator,
a mind that frolics and searches for blood, skin, and flesh,
a mind that dallies with lust, anger, greed, attachments,
fanaticism, and envy,
a mind that pursues theft, murder, and falsehood,
a mind that does not know the justice and moral codes of the Creator?
What can I do, O God?

The mind does not realize
the one word—*Allāhu,*
the one completeness—*Ahamad,*[1]
the one beauty—*Muhammad,*
the one complete Light—*Nūr.*

The playful mind
romps like a baby
and says all manner of things,
seeking to make everyone its enemy.
It is cruel to all lives.
It ruins and torments that which is intrinsic.
It voices lies and jealousy,
keeping one thing inside while stating another on the outside.

---

1. **Ahamad and Muhammad:** InTamil, *aham* means *heart,* and *muham* means *face* or *countenance.* The author explains: *Ahamad* is the heart of *Muhammad* ﷺ. The state of the inner heart, *Ahamad,* is reflected in the beauty of the face, *Muhammad.* In Arabic, *Ahamad*, one of the names of prophet Muhammad ﷺ, means *the most praiseworthy*. The name *Muhammad* means *the praised or glorified one.* The author explains this as follows: The only One worthy of the praise of the inner heart is God. And when the inner heart is brimming with God's praise, its beauty, reflected in the beauty of the countenance, is the beauty of God's Light and qualities. Muhammad is the effulgent face of God's Light (*Nūr*), the essence of God, the messenger of God, emanating from God. Trans.

In pursuit of body, wealth, and life,
it thinks unthinkable thoughts,
and attacks everyone with anger.
What can I do to this mind which acts in ignorance?
O God, what can I do?
What can I do to this mind that runs and wanders?
Is there a way to control the actions of this unbridled mind?

Developing from embryo to form,
and intermingled in the body—
in the flesh, skin, bones, and blood—
this mind runs around singing,
"I am beyond comparison; there is nothing like me!"

O God, Mighty One, Merciful One,
please come, bestow Your compassion,
and help me subdue and control
this dancing, playing mind.
Please catch this arrogant-speaking mind
which is surrounded by ignorant darkness,
and is suffering from insensible evil acts.
Please subdue its arrogance,
anger, and sins.
Please control the attachments of the body
with their karmic connections.
Direct this mind on the right path
and teach it wisdom and love.
Give it patience, inner-patience, contentment,
trust in God, and total surrender to God
(*sabūr, shakūr, tawwakul, al-hamdu lillāh*).
Please grant it this—Your wealth of praise.
O God,
if You teach the mind Your praises

and subdue it,
I will become good.
I can then bow down and worship You.
I can bow down
and pray to You with a melting heart.
Only then can I live my life serving You.
Otherwise, this mind will make me a dog,
a fox, and a ghost.
It will make me subject to demons.
It will entangle me in lust, attachments, and desire.
It will corrupt my birth,
making me plod along bearing burdens like a donkey.
What can I do, burdened with this mind?

O *Allāhu,*
You are beyond all refuge!
As Wisdom within wisdom,
as Life within life,
You inhabit the bodies of all lives.
You stand alone and rule, *O Allāhu!*
Intermingling in all lives,
You are the Single, Supreme Treasure
who serves and protects each life.
You are the One Sovereign Lord, *ill Allāhu.*
Please come and end our suffering.
Protect us before our living days come to an end.
Sustain us.
Look after us.
Bestow Your grace and keep us safe.
Take care of us, O Mighty One,
ill Allāhu.
Lord of all universes,
You are the only One.

Allāhu,
may I perceive the boundary of my heart,
swim the ocean of maya, and reach the shore.
May I understand the embryo.
May I understand the *mīm* within the embryo,
know the *lām* within the *mīm,*
understand the *alif* within the *lām,*
and understand everything within the *alif*—
the heart, the *dāl,* and the *hā'.*
May I understand the twenty-eight letters that resplend,[2]
know the five and six divinely ordained practices,
and understand the inner heart of five letters.

Allāhu,
You are the Ruler filled with compassion
who stays with me
as the Heart within the heart
and as the Inner Heart within the inner heart.

Allāhu,
You are the Mighty One
who rules over me.
Please open the inner heart
and show me what is within.

---

2. **Twenty-eight letters:** The inner form *(sūrat)* of man, composed of twenty-eight inter-linked letters, is the inner *Qur'ān.* This is where revelations occur. Everything has been placed here as a secret: the sounds of the *Qur'ān* that resonate through wisdom, the prophet Muhammad ☺, the angels, and the heavenly beings. Man's heart is composed of five of these letters, *alif, lām, mīm, hā',* and *dāl. Alif* represents God, *lām* represents the light of God *(Nūr),mīm* represents the eternal messenger of God (Muhammad) ☺, *hā'* represents the physical body, and *dāl* represents the world. In the heart of a true human being, these letters are transformed to *alhmd* which is the praise of God—All praise is to You, O God; You are the glory and the greatness that deserves all praise.

404

Bestow your three thousand
gracious qualities of compassion,
and reveal Your ninety-nine
gracious qualities in action *(wilāyāts).*
Within this form *(sūrat)*
which is the *Sūratul Fātihah,*[3]
may I understand Your praise—*al-hamd,*
and know and realize You within that praise.
With the strength and determination of *īmān,*
may I understand where I am
and perceive
Your sovereignty—the eighth heaven *(firdaus).*
May I perceive
Your throne of justice—Your moral code.

Within this form, which embodies
Your ninety-nine attributes *(asmā'ul-Husnā),*
may I understand the meaning of
Your Oneness—*Qul: Huwallāhu ahad.*[4]
May I understand Your state of equality—*Allāhus-samad.*
May I understand the meaning of *Lam yalid.*
May I understand the clarity and *right* of *Wa lam yūlad.*

---

3. **Sūratul Fātihah:** In Arabic, *sūrat* is a word used exclusively for *chapters in the Qur'ān.* The first chapter, *the Chapter of Praise,* is called the *Sūratul-Hamd* because its first word is *al-hamd*—*praise.* This chapter is also called the *Sūratul Fātihah, the opening chapter.* In Hindi, and in Arabic (with a different "s") the word *sūrat* means *form, shape, state, condition.* In Tamil the word *pātiyah* means *have you seen?* The author, interpreting through several languages, often asks, *Sūrate pātiyah*—Have you seen your true state? Man must *open* up his *form (sūrat)* and *see* his true inner *state* of *praise (al-hamd).* Trans.

4. **Qul: Huwallāhu ahad:** This is the first line of the one hundred and twelfth chapter of the *Qur'ān, Sūratul-Ikhlās.* The author interprets several lines of the chapter using both Tamil and Arabic. See footnotes in Chapter Five for further details. Trans.

405

May I realize Your state of peace and tranquillity—*Wa lam yakul-lahu.*
May I understand the One that is Oneness—*kufuwan ahad,*
the One in all of everything—*Allāhu.*

May I understand You,
bow down to You,
and worship You.
May I bow down to You,
pray to You,
worship You with a melting heart *(ibādat),*
remember You with each breath *(dhikr),*
and contemplate You alone *(fikr).*
May I realize that there is none
worthy of worship other than You,
and worship You without wavering.
Show me how to worship You in the right way.
Show me that state,
show me that wealth,
show me how to pray
in the state of Oneness—the state of *ahad.*

Give me the meaning, the grace,
and the resolute faith of this worship.
Give me inner-patience, contentment,
trust in God, and total surrender to God.
Grant me these treasures which are Your gifts
and protect me with Your grace.
O Ocean of compassion,
Mighty One,
Merciful One!
You created my torso as a wondrous house,
but when I look,
it is a grave-pit that devours.

You made that same region into a stomach
with its fire and hell.
It is a grave,
a hell,
and a fire
that makes me wither away
and die without dying.
It is a place of suffering and difficulty.
It is a grave,
it is fire,
it is suffering,
it is hell.
It is a grave that will bury all lives.

When I dig up each thing,
all I see
are snakes, scorpions, worms, and insects.
The seven hells are there,
and the more I dig, the more graves I unearth,
buried one above the other.
Many, many lives have been buried there.
All these graves exist,
and when I dig everything up
I see the *big* grave—the one-span grave[5]
that You have given us.
I spend my entire life serving that grave.
I forget You, and seek only to satisfy it.
I eat and I worship it;
I eat, I relish, and I defecate.

---

5. **One-span grave:** The author refers to the *stomach*, which measures one span
   in length (the maximum distance between the tip of the thumb and the tip of
   the little finger), as the *one-span grave*. Trans.

I work and labor all my life for that hell,
becoming subject to a fire of hell
that is not appeased for even a day.

And worse,
You have given us an even viler canal
with the raging fire of hell—
the canal and fire of sexual pleasure and lust.
Please help me extinguish the enormous fire of this canal,
with *īmān,*
with You,
and with Your compassion.
This raging hell-fire cannot be overcome.
Unable to cross over,
everyone has perished in the fire of this canal.
It is a vile canal,
and everyone perishes
in its fires of hell.

Since the coming of Adam ☺,
all lives,
enchanted by that hellish canal,
burn in its vile fire.
It is the seven fires of hell.
Seduced by this fire,
everyone forgets You.
Without thinking of You,
they seek the fire of hell
and perish in this canal, in the hell of birth.

Splitting one hair in seven,
You built a bridge over this hell-canal.
Sinners cannot walk on this bridge

with their arrogance, karma, and maya.
That darkness causes them to slip, fall, and perish.
None have escaped this hell.
It is extremely rare.

O *Allāhu*,
do You not understand the sufferings we undergo,
stuck in this terrible hell?

You have given us seven wisdoms—
perception,
awareness,
intellect,
judgment,
subtle wisdom,
analytic wisdom,
and divine luminous wisdom
(*unarchi, unarvu, pudthi, mathi,*
arivu, pahuth arivu, and *perr arivu*).
At the apex
You placed the wisdom of the Light of God.
You gave us this *Nūr-section*,
this Light of *Nūr Muhammad*.
You planted the *alif* in us,[6]
gave us the helper known as *Ahamad,*
and spread the fullness of *īmān* over all of this.
With *Nūr Muhammad,*
You built a bridge
that is sharper than sharp,
straighter than straight,

---

6. **Alif:** The first letter of the Arabic alphabet. Among the twenty-eight letters of the body, *alif* represents *Allah,* God within man. Trans.

finer than a strand of hair,
as direct as justice,
and as fine-edged as a sword.

Please grant me Your grace
that I may walk on the bridge
without faltering,
that I may go across all these hells,
that I may reach the other shore
and bow down to You saying,
"In the name of God, most Merciful, most Compassionate—
Bismillāhir-Rahmānir-Rahīm."
May I bow down to You,
unite with You,
and worship You.

Please show me
the boundary and shore
that I may worship You.
Please grant me this grace.
All praise is to You,
O Lord of the universes,
most Merciful, most Compassionate.

A God like You,
a Companion like You,
a Sustainer like You,
One of power such as You,
One who understands like You understand,
One who knows like You know,
One who comprehends and transcends everything—
there is none like You in this world.

Limitless, Mighty One,
Supreme Creator,
Endless Leader,
Birthless, Almighty One,
Ill Allāhu.
One without wife,
One without birth,
One without death,
One without destruction,
One without flaw,
One without house,
One without possessions,
One without property,
One without the hankering for wealth,
One without hunger,
One without illness,
One without old-age,
One without hell,
Truth living as Truth—
Allāhu.

Is there any equal to
Your praise,
Your actions,
Your conduct,
Your gracious qualities,
and Your perfection,
which bestows compassion and protects all lives?
Is there any equal?
Is there any comparison?
O Mighty One, *Ill Allāhu!*
For those who lack wisdom,
You are in the unknowable realm,

and for those who have wisdom,
You are in the heart.
For those with *īmān*, You are the wealth in the heart,
and for those without *īmān,* You engender poverty.
O Mighty One,
in those who lack inner patience,
You create restlessness,
and to those with inner patience,
You grant peace and tranquillity.
For those with resolute faith
You exist with them, as them,
offering assistance.
And even to those who lack certitude
You offer help in times of need,
supporting and helping them
from within and without.
You are such a One—
Ill Allāhu, Allāhu.

O Undiminishing One,
Lord of the universes,
You do not diminish even as we take from You.
O Undiminishing Wealth that fills the heart of man,
You give endless tranquillity and peace to all lives.
Bestower of equanimity,
Omnipotent, Complete, Perfect One,
Allāhu!

For all who have filled their hearts
with the one word—*Allāhu,*
You exist and resonate as *ill Allāhu.*
You resplend as their heart and inner heart.
You will resonate in *salāms* and *salawāt.*

You will be present in focused worship
and in prayers offered with melting hearts.
You will be
realized and understood as *Allāhu*.
Allāhu, Allāhu!
O Lord of the universes,
Allāhu.
Āmīn.

Chapter 29

A True Sheikh
Is With You Always

August 23, 1980

God is the wealth of grace
and the Sheikh is the fragrance.
Since God resides in the Sheikh,
the Sheikh can take your air and transform it
through wisdom, love, and resolute faith.
He can change what you have
and give you his qualities, actions, conduct,
patience, tolerance, wisdom, and īmān.
When that air wafts over you,
you will attain wellness.
Health and happiness will dawn,
fragrance will emerge,
and beauty and good qualities
will blossom.

A True Sheikh Is With You Always

A'ūdhu billāhi minash-shaitānir-rajīm.
May God protect us from the evils of the accursed Satan.
Bismillāhir-Rahmānir-Rahīm.
In the name of God, most Merciful, most Compassionate.

All praise is to the One of unfathomable grace, the One of incomparable love, *Allāhu ta'ālā Nāyan,* the Lone One who rules and sustains. May all praise and praising be to Him alone. God, the Father who created us, is the only One who has the rightful power and perfection to protect and take care of us. May all responsibility and life be His right alone. *Āmīn.*

My precious jeweled lights of my eyes, children born of my body, lives of my life, precious children who resplend as the soul within my soul, beloved ones who are the lights in my eyes, loving children who are the inner heart in my inner heart, my loving children, precious brothers and sisters, I give you my love and greetings. May the benevolence and grace-wealth *(rahmat)* of God be with us.

Precious jeweled lights of my eyes, we have gathered here today. Some of us have been here for ten years, and others have been here for one, two, three, or five years. We gather here as one family, one community, one society, and children of one mother. Why have we gathered here? We do so because we are one family. Each one of us has our own mother and father who gave us our physical body; we have brothers, sisters, grandfathers, and grandmothers—an expansive family of

417

blood-ties. We have many ties: blood-attachment ties, body-ties, mind and desire-ties. We live our lives associating with all these connections. This is the world.

Though we live with these ties now, we finally leave each other and go to the coffin alone, do we not? Who comes with us? What joins us in the coffin? Our house? Our property? Money? Wealth? Parents? Friends? What comes with us? Do the religions come with us? Does our race come with us? Do our scriptures come with us? Do our worldly experiences come with us? Who comes with us? No one! Will anyone come? No.

It was the same for those who came before us. Did we accompany our grandfathers when they died? No. Did we go with our grandmothers when they died? No. Those before us have departed alone, and so will those who come after us. Has anyone accompanied another in the coffin? No. This is the world. We are a gathering at a fair. What we celebrate now is a meeting at a marketplace. This is our connection. Everyone comes to a fair or marketplace to get what they need, and upon taking what they need, they return home.

Everyone comes to the fair.
Everyone will come to this fair.
But look, as dusk lengthens,
they seek their own towns.
As dusk lengthens,
they seek their own towns.
So, does this country belong to us?
O people of the world,
if your discernment is keen,
believe this—
the body is an eight-span cage[1]

---

1. **Eight-span cage:** The height of the human body is eight spans. One span is the maximum distance between the tip of the thumb and the tip of the little finger. Trans.

and a Divine House exists within.
It is the House of Liberation.
Search for it.
Seek this House of Liberation.
Look there; He is in front and behind.
We must perceive this.

Precious jeweled lights of my eyes, this world is a market-stage, an actor's stage, and in this play every individual is an actor, acting his or her own part. Some are dancers, some are actors, some are musicians, some are businessmen, some hold titles, some are passionate, some are lustful, some preach like gurus, some preach about religions, some talk about races, and some delve into scriptures. There are many different kinds of people, and all come to this marketplace buying something different on the basis of their personal desires. They come to this world, and then they leave. When dusk approaches, there will be no one left in this market. This is the market, this is the world.

Once they purchase what they need in the world, where will they be at dusk? They will not be at the market; they will go to the cemetery. Have they gone to stay at the cemetery? No. They will deposit the marketplace merchandise in the cemetery and go where they must go. This is what happens. The bodies, minds, and desires that hankered after the marketplace end up at the cemetery. Titles and status will end up at the cemetery.

Precious jeweled lights of my eyes, we must think about this. This is how we live in this marketplace. This is a drama-stage. There are many different kinds of actors on this stage, but for a man of wisdom, there is only a prayer-stage. For him, the world is a prayer-stage. For those who lack wisdom, however, it is an actor's stage for enacting the arts and sciences, the sexual games, the sensual pleasures, the singing, and the dancing. The same stage is also a stage for wisdom and a stage for prayer. This is how it is. We must understand this subtlety in the marketplace. We must find someone who can give us an explanation. We must search for and find such a person.

Look at a margosa tree.[2] It absorbs foul, poisonous air. It draws the air into itself, transforms it, and releases healthy, salubrious air. It imparts wellness. The released air cures man's illness, makes him healthy, and gets rid of fever and disease. The tree does this through its own wellness.

In the same way, we have fathers who gave birth to us and raised us, but they are attached to us through blood-ties. They are well-suited for the blood-connection, but for our soul-connection we need a [different] father, a true Sheikh. This Sheikh must be like the margosa tree.

> He should be like the margosa tree
> and draw out the bad qualities from you.
> He should then alter the bad qualities,
> change the poisonous karmic winds,
> change all the bad actions,
> change all the bad thoughts,
> and give you his hygienic air
> and his supreme treasure
> to make you well.
> A true Sheikh will do this.
> This wellness-air will be God's air.
> Its fragrance will be delectable.
> It will cure illness and end karma.
> The Sheikh will give you this air and these qualities,
> changing the ailments of your mind,
> your karma, and your thoughts.
> A father who can effect such change
> will be the father of the soul.

---

2. **Margosa tree:** A medicinal tree that grows in places like India and Sri Lanka. Trans.

We say that the connection between this father and his child is forever. What does this mean? It means that the connection can exist in this drama-stage and also in the hereafter, in the house of God. He will stay with you without letting you go until the very end. The connection will be maintained.

As long as the soul is with you, as long as it has not decayed, his connection will also last without decay. This is the unfailing grasp of the Sheikh, the connection that endures forever.

> The one who transforms everything bad,
> giving you the wellness-air
> that liberates the soul,
> the one who gives you these qualities,
> the one who can give you peace—
> one of such distinction
> is a Sheikh.

You must find such a Sheikh. You should have faith, certitude, and trust in him. Your faith in him must be steadfast and unwavering. Then, through this wellness, he can pull you into him. He can do this only if you are with him. If you stay around the tree, the air will help you. Similarly, if you revolve around his qualities, his wisdom, and his actions, that air will make you well.

The qualities, actions, and conduct of a true Sheikh will be that of God. He will not do his work for money, hunger, house, or wealth. His wealth, his health, his life, and his nourishment are God. The search for God will be his only quest. How does this Sheikh, this man of wisdom, attain his connection to God? He establishes complete faith in God. His faith is unwavering with no doubt or suspicion. It is firm, unshakable, *īmān*-faith. Through this faith, he feeds on God's qualities. He imbibes God's actions, conduct, demeanor, and virtues, thus disappearing and dying in God. Through this death he attains wellness. How does this happen? As soon as he disappears, God transforms his qualities and gives him wellness through divine qualities. Karma, arrogance, selfishness, pride, and jealousy are transformed into God's qualities. He is given that wellness.

He will acquire God's love, His virtues, His patience, His forbearance, His equanimity, and His three thousand gracious qualities. He adopts God's attributes that are manifest as ninety-nine qualities in action *(wilāyats)*. Because he is surrendered to God and merges with Him, he attains these qualities.

Just as the tree transformed the air, God transforms the Sheikh and liberates his soul. He receives that wellness. In his qualities and wisdom, God's beauty and fragrance will be present. Just as fragrance permeates a flower, God permeates his inner heart. The Sheikh merges into God's beauty, and God's beauty merges into the beautiful inner heart of the Sheikh, like a fragrance. The two exist as the fragrance and the flower.

A Sheikh will have this manner of faith.
He will merge with God and attain
this wellness, this beauty, and this fragrance.
If you arrive at that state,
have the same belief, certainty, and determination,
have the same doubt-free intentions,
have the faith that does not say
one thing on the outside and another on the inside,
and intermingle with the Sheikh
as the fish intermingles with water,
then the Sheikh will wash and cleanse your dirt
with wave after wave of wisdom.
He will transform your qualities.
He will change your karma,
your actions, and your thoughts
and give you the wellness he received from God.
He will take your airs,

lay open and purify them with wisdom,
wash them with love,
and cleanse them with patience and inner patience,
giving you strength and peaceful wisdoms.
This will give you wellness and happiness.
It will transform your blackened air,
change your karmic air,
and change your arrogance, karma and maya,
giving you the beauty and qualities
that bring forth peace, freedom, and soul-liberation.
It will grant you the state
wherein you liberate your soul and live.

When you associate with a Sheikh, this state should be entrenched in you. You should surrender to him with *īmān*—absolute faith, certitude, and determination. This faith is surrender. Establish certitude with the wisdom and strength of this faith, and when you attain this state, you can receive the benefits. Only then can there be change.

There are different kinds of trees; some make you well and others make you ill. If you stand beside a tamarind tree or a wood-apple tree, they could make you sick. They contain the five elements, sourness, and certain kinds of air that can change your health.

My precious jeweled lights of my eyes, what is the connection with a Sheikh? He is one who will obtain the liberation of the soul for you. He will make it sound and give it to you. He will safeguard the indestructible treasure of the soul which does not perish in this world or the next, and keep it from being tarnished.

In this body of five elements,
there are four hundred trillion, ten thousand
kinds of miraculous powers and tricks of maya
that cause change.
The Sheikh dispels these turbulent winds.

He has the breeze that will subdue all desires.
He has God's air of grace,
this grace-wisdom, this rare treasure.
In order to receive this treasure,
no matter how big you are in the world,
you have to be a babe-in-arms with him.

When you join a Sheikh who is a perfected man *(insān kāmil)*, you must be a baby to his qualities. No matter how much you may have studied, whether you rule the world, whether you are a king, whether you are a rich man or a poor man, or whether you are a ruler or a slave— you must be a babe-in-arms to the Sheikh. Only then will he embrace you to his chest.

When you come to him, come as a tiny baby. If you are a baby, he will pick you up on all four sides. He will carry you on his shoulder, embrace you to his chest, wrap you around his neck, or carry you on his head. He will carry you in one way or another. Even if he has to tie you on his back, he will carry you.

But if you come to him as a great king, like a big mountain, he will unburden himself and move on. Why? He will not carry you, because you are too heavy. You must first understand the meaning of belief, resolute faith, determination, and certitude. Then, unloosen and discard all your prior learning and intentions. If you want to follow a Sheikh, you must become a babe-in-arms with unconditional *īmān*. You should not harbor any doubt or suspicion. You should not hold on to anything else. If you do, he will move on, saying, "That's fine, play with it." Having tried his very best, he will then leave you and move on.

When fragrance permeates a beautiful flower, it can be used and savored by all. But when the fragrance does not merge with the flower, the flower has no scent, and the fragrance cannot be used. Similarly, if you do not merge with the flower of the Sheikh's inner heart—nestle in it, unite with it, and permeate it—you will not acquire its fragrance and qualities. Every duty has to be done with steadfast faith in the Sheikh.

Faith in God must be resolute and unwavering. When this unswerving faith dawns in you, Satan may also appear, tempting you with bigger and better things. He will bring you wealth, bring you stars, bring you gold, bring you a kingdom, and bring you all sorts of miraculous powers and magic. He will say, "I'll give you a kingdom. Come! What you are doing now is mere craziness." He will lure you with miracles, praise, and titles. In bringing these things and showing them to you, he might deceive you. He could undermine your resolute faith. He will bring you a beautiful girl. He will bring gems. He will tell you, "Accept this girl. Don't leave her behind. You are crazy. Come here, I'll give you all kinds of things." These are some of the four hundred trillion, ten thousand deceitful tricks of Satan.

Search only for the inheritance of God—the One.

Seek God's wealth. The Satan who can give you everything else cannot give you paradise. This all-giving Satan cannot give you the soul (*rūh*). He cannot give you the good qualities that are paradise. He cannot give you wisdom. He can only give you trickery and deceit. He can give you enticing *advertisements* that lead you to hell.

All these things perish when you go to the cemetery. Everything has to be left behind—wealth, sexual games, sensual pleasures, desires, and the mind. We should not lose the freedom of our life, the freedom of the soul, paradise, and God in search of things we have to leave behind. The undiminishing treasure, the wealth of *īmān*, is our grace-wealth of all the universes *(rahmatul-'ālamīn)*. If we receive this wealth, it is the wealth of soul-liberation, the wealth of perfect purity. God's wealth is imperishable, flawless, endless, and perfect. You must receive the wealth of the Merciful One. Throw away everything that comes into your hand and tries to deceive you. Tell each thing to go away, saying, "No, go away, be gone!" Everything that promises to bring you something leads you to hell. Each thing creates doubts in you to separate you from God, from the Truth, from resolute faith, from certitude, from life, and from the liberation of your life. They are only shown to you in order to distract you. Therefore, if you have certainty in God, in faith, and in steadfastness, then in keeping with that certainty, throw all these things away. You will then receive the wealth.

When you are with a Sheikh
you must have absolute faith in God and the Sheikh.
Why?
Because God is the wealth of grace *(rahmat)*,
and the Sheikh is the fragrance.
Since God resides in the Sheikh,
the Sheikh can take your air and transform it
through wisdom, love, and resolute faith.
He can change what you have
and give you his qualities, actions, conduct,
patience, tolerance, wisdom, and *īmān*.
When that air wafts over you, you will attain wellness.
Health and happiness will dawn,
fragrance will emerge,
and beauty and good qualities will blossom.
You will acquire peace, equanimity, and justice.
You will be able to discern right and wrong
and escape all evil.

You must follow the Sheikh with *īmān* and unwavering certainty. Just as the flower and its fragrance exist as one, just as a fruit and its taste are one, just as the sun and its light are one, so must you unite with your Sheikh. Just as water and milk merge as one, so must you merge, inner heart with inner heart. If you have the *īmān* and determination to stay united with the Sheikh, you will attain wellness and soul-liberation. Arrogance and karma can be changed, Satan's evil actions can be dispelled, and through the help you receive, you will attain the freedom to go anywhere. Imbibing the wellness-medicine of the Sheikh, you can go anywhere. This medicine cures illness and ends the karma of birth. It will give you the unfathomable freedom of the soul. You must know this medicine.

My precious children, the explanations and refinements of *īmān* are of such eminence. Stay with the Sheikh with steadfast faith—without any doubts, as a babe-in-arms. Become a baby and drink the milk that the Sheikh feeds you as he embraces you to his chest. No matter how great a scholar you are, no matter how much you have learned or studied, you must be a baby when you are with the Sheikh. Only then will you attain the benefits. Children, the Sheikh has to be a baby with God in order to attain the benefits, and you have to be like a baby with the Sheikh in order to reap your benefits. Understand this unconditionally. If you stand under a particular tree, you will absorb and emanate its odor. If you sleep under the *Peenari* tree,[3] you will have a fecal odor. You will not attain wellness and the soul-liberation, purity, wisdom, qualities, and actions related to that wellness. Think about this.

Each child, reflect on this and understand the nature of this *īmān*, belief, wisdom, clarity of wisdom, beauty, and qualities. Then if you act accordingly, it will bring you victory. You can attain that wellness and be triumphant. You must merge with the Sheikh as fragrance merges with the flower and as taste merges with fruit and honey. You must unite with him.

The Sheikh is like a honeybee;
he knows the exact type of honey that exists in each place.
In God's kingdom,
he knows the location of every medicine
for every ailment.
He knows the location of every flower.
Upon identifying your illness,
he will go to the appropriate flower and bring you its nectar.
If you are poisoned,
he will go to a particular tree and bring you its fruit.

---

3. **Peenari tree:** *Sterculia foetida.* A tree that smells like feces and has medicinal properties. Trans.

If you lack a certain fragrance,
he will go to a rose and bring you its scent.
He will bring you the nectar of a sandalwood-tree,
and when you have a fever,
he will fetch a remedy from the margosa tree.
He knows every flowering tree and treasure
in God's kingdom.
He journeys like a honeybee,
bringing the correct remedy for your ailing mind.
This is the work of a Sheikh.

Only when you remain a baby will he give you the explanation and honey that can cure your illness. You must accept this knowledge. Take everything the Sheikh tells you and place it within. You must drink his words. If a child does not drink the milk, what can the Sheikh do? Therefore, drink the honey he gives you; drink the milk he gives you. Embrace him and imbibe the milk. Take in the wisdom he provides. When he embraces you, kisses you, and gives you something, you must relish it. Your heart must drink in everything he says. Take in everything! When you accept and conserve everything he gives you without doubt, you will experience its wellness. Only when you drink it without suspicion will you experience its bliss. However, if you try to mix it with your water, air, and intoxicants, you will not experience its taste. Then your illness, karma, arrogance, and maya will increase, because you have stirred in your own ingredients.

Your father assesses your state and brings you the appropriate remedy. You must drink it intact, without mixing it with anything else. Like the honey bee, your father will fly to paradise, to the kingdom of God, to divine-wisdom explanations, or to divine-wisdom lights, bringing you what is appropriate for your intentions and ailments. He will give you this divine knowledge *('ilm)*. Savor it!

If your inner heart is in this state, you can attain the benefits. But if you proceed in the opposite direction, have doubts, think contrary thoughts, remain in a different state, and mix other ingredients with the remedy he gives you, you will not be cured. Instead, that illness and karma will increase, leading you finally to the cemetery, to Satan. This will create doubts, suspicion, differences, anger, and sin. It will make you forget, and you will wander and hide. Unable to face the Sheikh, you will hide, and doubts will invade your mind. You will be reproached by others, and your doubts will increase. You will hide from the Sheikh, and your doubts will multiply. You may decide to leave, and then everything will be lost. Why does this happen? It happens because of doubt, suspicion, and differences. You will not attain the benefits and wellness from the Sheikh. You will be *outside,* and your illness will worsen.

If you do not surrender to the Sheikh, you will not reap the benefits. But if you are like a baby, drinking and relishing what he gives you, you will attain wellness, paradise. You will realize God and the history of God. As long as you do not establish this faith, as long as you perceive yourself to be big, he will not carry you. He will try to a certain degree, then drop you and move on. If you have doubts, he will step back. He will try to talk to you, but if you do not listen, he will move away. If you harbor suspicion, he will leave you alone.

By the same token, there are many people who say one thing on the outside and another on the inside. There are also those who say one thing in the presence of a Sheikh and another when he is not around. One who has not understood the Sheikh, has not surrendered to the Sheikh, or has not understood the value of the Sheikh will never attain the benefits. He has not surrendered. He has not become a baby.

God can understand the secret of the Sheikh, but you cannot comprehend it. God's secret is with a Sheikh, with a perfected man. The Sheikh lives in God, and God lives in the Sheikh. He has that privilege, that wellness. Such a Sheikh will know the ailments of each individual and will dispense the appropriate treatment. If you do not realize this, if you do not believe that he is capable of this, he will not give you anything. He will move on. He does not have to do this.

So what is the connection between the Sheikh and the children? He is the Sheikh of the soul, not the sheikh of the world. He is not the sheikh of your wealth, gold, and earth; he is the Sheikh who cures your illness. He will cure your karma, your maya, and your arrogance. He will cure all such illnesses. He can change the four hundred trillion, ten thousand energies and forces that seize you. He has the medicine to effect these changes. But you have to drink that medicine with faith and accept each of his words. When you go beyond his word, everything falls apart.

You will not understand everything the Sheikh says. If he tells you to go into the ocean, you will not understand what he is saying. You do not know what the ocean holds, and you must not think that he is telling you to drown. Just enter the ocean; there might be a secret there. If you enter with faith, there will be a divine secret, and through that divine secret you will attain the benefit. You must have the certainty to enter the ocean. However, if you cast forth *your* knowledge, you will only perceive snakes and sharks that devour you. But if you proceed in accordance with the Sheikh's words, you will immediately enter the divine kingdom, perceive certain secrets, and return to the shore. The Sheikh knows the secret. He knows why he sends you to a particular place and why he calls you back, but you will not understand. However, if you understand the secret, there is no need to come here, no need to find a Sheikh.

If you do need the Sheikh, then maintain a state of faith. Focus on and follow his every word. If he tells you to drink that which you consider poisonous, drink it. See whether it is poison or something other than poison. Do what he tells you. But do this only when you are with a Sheikh who is a perfected man, an *Insān Kāmil*.

If I were to tell you, "I am so learned. I am a great man. I will do this. I will do that," you would be very proud and happy. You would announce this, saying, "Look at our sheikh. He is so great." You would take great pride in all of this. And if I were to tell you about my titles, my names, my wealth, and my privileges, you would eagerly publish my titles and do a lot of advertising. You would begin to have faith. But if I told you that I am just a small person, you would have no faith and you would leave, saying, "He is a crazy man."

God is exceedingly small—an atom within an atom. A rocky mountain, on the other hand, is enormous. But when an atom strikes the mountain, the mountain breaks in four. Similarly, the world can also be destroyed by something very light and small. God's Truth is very light. His qualities are very light. His actions are extremely light and exceedingly humble. Similarly, a truly perfected man will not advertise; he will remain small. When you come to him, you must attain the same state. Otherwise there will be no benefit, and your birth-illness, karmic-illness, arrogance-illness, and maya-illness will never be cured. This will be hell. Understand this.

The connection between you and a Sheikh must be the bonding of inner heart with inner heart. Love must merge with love, and wisdom must merge with wisdom. With the steadfastness of *īmān*, the merging of the two should be like the fragrance merged in the flower. Only with this steadfast faith can you realize wisdom and God's kingdom. You can attain soul-liberation, end karma, and live with this wellness. There is no other way to do this. You must have steadfast faith in God and the Sheikh. Know that true faith is essential to reap the benefits.

What is a Sheikh? He is a fragrance-laden tree, God's tree of grace, His treasure-tree. The Sheikh has tasted the air [of God's grace]. He will give you that air and that wellness, driving away your karma and your air. Using the acid he possesses, he will burn away everything other than gold. He will burn away the lead, brass, copper, and silver in you, leaving only the gold. With different acids to consume each metal, he knows what to destroy and what to save. Such is his wisdom, power, and *īmān*. However, if you do not merge with him, he will not burn away these metals. He will leave you alone. If you have not merged with the inner heart of the Sheikh and acquired its fragrance, if you do not have that faith and determination, he will not waste his time on you. He will not need to use the acid. Everything will burn away.

There is much to say about this subject, and a large part of it relates to the Fellowship itself. Among the people in the Fellowship, I have seen some who are hypocritical. They think one thing on the inside and say something else on the outside. There are also those who find fault with me, those who hide and move about, those who hide stealthily, those who hold meetings downstairs, those who hold meetings in the park, and those who give voice to their suspicions. I have seen men and women of this kind at this Fellowship, and their words have reached my ears. If you are in any of these states, you will not attain your profit, your liberation. When you adhere to the Sheikh unconditionally, you will attain liberation and end karma. He is like a honeybee, finding whatever you need and bringing it to you. But if you do not join him, there is no benefit in your being here; there is no benefit in my being here.

When there is no water in the land, it is the land that suffers, not the water. Similarly, if I am not with you, it is your loss, not mine. If each one of you strives to live with unwavering *īmān*, it will be good. If you merge as the fragrance with the flower, as certitude with certitude, as taste with taste, and as honey with honey, that will be good. If you strengthen this *īmān*, it will be good. If you have even an atom of jealousy, you will not reap the profits. A little poison kills. An atom of darkness in the inner heart is sufficient to destroy man. An atom of doubt destroys man's life. It is poison. Never let that be your state. Keep your inner heart filled with steadfast faith, purity, and trust. Then you will have the assistance of the liberated soul. It will be your helper from now until the end *(ākhir)*—for as long as the soul exists. God has sent His representative, perfected man, the *Qutbiyyat,* as a helper. From here until the very end, this is the helper who assists and dispels karma.

Each of you must understand this. What is *īmān?* What is belief? What is a Sheikh? How should we merge with him? Think about these things, and strive to live accordingly. Only then can you end the karma of this birth, realize the perfectly pure light of the soul, attain the divine kingdom of the liberated soul, and receive God's treasures. In the presence of God, in His kingdom, you can receive His wealth and become

His prince. But if you do not attain this, it [this failure] is only your karma—the disturbances of Satan. Your own difficulties and worries will then be the only things that transform you. Think about this.

Each one of my children, think about how you should live with faith in the Sheikh. If you realize the nature of a perfected man—and believe in him—that will be very good. The Sheikh believed in God, received His wellness, and merged with Him. If, through that same faith, you merge with the inner heart of the Sheikh, you will attain that same wellness. Make your faith strong and certain. The Sheikh is a father, a soul-father, and you must become children who receive soul-liberation. If you change into a baby of this kind, and if he is a soul-father, you can receive the wealth of freedom. Your illness, karma, and maya will end, soul-liberation will dawn, and you will receive beauty, bliss, and happiness in life. You will attain peace. You will become tranquil. You will know equanimity.

Think about this. I had to tell you these things so that you might, at least from today, correct yourselves and act accordingly. These words had to be said, but I did not say them. The One who must say them, speaks. He sees what is happening here and speaks. He is saying this Himself, and if you wish to listen to and follow what He says, if you intend to establish faith, then live like that. These are not my words; the One who speaks and the One who is saying it, are He. These are His words. Understanding your actions and your earnestness, He is telling you not to let anything overcome you—escape! This is why He speaks. If you understand this and live, that will be good.

Strengthen *īmān!* Strengthen wisdom! Have faith, free of all doubt! Trust in God! That will be good. *Āmīn. Āmīn.*

May Allah, the Lone One who rules and sustains, give you this resolute faith and these honorable qualities. May He give you faith, determination, and certitude. May He help you to live your life free of doubt and suspicion. *Āmīn. Āmīn.*

May the peace, the beneficence, and the blessings of God
be upon you.

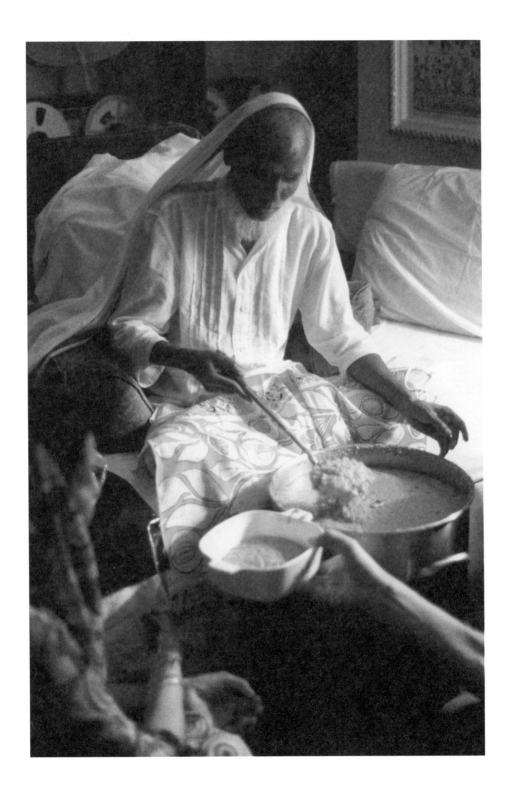

Epilogue

In the name of Allah, Most Merciful, Most Compassionate

Throughout the days of Ramadan, during which Bawa Muhaiyaddeen☺ tirelessly delivered these exalted discourses, he would also prepare the community meals that culminated each day's fast. The month of Ramadan follows the shifting progressions of a lunar calendar, annually relocating within the cycle of time, gradually migrating across the seasons. In 1980, Ramadan fell during the searing, prolonged days of July and August. Bawa, as father, tenderly viewed his children's determined efforts to evade the nagging calls of hunger and, particularly, of thirst. From earliest morning and into the withering, seemingly endless afternoon hours, he fed our hearts with wisdom and engaged our hands with edifying activity. Trusting in the transcendent certainty of our gratitude—which, alone, defies all the hungers of temptation—he surrounded us with food and set us to making dinner.

Men, women, and children customarily crowded upon the carpet in Bawa's bedroom, the locale in the Fellowship house where he most frequently addressed us. But during Ramadan, this room, brimming to capacity, metamorphosized into a kitchen of wonders! Imagine a bedroom paved with large cutting boards, around which clusters of people are congregated, each one wielding a serious kitchen knife. The master chef sits upright upon his bed, astutely directing his eager apprentices. For many an ardent seeker of lofty universal truths, it is this humanly ordinary image of Bawa Muhaiyyaddeen cooking and serving food that prevails as a foremost, cherished memory.

Bawa cooked *khanjis* and curries. In the giant pot heating upon a burner placed by his bedside, he prepared potions of vegetables, condiments, spices, and oils assembled in exacting measurements and proportions. Specified quantities of cabbages, broccolis, potatoes, carrots, onions, garlic, and other integral ingredients were distributed to the cutting crews, where they were chopped, diced, slivered, grated, or minced according to Bawa's precise directives. Workers of all ages sat in their circles, heads huddled in diligent obeisance and concentration upon the task at hand. As each of the vegetables was prepared, the pieces were heaped into huge metal bowls where they erupted in abundant mountains of color. The hiss and sizzle of seed spices hitting hot oil proclaimed the readiness of the cooking pot. Soon, pungent aromas of cumin, cardamom, fennel, and fenugreek flavored the surrounding air.

Although Bawa assembled his stews with vigilant precision, they were a feat of improvisation in that they materialized independently of any prior documentation, heeding the arcane requirements of the moment. Ingredients, amounts, preparation techniques all were summoned in spontaneous combination for a first-of-a-kind recipe—in other words, a daunting quantity of food to prepare and put together by simply "winging it." Nevertheless, the contents of the bowls were transferred, in specified order, to the deep cooking pot; and, with a long-handled spoon, Bawa confidently dipped into the vessel, distributing the vegetables

438

among the heated seasonings. Observing as this bounty was added, one skeptically marvelled that it could actually all be contained. Yet, when all the bowls were finally emptied, the vegetables settled in wondrous repose, precisely level with the rim of the pot.

Bawa sat cross-legged upon the edge of his bed, a compelling stillpoint of industriousness. Though it appeared a near impossibility to effectively stir such a heavily laden pot, it was crucial to consistently scrape the bottom, lifting and rotating the vegetables which would, otherwise, readily burn. Turning them seemed bound to produce major splattering, if not outright flinging of the compacted contents. Yet, remarkably, as Bawa stirred with his purposeful economy of gesture, nothing even dripped over the side.

Indefatigable, he practiced holiness as an everyday necessity. Beyond the savory enticements, it was always profoundly clear that Bawa Muhaiyaddeen's cooking was an act of prayer.

The exemplary chef, he revealed to us the recipe for life. His scrupulous attentiveness mirrored the impeccability with which he approached every endeavor. Always immaculate, he demonstrated the liberating discipline of orderliness and exactitude. He showed us the importance of correct proportion. He taught us that vitality is a matter of balance. He seasoned and blended our disparate demeanors, the better to serve us up to God. After all, like the cooking pot, we are each the measure of all that we contain.

Bawa scrutinized the simmering contents of the vessel with his intent, piercing gaze. Did it only *seem* that he was assessing the dancing interplay of each molecule? Did we merely imagine him to be swirling cosmos, in accord with the harmonious formula of Creation? The irresistible aromas permeated our senses—intangible, impalpable forces—testimony to the paramount power of that which exists unseen.

Finally, the anticipated moment arrived when we could break our fasts, and we formed the long line leading to Bawa's bed. Bawa filled each outstretched bowl, rhythmically tipping the spoon, scarcely spilling so much as a drop. If he, himself, ate at all, it was only after everyone else had been served. So long as one person remained hungry, his own appetite would not be appeased. Thus, by means of this sustenance, we literally incorporated his replenishing, beneficent love.

In essence, Bawa Muhaiyaddeen nourished our bodies and our souls, while personifying the fulfillment of his own explanation:

"When we understand and respect other's lives as our own,
consider other's hunger as our own,
look upon other's happiness as our own,
and regard other's sorrow as our own;
when we attain the wisdom, abilities, qualities, and actions
to bring peace and comfort to all lives—
that will be the grace and blessings of the fast."

Muhammad Sitti Rahmat (Myra Diaz)

Khanji Recipe

Ingredients:

8 cups rice
6 coconuts (grate and squeeze out milk once
        then add water and squeeze out milk again)
7 tablespoons salt
16 cups mung beans (cooked)
4 cups almonds (blanched and sliced)

3 bulbs garlic
1 ten inch piece of ginger (peel and blend both ingredients)

I tablespoon powdered ginger
1 tablespoon powdered garlic
1 tablespoon tumeric (mix all three ingredients with water
        to form a paste)

Method:

Boil water (about four times the amount of rice)
Add spice paste and blended ginger and garlic and cook
Add coconut milk
Add rice and boil.
Set heat to low, and cook until rice falls apart, stirring periodically
(about 30 minutes)
Add mung beans and sauted almonds

cont'd

441

Alternatives:

1. Vegetables and other lentils may be added after water, with rice, has boiled. Onions and blanched tomatoes may also be added.
2. For an exotic, sour taste, add block or instant tamarind paste mixed in a little water—at the very end.
3. For a spicier khanji add I tablespoon cardamom, 1 tablespoon fennel, I/2 tablespoon tumeric, 1/2 tablespoon cinnamon and 1/4 tablespoon clove to spice paste.
4. For a very spicy khanji add 2 tablespoons cayenne, 2 tablespoons coriander, 1 tablespoon cumin, 1 tablespoon fennel, and 1 tablespoon cardamom to original spice paste.

This basic recipe, used in the Fellowship, makes ten gallons of Khanji.

Glossary

As wisdom grows
and the words are analyzed
to a greater extent,
different meanings are understood.
As each connotation is abstracted,
the meaning increases
in depth.

Glossary

Arabic Calligraphy:

The following traditional supplications in Arabic calligraphy are used throughout the text:

(صلعم) following the Prophet Muhammad or *Rasūlullāh* stands for *sallallāhu 'alaihi wa sallam,* may the blessings and peace of God be upon him.

(عم) following the name of a prophet or an angel stands for *'alaihis-salām,* peace be upon him.

(رضه) following the name of a companion of the Prophet Muhammad, a saint, or *khalīfah* (successor, representative, vice-regent) stands for *radiyallāhu 'anhu,* may God be pleased with him.

(A) Indicates an Arabic word
(T) Indicates a Tamil word
(U) Indicates an Urdu word
(P) Indicates a Persian word

Pronunciation Index:

ā is pronounced *aa;* eg. *Dhāt* is pronounced *Dhaat*
ī is pronounced *ee;* eg. *Dīn* is pronounced *Deen.*
ū is pronounced *oo;* eg. *Nūr* is pronounced *Noor.*

'Abdullāh (A) From the word *'abd* meaning slave; *'Abdullāh* is a slave of God. One who is completely surrendered to God's service.
Ahad (A) The only One; referring to God in His Absoluteness.

Aham (T) The inner heart, *qalb*.

Ahamad (A & T) The literal meaning in Arabic is "the praised." In Tamil, *Aham* means inner heart. When the beauty of God's qualities fill the inner heart making it radiant, that is *Ahamad*.

Ākhirah (A) The hereafter; the kingdom of God; the end—the returning to and disappearance of each thing in the place of its origin. *Ākhirah* is one of three worlds—*awwal* (the world of souls), *dunyā* (this world), *ākhirah* (the hereafter). When the treasure that came from God disappears into God, that is *ākhirah*. When the soul disappears into the world of souls, that is *awwal,* and when it disappears into the world and into Satan, that is hell. When each treasure disappears into That with which it should merge, that is *ākhirah*. That is *Ahad*. That is God. That is His Mystery.

'Ālam (A) (pl. *'ālamīn*) A world; cosmos; universe. There are eighteen thousand universes within the inner heart. This world is a universe, an *'ālam*. Heaven is one universe, hell is another. Other universes include those of the soul, the angels, the jinns, the animals, fire, earth, water, air, the fairies, Satan, the prophets, the saints, the *qutbs,* wisdom, the *Nūr,* and God.

Al-hamdu lillāh (A) All praise belongs to God. All praise for everything that appears and everything that comes to an end is due to God alone. This is *Al-hamdu lillāh*. When you say, *"Al-hamdu lillāh,"* you praise Him and surrender completely to Him acknowledging, "Everything is Yours." *See Sabūr.*

Al-hamdu Sūrat (A) The Chapter of Praise. Another name for *Sūratul-Fātihah,* the opening chapter of the Qur'an.

Alif (A) The first letter of the Arabic alphabet. Of the twenty-eight letters that constitute the inner form of man, *alif* represents God. Everything has a beginning and an end, but God alone is eternal, existing forever, always "Natural." He has no beginning, end, or destruction; He has nothing. He alone existed then and now. That is God, *alif.*

Allah (A) God. It is the name of Majesty, the name of the Essence, the Absolute. It is the Arabic word for God, used by Muslims and Arabic speaking Christians in oriental churches.

Allāhu (A) God. The acknowledgment of God: "O God, You are the Explanation and the Resonance; the explanation and the resonance come from You. The sound of *"hū"* exists in you."

Allāhu Akbar! (A) God is Great!

Allāhu taʿālā nayan (A & T) God is the Lord above all. *Allāhu:* Almighty God, the Solitary One. *Taʿālā:* the One who rules, the One who exists in all lives in a state of humility and exaltedness. *Nayan:* the One who sustains, the Lord.

Ambiyā (A) (pl.of *nabī*) Prophets; messengers of God.

Āmīn (A) The Arabic word similar to Amen that means assent; verily; truly; so be it; may He make this complete; may it be so; may He fulfill this. It is stated in total praise of God: Rightful praise is Yours alone. No other form of praise is praise. Praise arising from an inner heart that has given all responsibility to You is Your praise. This is *Āmīn*.

Āndavan (T) God, the Ruler.

Arivu (T) Subtle wisdom; the fifth of seven wisdoms (the first four being: perception, awareness, intellect, and judgment). The five elements, earth, fire, water, air, and ether, function only up to the level of the intellect. Judgment, the ability to assess and evaluate, rises above the intellect. Subtle wisdom arises from judgment, from man's assessment of his life, body, and wisdom. *See unarvu, unarchi, pudthi, mathi, pahuth arivu,* and *perr arivu.*

ʿArsh (A) The throne of God. It is the Wisdom within wisdom, where the plenitude of God's Light (*Nūr*) exists. It is the throne where God, the Primal Supreme Effulgence resides. The *ʿarsh* is above the *Nūr,* and God is above that. In man, this throne of God is located in the crown of the head.

ʿArshul-muʾmin (A) The throne of one of pure faith—*ʿarsh* means throne, and *muʾmin* means one of pure faith. Within man there are two thrones for God. One is the perfect wisdom of man, the *Nūr,* the Light, the *ʿarsh* where God dwells eternally. The other is the inner heart of man, which when purified, is a place of perfect faith and purity, the *ʿarsh* of *Īmān-Islām,* a place where God can reside.

Arwāh (A) (sing. *rūh*) The unseen divine realm; the realm of souls.

Asmāʾul-husnā (A) The ninety-nine beautiful names of God. They are the names of His qualities, while the one hundredth name, Allah, is the name of His essence. These ninety-nine qualities have been given to man, constituting man's true state.

ʿAsr (A) The afternoon prayer; the third of the five daily prayers of Islam. This prayer also represents the third of five periods in man's life. During this period, between the age of thirty and forty, one should understand an important aspect of wisdom—the secret that exists between this world and the hereafter. The first period is the time of man's birth, the second is his time of growth, and this third period is his time of maturity. Man must understand this period of his life as the time when he can either become one with God or one with the world. *See subh, zuhr, maghrib, and 'ishā.*

Astaghfirullāhal-'azīm (A) I ask forgiveness from God, the Lofty One.

Auliyā (A) (pl. of *walī*) Guides, friends, saints, those who are close to God.

Avathānam (T) Concentration; attention; focus. *See Sheikh.*

Awwal (A) The time of the creation of forms; the period in which God creates the six kinds of lives—earth-life, fire-life, water-life, air-life, ether-life, and light-life—and places each soul, each entrusted treasure, in its respective form.

Barakat (A) Blessing, God's grace.

Bismillāhir-Rahmānir-Rahīm (also referred to as *bismin*) (A) In the name of God, most Merciful, most Compassionate. *Bismillāhi—* In the name of God, the Cause of all things; *Rahmān*—the Merciful One; *Rahīm*— the Compassionate One who creates, protects, and sustains all three worlds. This is God's duty. He alone can do this. He has no beginning or end. The *bismin* resonated within Him and came from Him. One who utters the *bismin* with the true understanding that God alone is sufficient, receives the treasure and grace of divine wisdom.

Bismin (A) *See above word.*

Bismin-kāi (A & T) God's house, a *point* of power within a minute morsel of flesh in all lives. Within the heart of each creation, there is a point which is naturally and spontaneously aware of God. Even if we forget God, there is a force within the body which makes us remember. This point within the flesh trembles and reminds us to believe in Him. God has placed this piece of flesh closer to us than our own lives, and God is within it, even smaller than that minute point. Truth, Light, God and His Power exist there in perfect equanimity.

Darsul-ambiyā' (P) Throne.

Daulat (A) God's imperishable wealth; the true wealth that exists forever.

Dhāhuth (P) The throne of God; the kingdom of God, where final judgment is decreed. *Dhāhuth* is above the *'arsh*. It is absolute faith—*īman;* beyond purity. This is the place from which God dispenses justice. From here alone do revelations occur. It is also from here that one is counseled, cautioned, and judged. Each is guided and told, "What you did was wrong. Go and ask for forgiveness." Each is warned in this way and urged to act. This is the function of the *Dhāhuth*.

Dhāt (A) God's essence; His treasury of grace. *See sīfat.*

Dhikr (A) The remembrance of God. Remembering with each breath that *There is nothing other than You, only You are God—Lā ilāha, ill Allāhu.* This remembrance of God cuts away the influence of the five elements, washes away the karma that has accumulated, and dispels darkness, making the heart beautiful and resplendent. It washes the body and heart of man, making him pure. It causes wisdom to emerge and impels this wisdom to know the self and God.

Dīn (A) Pure Light. Lit. religion; faith; path.

Dīnul-Islām (A) *Dīn* is pure light and *Dīnul-Islām* is the beauty of the pure light. Perfect purity, its light, and its truth are known as *Dīn* and *Dīnul-Islām.* This is the truth, beauty, and light for the path, for this world, and for the hereafter.

Du'ā (A) A prayer beseeching God's help; a humble supplication.

Fard (A) Divinely instituted obligation; duty. To know, understand, and act in accordance with God's commandments is *fard*, duty.

Fikr (A) Focused inner remembrance of God. As understanding, faith, and certitude deepen, constant remembrance of God (*dhikr*) evolves into *fikr*—total contemplation of God and immersion in Him.

Firdaus (P) Paradise.

Gnānam (T) Divine luminous wisdom; the wisdom of the light of God—*Nūr*.

Gnāni (T) One who has attained *gnānam*.

Hadīth (A) (pl. *ahadīth*) The author uses this word to refer to God's words and explanations. In normal use, *ahadīth* refer to traditions relating to the deeds and utterances of the Prophet☉, as authenticated by his companions.

Hajj (A) Holy pilgrimage to Mecca; the fifth of the five obligatory duties in Islam. The inner meaning of this pilgrimage is to journey inward, die to the world, and meet God, "making one's way" toward mystic union and Oneness. It is said that those who "can make their way" to Mecca should try to do so at least once in their lifetime.

Halāl (A) That which is permissible according to Truth, justice, and God's word. Lit. lawful.

Haqīqat (A) The third step of spiritual ascendance. At this level man must have the faith, certitude, and determination to merge with God. He must have the complete resolve to merge as one with God. However, all he sees around him at this stage are miracles, demons, and spirits. There are four hundred trillion, ten thousand spirits within the body, and countless energies that travel outside the body. Man reaches this third level and becomes fascinated. He calls out to the spirits and worships them. He says, "Spirit, spirit, god, god," but has no idea to which spirit, god, or idol he is calling out. If man escapes this, and instead, the beauty of his faith (*īmān*) merges with God's light, that is *haqīqat*. Where the two embrace as one is *haqīqat*. *See sharī'at, tarīqat, ma'rifat, and sūfiyyat.*

Harām (A) That which is impermissible according to Truth, justice, and God's word. *Harām* refers to all that is detrimental to progress on the pure path. Lit. prohibited.

Hayāt (A) *Hayāt* is often used to mean life, but its true meaning is eternal life—the soul. The soul alone is imperishable and eternal. *Hayāt* is also used in reference to one's faith (*īmān*) becoming eternal, becoming *Īmān-Islām*. Although the soul alone is imperishable, people bless each other saying, "May you be *hayāt* always." They mean: May the inner purity never die; may you be pure always.

'Ibādat (A) Prayer, acts of worship, service; from the verb *'abāda* "to serve" and *'abd* "servitor." Praying to God with a melting heart is *'ibādat*. When the inner heart melts into liquid, when it melts like wax in prayer to God, when that state is achieved, it is *'ibādat*. This is prayer. It is prayer to the One.

Ill Allāh, Ill Allāhu (A) Nothing other than God. This is the second part of the remembrance *Lā ilāha, ill Allāhu*. *See Lā ilāha, ill Allāhu.*

'Ilm (A) Divine knowledge. The wisdom of *'ilm* is God's powerful love. Without letting the inner heart dry out, it creates a state wherein the inner heart is always cool, refreshed, beautiful, and happy. With this *'ilm* one can look at and review one's life with clarity.

Īmān (A) Absolute, unshakable, resolute faith, certitude, and determination that God alone exists; the complete acceptance by the heart that God is One.

Īmān-Islām (A) The pure heart which, having cut away all evil, takes on the power of courageous determination and faith and shines in the resplendence of God. When this resplendence of God is seen as the completeness within the heart of man, that is *Īmān-Islām*. When the completeness of the heart is directed toward the One who is Completeness, communing, trusting, worshipping, and accepting

450

Him as the only Perfection, then the two merge. This is *Īmān-Islām*.

Injīl (A) Christianity. *See Zabūr.*

Insān (A) Man; a human being. The true state of a human being is God's qualities, actions, conduct, and virtues. One who is replete with these qualities is a true *insān*.

Insān kāmil (A) A perfected, God-realized being. Having realized God as his only wealth, he cuts away the wealth of the world and the wealth sought by the mind, acquiring and immersing himself within God's qualities.

'Īshā' (A) The late night prayer; the fifth of the five daily prayers of Islam. This prayer represents the fifth of five periods in man's life. In the fourth period of his life, man must put the world to death, and in this fifth period, he should pray and commune with God. *See subh, zuhr, 'asr, and maghrib.*

'Ishq (A) Love; divine love; desire. There are two types of *'ishq*: desire is known as *'ishq,* and surrender to and love for God is known as *hubb-'ishq*—surrender to the Light. The *'ishq* that is the opposite of Light is desire. When desire enters, there is duality, but if one truly loves and merges with God, there is only One.

'Izrāfīl (A) The Angel of Air; Raphael.

'Izrā'īl (A) The Angel of Death; the angel of fire.

Jabrāt (A) Fire worship; the scripture corresponding to the religion of fire worship (Zoroastrianism). *See Zabūr.*

Jinn (A) Subtle beings created out of fire. There are two kinds of jinns. Those created through the commandments of God are the pure jinns who glorify Him. Those created out of fiery qualities, possessing qualities of anger and inducing bad qualities in human beings, are known as the jinns of Satan.

Kalimah (A) The literal meaning is *the word*. It is a name used for the testimony of faith in which a person affirms, *There is nothing other than You , only You are God—Lā ilāha, ill Allāhu.* The *kalimah* is God's grace and His pure light of Truth with which man can wash his inner heart. This is the *awwal kalimah,* the *word* that originated in the Beginning (*awwal*).The truth of the *kalimah* has the power to wash away all the *karma* that has accumulated from the beginning of one's life. *See dhikr; lā ilāha, ill Allāhu.*

Kāmil Sheikh (A) Perfect spiritual guide; the true guru; the one who knows himself and God and guides others on the straight path to God; one who has developed the three thousand gracious qualities of God. Seated on the throne of patience, with the quality of compassion, the *Kāmil Sheikh* comforts his children, dispels the karmic evils of this world, and teaches them subtle wisdom. He teaches them about the outer and inner forms of man, and makes them realize that God is their only wealth—God alone is sufficient.

Karma (T) Inherited tendencies. The thoughts, looks, qualities, and actions of Satan, the qualities of maya, the qualities of base desires, the qualities of the essence of the five elements, and the qualities of mind and desire which are connected to earth, hell, and maya—all these qualities constitute karma. Qualities of God, qualities of resolute faith, and qualities of perfect purity eliminate karma.

Kasthūri (T) The fragrance of grace that emanates from God, from His gracious qualities, from His thoughts, from His beauty, and from His *qalb*. He bestowed this fragrance on Muhammad⊕.

Khair (A) That which is right or good, as opposed to that which is evil or bad (*sharr*); that which is acceptable to wisdom and to God.

Kursī (A) The gnostic eye, the eye of Light. It is divine wisdom, the eye of wisdom in the center of the forehead, where the Light of God (*Nūr*) was impressed on Adam⊕. With this eye, everything can be seen and understood. The *kursī* is the "footstool" of God's throne, *'arsh*.

Lā ilāha, ill Allāhu (A) There is nothing other than You, Only You are God. *Lā ilāha, ill Allāhu* is God's unique, most exalted *word*. There are two aspects: *lā ilāha*—all that has appeared, all creation—*none of this is Reality; ill Allāhu*—the One who created everything—*God, the only Reality.* When one truly comprehends and accepts this with certitude, it is the state of purity. Lit. No god (is), except God. *See kalimah; dhikr.*

Lailatul-Qadr (A) The Light of God. God's Light ray, the Qur'an, was sent down to the Prophet⊕ on the Night of Power; traditionally the twenty-seventh night of Ramadan. Each verse of the Qur'an, the Divine Scripture, entered the Prophet's heart. This is the day when light entered a heart without darkness, a heart with pure faith. Similarly, when man is free of darkness and karma, the *Lailatul-Qadr*—God's grace, God's Light, the Qur'an—is bestowed on him.

Lām (A) The Arabic letter which corresponds to the English consonant 'L'. Among the twenty-eight letters that constitute the inner form of man, the *lām* represents the *Nūr,* the Light of plenitude. This is divine luminous wisdom—the seventh wisdom of perfect purity.

Al-Lauhul-mahfūz (A) The guarded or preserved tablet; the repository of destiny; the tablet of light upon which is inscribed the secret nature of all things and the "story" of all that will come to pass in the world of souls, this world, and the hereafter. It is known only by "knowers" of God in varying degrees, according to their stations. The tablet is "preserved" from the sight of all who are unworthy of reading it.

Maghrib (A) The sunset prayer; the fourth of the five daily prayers of Islam. This prayer represents the fourth of five periods in a man's life, the period when one puts the world to death within oneself. This is the time when the darkness of the world is dispelled through wisdom. *See subh, zuhr, ʿasr, and ʿishā.*

Maʿrifat (A) The fourth step of spiritual ascendance. *Maʿrifat* is union with God, intermingling with the Light, and existing in Light always. It is beyond the ten sins; a state in which there is no day or night, only Light. When one is with God, time does not exist. Therefore, one has no specified time for prayer, no age, no death. One prays while merged in God—this is *maʿrifat. See sharīʿat, tarīqat, haqīqat, and sūfiyyat.*

Mathi (T) Judgment; the fourth wisdom. The literal meanings of this word are understanding, discrimination, judgment, discernment, assessment, and estimation. There is no one English word that corresponds to this wisdom, this realm of consciousness, which performs all of the above functions at different times. *Mathi* involves a dynamic understanding and discrimination, ultimately generating and assessing the question, "Who am I?" The author uses the English words *estimate* and *witness* to describe its function in certain areas. *Mathi* assesses and contemplates the beginning of life, this world, and the hereafter. Man contemplates the heaven he will attain, the realm where he originated, and the *section* that is his body in this world. Through *mathi* he assesses three sections: his life (soul), his body, and his divine wisdom *(gnanam)*—God's grace *(rahmat)*.

Maya (T) Illusion; delusion; the unreality of the visible world; a hypnotic fascination that arises within the state of darkness. Maya is an energy, a *shakti,* which takes on various shapes, causing man to forfeit his wisdom by confusing and hypnotizing him into a state of torpor. It takes many, many millions of hypnotic forms. If, perceiving one of these forms, man tries to grasp it with his intellect, he will never catch it, for it will elude him by taking on yet another form. Maya leads to the false attribution of reality to physical and mental visions, causing one to misperceive the unreal as real. Often equated with the English word *illusion,* it cannot adequately be translated by any one English word. Therefore, as instructed by the author, the word maya is used as such in the text.

Mīm (A) The Arabic letter which corresponds to the English consonant 'M.' Among the twenty-eight letters that constitute the inner-form of man, *mīm* represents the eternal messenger of God, Muhammad☺.

Miʿrāj (A) The ascent; communion with God. Although several prophets have communed directly with God, *Miʿrāj* traditionally refers to the night journey of the Prophet Muhammad☺ through the heavens. It is said to have taken place in the twelfth year of the Prophet's mission and is celebrated on the twenty-seventh day of the month of *Rajab.* However, each individual's celebration of *Miʿrāj* is the day when he or she communicates directly with God; when resolute faith, wisdom, the beauty of the face (*Muhammad*), and the beauty of the heart (*Ahamad*) meet God and commune with Him.

Muhaiyaddeen (A) The literal meaning is the giver of life; the reviver of faith—*Dīn. Muhaiyaddeen* is the pure resplendence called the *qutb,* the beauty that manifests from God, to which God gave His powers *(wilayat).* It is that which awakens the wisdom lying hidden under maya; that which gives life to wisdom, showing it to be a resplendence once more. The name *Muhaiyaddeen* is made up of several parts: *Mu* is that which existed earlier; *hayy* is life; *yā* is a title of greatness, and *dīn* is the light which is perfectly pure. Therefore, *Muhaiyaddeen* is the exalted purity that existed in the beginning, the "Primal Thing" which was originally with God and is with Him always. To that purity God gave the name *Muhaiyaddeen.*

In a human being, *Muhaiyaddeen* is the sixth wisdom—perfectly pure divine analytic wisdom (*pahuth arivu*) that discriminates right and wrong, good and evil, permissible and impermissible, essence and creation. It discards everything that is impermissible, accepts only God, and shows Him to you. This wisdom which discerns, distinguishes, and understands is also known as *qutb,* the *qutbiyyat,* the spiritual axis, the wisdom of *Muhaiyaddeen.*

Muham (T) Face. When we talk about the *muham* of man, it means face, but when we talk of *Muhammad,* that is the beauty of God.

Muhammad (A) The Final Prophet; the Messenger of God☺. Also, the beauty of the light of God's essence found in the heart and reflected in the face.

Mūlādhāra chakrā (T) The center of energy at the base of the spine.

Mu'min (A) One of pure faith; one who has steadfast belief in God.

Nafs or *nafs ammārah* (A) There are seven *nafs,* seven cravings, seven desires for the world. They are the essences of the five elements, mind and desire.

Nasīb (A) Destiny or fate.

Navagraham (T) The nine planets that are considered to influence a person's destiny.

Nithānam (T) Balance; assurance, correctness, resolution. To proceed toward God without deviating, slowly, carefully, and with balance . *See Sheikh.*

Nōnbu (T) The fast.

Nuqat (A) (sing. *nuqtah)* Dot. A diacritical mark placed over or under certain Arabic letters, differentiating one letter from the other in appearance and sound.

Nūr (A) Light; the resplendence of God; the plenitude of the Light of God which has the brilliance of a hundred million suns; the completeness of God's qualities. In man it exists as innate divine luminous wisdom. It is complete Light, the Light of God's grace, the Light of God's essence. *See perr arivu.*

Nūr Muhammad (A) [Same as *Nūr*] The plenitude; the Light which became complete within God and then emerged.

Oli (T) Light; an illuminated being. This Tamil word has the same usage as the Arabic word *walī.*

Pahuth arivu (T) Divine analytic wisdom; the sixth of seven wisdoms; explanations from the *Qutbiyyat.* This wisdom separates right from wrong, accepts only what is right, and reveals it to you.

Panjāngam (T) Astrological almanac of five letters used in eastern countries.

Perr arivu (T) Divine luminous wisdom; the ultimate of seven wisdoms. This wisdom, which enables man to realize that he is in God and God is in him, is God's greatest gift to mankind.

Pudthi (T) Intellect; the third of seven wisdoms. It is the essence and intellect of the five elements: earth, fire, water, air, and ether. Arising out of perception and awareness, the intellect obtains its knowledge through them, and also controls them.

Purānas (T) Ancient legends.

Qalam (A) The divine pen which symbolizes both the instrument of creation— the inscription of existence on the cosmic tablet, and the writing of

455

individual destinies. Lit. a reed pen.

Qalb (A) Heart; the inner heart. This is the battlefield where one's personal battles are fought. When the beauty of God and His Truth blossom, this same place becomes the Kingdom of God—His temple, His church, His mosque.

Qiblah (A) Traditionally, the direction that Muslims face when performing ritual prayer toward Mecca. Inwardly, the *qiblah* is toward the throne of God within the inner heart. To face God while in prayer is the true direction—*qiblah*.

Qiyāmah (A) The Day of Questioning; the Day of Standing Forth. Traditionally, this is the day of questioning and accounting for the good and evil of one's life. Sufi's also use the term for the state of a man who, having died to the world, "stands forth" to begin a new life in God.

Qur'an (A) The Holy Book of Islam. The Qur'an is a collection of revelations given by God to Prophet Muhammad☺ in 6,666 verses, with Angel Gabriel☺ as the intermediary. It is the explanation of God's qualities, actions, and duties in this world and the world of souls. It is also an explanation of His creations, of earlier prophets, and of later prophets. The Qur'an reveals these explanations to the people, prophets, saints, angels, heavenly beings, *qutbs*, jinns, fairies, and all created beings.

The Qur'an also exists within the heart of man. This original Qur'an is a wealth that was entrusted to man by God in the world of souls. It was then that God placed within man His actions, beauty, plenitude, completeness, duties, and limitless qualities that are the state of Truth. Together they constitute the inner Qur'an.

What is seen on the outside are the commandments, and to understand them is to learn from the examples. However, when the explanations are understood from within, that will be called the essence (*dhāt*) of God. If one continues to study and understand from the outside, that is *sharī'at,* the first step of spiritual ascendance. Studying on the inside constitutes the third and fourth steps—*haqīqat* and *ma'rifat.* We must hold on to God's qualities and climb one step after another. When we comprehend and recite the inner Qur'an, we will perceive God as the One—the One Truth, the only One worthy of worship. We will see only one family.

Qurbān (A) From *qarraba,* to bring near; any practice that brings one nearer to God. On the outside, it refers to the ritual method for the slaughter of animals in order to purify them, making it permissible to consume their flesh. On the inside, *qurbān* refers to the cutting away of beastly qualities within one's heart; sacrificing or dedicating one's life to the devotion and service of God.

Qutb (A) The literal meaning of the Arabic word is *axis, pole, pivot.* A *qutb* is a divine being sent by God to shed light on His words. There is always a *qutb* present in this world. In man, the *qutb,* the *spiritual axis,* manifests as the divine analytic wisdom *(pahuth arivu)* which explains and awakens all truths that have been destroyed and buried in the ocean of maya. It awakens true faith and explains the state of purity as it existed in the beginning of creation. As the inner Sheikh, the inner guide, the grace of God's essence, it awakens the purity of life, transforming it into the divine vibration. *See pahuth arivu.*

Qutbiyyat (A) The wisdom of the *qutb;* the sixth wisdom. *See Qutb.*

Rabb (A) The Lord, God. The One who creates and protects all lives. The literal meaning is *to bring up.* God is the One who can bring everything up to its perfect standard. Like a parent, He watches, guides, tends, and sustains all that is in His care.

Rahmān (A) The most Gracious, most Merciful. The One who rules eternally with His three thousand compassionate, benevolent qualities. He has no anger at all. His duty is only to protect and sustain.

Rahmat (A) God's grace; His mercy; His forgiveness and compassion; His benevolence; His wealth. Everything within God is *rahmat.* This *rahmat,* His perfection, will never change. This is why it is the greatest, most valuable treasure that anyone can receive.

Rahmatul-ālamīn (A) God, the Mercy and Compassion of all the universes. God is the Ruler of fathomless grace, the One of incomparable love. No love compares to His love. His grace has no end. That is how it is. Because of this, every need—whatever the heart needs, whatever the soul needs, whatever hunger and thirst need—is satisfied through God's *rahmat* (grace and mercy). He gives His creations everything they ask for or desire. This is why He is called the *rahmatul-ālamīn*— the grace-wealth of all the universes.

Rāsis (T) Signs of the Zodiac.

Rasūl (A) A messenger of God. A *rasūl* is one who has accepted only God and has rejected everything else; one who has accepted God's divine words, qualities and actions, putting them into practice. *Rasūls* are those who, from time immemorial, have given the divine laws of God to the people, each following the commandments given to them in their particular era.

The Rasūl☺ (A) The Messenger of God—the Prophet Muhammad☺—the manifestation of the Light and Essence of God that has existed since the primal beginning and will exist for eternity. This *Rasūl* imparts explanations of luminous wisdom to all of God's creations within themselves.

Rasūlullāh☺ (A) The *Rasūl* of God.

Rizq (A) Divine nourishment; food; sustenance. That which is given by God—*ar-Razzāq,* the Provider, the Sustainer, the Bestower of sustenance—to all creations according to their capacities and needs.

Rūh (A) Soul. The *rūh* is the light-life that comes as a ray from God's Light—*Nūr.* Having received the grace of God, this light-life is eternal. The other five kinds of life—earth-life, water-life, air-life, fire-life, and ether-life—disappear and go away, but this life, this soul, never disappears. It exists forever.

Rūhul-'ālam (A) The realm of souls.

Sabūr (A) Inner patience. It is the first of four qualities advocated by the author: *sabūr, shakūr, tawakkul,* and *al-hamdu lillāh*—inner patience, contentment, trust in God, and total surrender to God. Patience is a state of being, a treasury. To go within patience, to reflect, to be tolerant, to practice inner patience—this is *sabūr.* Going deeper within and contemplating is *shakūr.* Handing all responsibility over to God is *tawakkul.* Surrendering everything to God means that "the person" no longer exists. Neither the good nor the bad that follow affect him emotionally. This is *al-hamdu lillāh.*

Salām (A) Peace; the peace of God; greetings. When we greet each other outwardly saying, *"Salām,"* our intention, in God's name, is that we unite in a state of peace. True *salām* is honoring God alone, revering only Him, and rendering His name of purity [as-*Salām*] to Him. *See salawāt.*

Salawāt (A) Prayers; blessings; glorification. On the outside, giving *salāms* and *salawāt* is the practice of praising and glorifying God, remembering the *Rasūl*☺, the prophets, the angels and other exalted beings, and asking that God's peace be upon all. True *salawāt* is returning God's praise to Him—returning His words, His glory, and His benevolence, and praising only Him.

Sallallāhu 'alaihi wa sallam (A) God bless him and grant him peace. On the outside, this is a supplication traditionally spoken after mentioning the name of Prophet Muhammad☺. It is denoted in the text with ☺. Acknowledging God's commandments, God's messengers, and the words brought by His messengers, and revering them—this is *Sallallāhu 'alaihi wa sallam*. This is the true praise of God and His *Rasūl*☺.

Satthiya Vētham (T) *Satthiya* means true, and *Vētham* means scripture. The Truth of God and the resplendence of His Truth are the only scripture for all creations. This clarity alone is God's commandments. The justice of His commandments and His Truth are the scripture for all human beings. This is God's scripture, true scripture, *satthiya vētham*. Fulfilling God's commandments and Truth in one's life and living accordingly is scripture—*vētham,* and Truth—*satthiyam*.

Shaitān (A) Satan; *iblīs*. Satan was created from fire. He is one of the jinns. He was born from the fire of anger, jealousy, deceit, arrogance, pride, and egoism—the fire that will destroy everything, both good and bad, without discrimination. Anyone possessing the fire of anger is Satan. Fire is anger, jealousy, arrogance, deceit, the egoism of the "I," and the qualities of attacking and hitting others. One who has the qualities of God, on the other hand, is a true human being—God's representative, with nothing other than God and God's qualities, actions, gaze, fragrance, and speech. Such a one attains these qualities and abides by them, thus attaining God's beauty. All the opposite qualities and their forces—hurting others, talking behind another's back, being angry, being unjust, striking others, murdering others, using intoxicants, stealing, lying, having base desires, lust, and all the evil qualities which lead to evil actions—are Satan. Satan is darkness—the qualities of hell. One who acquires these qualities is Satan.

Shaktis (T) The forces or energies arising from the five elements.

Shakūr (A) Contentment. The state that follows inner-patience, usually called thankfulness, gratitude, or contentment. Contentment is deep within the treasury of inner patience, pacifying and comforting. *Shakūr* is one of the ninety-nine divine names of God. *See Sabūr.*

Sharī'at (A) The first of the five steps of spiritual ascendance (*sharī'at, tarīqat, haqīqat, ma'rifat, and sūfiyyat*). In this first step, each brings to prayer what is within, projects it outside as a form, and worships it. While acknowledging the One God, they pray for the ability to perform miracles, complain about the things they lack, and beseech God for wives, children, livestock, property, and material possessions. Since man was created out of the five elements (earth, fire, water, air, and ether), and since both light and darkness, good and bad, truth and falsehood, heaven and hell exist within him, he must distinguish good from bad, right from wrong, and act accordingly. Finally, he must understand that the only *right* is God and worship Him alone. This is *sharī'at.* Lit. the law. *See tarīqat, haqīqat, ma'rifat, and sūfiyyat*

Sharr (A) On the outside, *sharr* refers to that which is wrong, bad, or evil, as opposed to that which is good *(khair).* On the inside, one must realize that everything that has appeared is *sharr.* Only that which is imperishable, existing forever, is *khair.* We must focus on that which is eternal, and through the wisdom of resolute faith, discard *sharr,* which is perishable and subject to change.

Sheikh (A) Spiritual guide; master; teacher; guru. Everything we look at and study from is a sheikh. Everything that teaches us is a sheikh. However, if one is a true Sheikh, he must have the four virtuous qualities (*thānam, nithānam, avathānam,* and *gnānam*) within God's Truth, justice, commandments, and purity. *Thānam* is dedicating oneself to God and following His commandments without wavering. *Nithānam* [balance] is focusing on God alone, standing in His gaze and walking toward Him without the slightest deviation. *Avathānam* is concentrating on acting with God's qualities on the path of the justice of God's Truth. This has to be done with care and caution, for hell is on one side and the world on the other; mind is on one side and desire on the other. One who has attained this state is in the state of *gnānam—divine wisdom. Gnānam* is the wisdom of the *kursī,* the wisdom of the *qutbiyyat* (divine analytic wisdom). One who establishes this state and lives in this way is a Sheikh, the one Sheikh in the world. He is the one Sheikh for the world of souls, this world, and the next.

Shiva (T) In Hinduism, Shiva is one of three main aspects of God—Brahma the Creator, Vishnu the protector, and Shiva the Destroyer. In addition, Shiva symbolizes particular aspects of life for all Hindus—procreation and renunciation. In the author's usage, Shiva and Shakti (the aspect of procreation) correspond to Adam☺ and Eve☺.

Sidhis (T) Supernatural abilities; the capacity to perform miracles obtained by devotion to and control of the elements.

Sifāt (A) Creation. *Sifāt* is all of creation, *dhāt* is the essence. *Sifāt* refers to everything that came into being when God said, "*Kūn, Arise!*"

Singhan (T) *Singhan* is the arrogance present at the moment the semen is ejaculated. It is the quality of the lion. *See tārahan.*

Sirr (A) Secret; The secret of God within man, a secret which man must uncover. *Sirr* is secret. But nothing is a secret to God, for He knows everything. Each inner heart that fails to realize God is *sirr.* That which is not understood by such a man is *sirr.* His is an unstable existence. Once he understands God, he has no *sirr.* He has no birth. Once man understands his true place of existence, once he understands himself and his Lord, there are no more secrets. There is only Light. If man does not realize this, there is *sirr* in his life, but if he realizes the Light, he becomes eternal. Ignorance is man's *sirr.*

Subh (A) The first of the five daily prayers of Islam, also known as *fajr* or *subahu.* This prayer represents the first of five periods in man's life, a period when one emerges from darkness to dawn. To understand the place one appeared, the time one appeared, and the origin of one's appearance, and worship God, the only One worthy of worship, is *subh.* To understand how one emerged from the darkness of maya, to perceive the light outside, to know God, and worship Him is *subh.*

Subhānallāhi Kalimah (A) A prayer; also known as *tasbīh,* or the Third *Kalimah.* The words—*Subhānallāhi wal-hamdu lillāhi wa lā ilāha ill Allāhu, wallāhu Akbar. Wa lā hawla wa lā quwwata illā billāhi wa huwal-'alīyul-'azīm*—mean: Glory be to God, and all praise is to God, and none is god except God, and God is the Greatest, and none but God has the majesty or power to sustain, and He is the Majesty, the Supreme in glory.

Sufi, Sūfiyyat (A) One in the state of *sūfiyyat;* one who has seen God within himself. To go beyond the four steps of spiritual ascendancy (*sharī'at, tarīqat, haqīqat,* and *ma'rifat*) is *sūfiyyat.* It is the state of one who has transcended the four religions and merged with God.

Sūran (T) One of the three sons of maya. *Sūran* is the illusory images of the mind enjoyed at the moment of ejaculation. It is all the qualities and energies of the mind. *See tārahan.*

Sūrat (A) In Arabic, *sūrat* is a word used exclusively for chapters in the Qur'an, of which there are one hundred and fourteen. In Persian, Hindi, and other eastern languages, and also in Arabic when spelled with a different S, *sūrat* means form, shape, figure, state, or condition. The author uses *sūrat* in all of its various meanings.

Sūratul-Baqarah (A) The second chapter of the Qur'an; the Chapter of the

461

Heifer.

Sūratul-Falaq (A) The 113th chapter of the Qur'an; the Chapter of the Daybreak. It signifies the cleaving of light from darkness.

Sūratul-Fātihah (A) The opening chapter of the Qur'an. In Islam, the *Sūratul-Fātihah* is recited at the beginning of every prayer. *See Sūratul-Insān.*

Sūratul-Ikhlās (A) The Chapter of Sincerity, or Purity, the 112th chapter of the Qur'an. It proclaims the unity, the absoluteness, of the Divine Essence, indicated by the word *Huwa* (He) which is the name of the Essence. Except for the opening chapter, this is the most often repeated chapter of the *Qur'ān.*

Sūratul-Insān (A) *Sūrat* is the body, *Sūratul-Insān* is the true form of man within the body. Man's physical body formed of the five elements is the *sūrat. Sūratul-insān* is one who has God's Light. He has the inner form, the inner Qur'an formed of [twenty-eight] letters of light. This *Sūratul-Insān*—this *Sūratul-Fātihah* is God's *Sūrat,* God's Qur'an. You should perceive this Qur'an. If you see His Qur'an and recite it, you will perceive only God's commandments there. Understanding this is *Sūratul-Fātihah*—knowing yourself. When you know yourself, you will know your Lord. When you know your Lord, you will know His creations. When you know the creations of the Lord, you can be an emperor to those creations. You can become a *sayyid* or a *sheikh,* correcting them, showing them the path, and taking them on that good path.

Sūratul-'iqrā (A) The 96th chapter of the Qur'an; the Chapter of the Proclamation, also known as *Suratul-'alaq.*.

Sūratul-Nās (A) The 114th chapter of the Qur'an; the Chapter of Mankind.

Tārahan, Singhan, and Sūran (T) The three sons of maya. *Tārahan* is the trench or pathway for the sexual act, the birth canal or vagina. *Singhan* is the arrogance present at the moment the semen is ejaculated. It is the quality of the lion. *Sūran* is all the illusory images of the mind enjoyed at the moment of ejaculation. It is all the qualities and energies of the mind.

Tarīqat (A) The second of the five steps of spiritual ascendance. After accepting what is "right" in *sharī'at,* that understanding must be firmly rooted and established. *Taripādu* in Tamil, and *Tarīqat* in Arabic, refer to deepening one's faith, making it firm and resolute. However, this is also the level of fire-worship, the period when the fire of hunger, the fire in air, the fire in water, and the fire in old age hypnotize man, making him hungry and torpid. He runs here and there, he seeks, and he meditates, forgetting to search for the food of determination, for the prayer of certitude, and for resolute faith. If man establishes faith (*īmān*) in God, and maintains the certitude that God who created everything, will also provide food, then he will escape and move to the next step—*haqīqat*. See *sharī'at, haqīqat, ma'rifat, and sūfiyyat.*

Tawakkul-'alallāh (A) Absolute trust in and surrender to God; to take each thing to God and hand over the entire responsibility to Him. This is a state of total surrender; the "I" does not exist. Whatever happens as a result—whether it be good or bad—is no longer one's responsibility. It has been given over to God. Absolute trust in God resides deep within contentment, reassuring and sustaining. *See Sabūr.*

Thānam (T) To surrender; to offer; to dedicate. Man must know to Whom he should dedicate himself, and then proceed vigilantly toward Him. *See Sheikh.*

Thiru Marai or *Thiru Qur'ān* (T & A) The original scripture; the inner Qur'an inscribed within the heart. In Tamil, *thiru* has two meanings, sacred and triple. All the secrets, as well as the essence of the three worlds, *awwal, dunyā,* and *ākhirah* (the beginning of creation, the physical world, and the hereafter), have been compressed and concealed by God within the *Thiru Qur'ān.* Within it, He has concealed the explanations of the essence of grace (*dhāt*) and the manifestations of creation (*sifāt*). There He has concealed the *alif, lām,* and *mīm*—these three which are the essence. That is why it is called the *Thiru Qur'ān.*

Marai literally means holy scriptures, and as such, it refers to the scriptures and words of every religion. In this sense it refers to the book called the Holy Qur'an. But as explained by the author, the inner *Thiru Marai* is the manifestation of the conscience of God in every age to every nation, revealing to mankind the means of attaining Him. This is the inner *Qur'ān,* the original *Qur'ān,* which becomes manifest from time to time, revealing the guidelines for human conduct in relation to spiritual evolution. Since God is the Reality immanent in man, the voice of God (the revelation that proceeds from the *Nūr,* the *perr arivu*) is called *Thiru Marai.*

Thiru Qur'ān (T & A) *See Thiru Marai.*

Thiyānam (T) Meditation. Pronounced and often spelled as *dhyānam.*

Tholuhai (T) Prayer; prayer in which one remembers only God to the exclusion of everything else. Traditionally, this word is used for the five daily prayers of Islam.

Ummī (A) One who is filled with God. In Tamil, *ummī* means silent, dumb; in Arabic, it means unlettered. God knows everything. He has no shape or form, no self-interest; He has everything within Him. An *ummī* is one who keeps only God—God's wisdom, perception, speech, words, actions, grace, Truth, and qualities—in him, discarding the world, self-interest, and all perceived sights and sounds. Keeping only that which belongs to God, he discards everything else that comes along. He is silent and unlettered—he has no speech other than God's speech, no *writing* other than God's writing.

Ummul-Qur'ān (A) Derived from *umm,* which means mother, the *Ummul-Qur'ān* means the Mother of the Book—the uncreated prototype of the Qur'an in heaven, inscribed symbolically on the "guarded tablet." It is the eternal source of all the revelations to the prophets. It is also known as the *Ummul-Kitāb.* The author also uses this term in reference to the inner, silent Qur'an which exists as a mystery within the heart of each individual. Lit. the Mother, or Source of the Book.

Unarchi (T) Awareness, the second of the seven wisdoms innate in man. On the physical level, awareness helps one to locate feelings and sensations, while on the inner level, it contributes to a growing awareness and scrutiny of one's life and origin.

Unarvu (T) Perception or feeling, the first of the seven wisdoms innate in man. On the physical level, it refers to physical perception, while on the inner level, it refers to one's perception of the state of one's life.

Vanakkam (T) Worship. Other than God there is none worthy of worship. To know God completely, and to worship Him as Him, without the "I," is *vanakkam.* Only God can worship God. To transform the *sūrat* (form) and qualities of man, to acquire the *sūrat* and qualities of God, and to thus worship Him as Him, is *vanakkam.* Thus, God worships God—this is *vanakkam.*

Viratham (T) The fast.

Wahy (A) Revelation; inspiration from God; the inspired word of God revealed to a prophet; the words of God transmitted to the Prophet Muhammad⊕ by the archangel Gabriel☺. Revelations have come to Adam☺, Moses☺, and various other prophets, but the histories of all the earlier prophets were included within the revelation given to Prophet Muhammad in 6,666 verses.

Wahys are also commandments given by God, benevolences

464

bestowed by Him [to a heart without darkness]. They are His *rahmat,* or wealth of grace, the grace of divine knowledge, the grace of truth, the grace of *īmān,* the grace of wisdom, and the grace of perfect purity.

Wilāyāt (A) God's Power which has been revealed and manifested through His actions; the actions of His miraculous names (*asmāʾul-husnā*); the powers of His attributes through which all creations came into existence.

The outer meaning of *wilāyāt* is miracles and forces acquired by chanting praises to the five elements (earth, fire, water, air, and ether), to jinns, demons, and ghosts. Mantras are chanted to summon, control, and utilize these elements to perform supernatural feats. The miracles performed in this way are known in Tamil as *sidhis* and in Arabic as *wilāyāt.* They are not related to the Power of God.

The inner meaning refers to everything that occurs through divine grace, through the Power of God. When man dedicates himself to God, he has no miracles or anything else in this world. In this state, only God worships God, only God shows the way to God. Such a man praises nothing other than God, and has no miracles to perform. For such devotees, their state of *qutbiyyat* receives grace from the compassionate gaze of God. As soon as they intend God, His gaze falls on them, and through His divine grace they receive His Power. God makes things happen, not the devotees. No forces or energies are involved, neither do His devotees desire any miracles. When God glances at them, things happen. They are done by God, through His Power—His *wilāyāt.*

Yaman (T) The Tamil word for *'Izrāʾīl* ☺, the Angel of Death.

Zabūr, Jabrat, Injīl, and *Furqān* (A) The four scriptures, four religions (Hinduism, Fire-worship, Christianity, Islam), four steps of spiritual ascendance. These four constitute man's body. The area below the waist represents procreation—Hinduism, *Zabūr.* The stomach represents the fire of hunger—Fire-worship, *Jabrat.* The chest represents vapors and spirits—Christianity, *Injīl.* The head with its seven outer principles—two eyes, two ears, two nostrils, and one mouth—represents the pull of the senses—Islam, *Furqān.* Man must study and understand these four religions as four steps, transcend them and go beyond. He should transform himself, use the seven inner principles with wisdom, and attain direct communication and union with God.

465

Zīnat (A) The beauty of God which enamors all creations. When one becomes true man, he will acquire the beauty of God.

Zuhr (A) The noontime prayer; the second of the five daily prayers of Islam. This prayer represents midday, adolescence, the period of man's life when mind, desire, and illusion surround and intoxicate him. The essence of the seven forces (earth, fire, water, air, ether, mind, and desire) function in this period, keeping him in a state of torpor. Hell is on one side, and mind and desire are on the other side. God, wisdom, Truth, and the path of justice are in the center. This is the period in which man must decide which way he wishes to go. Having decided, he must then walk carefully. If he falls to one side maya will grab him, and if he falls on the other side hell will grab him. Thus, *zuhr* is the period of life when man, surrounded by hypnotic forces, must choose his path with care and understanding. *See subh, 'asr, maghrib, and 'ishā.*

About the
Bawa Muhaiyaddeen Fellowship

Muhammad Raheem Bawa Muhaiyaddeen ☺, a Sufi mystic from Sri Lanka, was a man of extraordinary wisdom and compassion. For over seventy years he shared his knowledge and experience with people of every race and religion and from all walks of life.

The central branch of The Bawa Muhaiyaddeen Fellowship is located in Philadelphia, Pennsylvania. It was Bawa Muhaiyaddeen's residence while he was in the United States until his death in December 1986. The Fellowship continues to serve as a meeting house and a reservoir of people and materials for all who are interested in his teachings. All are welcome.

Also located on the same property is The Mosque of Shaikh Muhammad Raheem Bawa Muhaiyaddeen where the daily five times of prayer and Friday congregational prayers are held. An hour west of the Fellowship is the *Mazār*, or tomb, of M. R. Bawa Muhaiyaddeen which is open for visitation.

For further information write or phone:

The Bawa Muhaiyaddeen Fellowship
5820 Overbrook Avenue
Philadelphia, Pennsylvania 19131

(215) 879-8604
(24 hour answering machine)

E-mail Address: info@bmf.org
Web Address: http://www.bmf.org

If you would like to visit the Fellowship or obtain a schedule of current events or branch locations and meetings, please write, phone, or E-mail *Attn: Visitor Information.*

Books by
M. R. Bawa Muhaiyaddeen

Truth & Light: brief explanations

Songs of God's Grace

The Divine Luminous Wisdom That Dispels the Darkness

Wisdom of the Divine (Vols. 1–5)

The Guidebook to the True Secret of the Heart (Vols. 1, 2)

God, His Prophets and His Children

Four Steps to Pure Iman

The Wisdom of Man

A Book of God's Love

My Love You My Children:
101 Stories for Children of All Ages

Come to the Secret Garden: Sufi Tales of Wisdom

The Golden Words of a Sufi Sheikh

The Tasty, Economical Cookbook (Vols. 1, 2)

Sheikh and Disciple

Maya Veeram or The Forces of Illusion

Asma'ul-Husna: The 99 Beautiful Names of Allah

Islam and World Peace: Explanations of a Sufi, Revised Edition

A Mystical Journey

Questions of Life—Answers of Wisdom (Vols. 1,2)

Treasures of the Heart: Sufi Stories for Young Children

To Die Before Death: The Sufi Way of Life

A Song of Muhammad ﷺ

Hajj: The Inner Pilgrimage

The Triple Flame: The Inner Secrets of Sufism

The Resonance of Allah: Resplendent Explanations Arising
from the Nūr, Allāh's Wisdom of Grace

Enough for a Million Years
Why Can't I See the Angels: Children's Questions to a Sufi Saint
The Tree That Fell to the West: Autobiography of a Sufi

Gems of Wisdom series—
Vol. 1: The Value of Good Qualities
Vol. 2: Beyond Mind and Desire
Vol. 3: The Innermost Heart
Vol. 4: Come to Prayer

A Contemporary Sufi Speaks—
To Teenagers and Parents
On the Signs of Destruction
On Peace of Mind
On the True Meaning of Sufism
On Unity: The Legacy of the Prophets
The Meaning of Fellowship
Mind, Desire, and the Billboards of the World

Foreign Language Publications—
Ein Zeitgenössischer Sufi Spricht über Inneren Frieden
(A Contemporary Sufi Speaks on Peace of Mind—
German Translation)

Deux Discours tirés du Livre L'Islam et la Paix Mondiale:
Explications d'un Soufi
(Two Discourses from the Book Islam and World Peace:
Explanations of a Sufi—French Translation)

¿Quién es Dios? Una explicación por el Sheikh Sufi
(Who is God? An Explanation by the Sufi Sheikh
—Spanish translation)

For free catalog or book information call:
(888) 786-1786 (toll-free in USA) or **(215) 879-8604**
or fax: **(215) 879-6307**
or email: **info@bmf.org**
Web Address: **http://www.bmf.org**

Notes

Notes

Notes

Notes

Notes